To. Mario
With thanks for
your AC.

Bob Reich

May '09

REASON

REASON

WHY LIBERALS WILL WIN
THE BATTLE FOR AMERICA

ROBERT B. REICH

ALFRED A. KNOPF   NEW YORK   2004

THIS IS A BORZOI BOOK PUBLISHED BY ALFRED A. KNOPF

Copyright © 2004 by Robert B. Reich
All rights reserved under International and Pan-American Copyright Conventions.
Published in the United States by Alfred A. Knopf, a division of Random House, Inc.,
New York, and simultaneously in Canada by Random House of Canada Limited, Toronto.
Distributed by Random House, Inc., New York.
www.aaknopf.com

Grateful acknowledgment is made to Farrar, Straus and Giroux, LLC, for permission to
reprint an excerpt from "Annus Mirabilis" from *Collected Poems* by Philip Larkin.
Copyright © 1988, 1989 by the Estate of Philip Larkin.
Reprinted by permission of Farrar, Straus and Giroux, LLC.

Knopf, Borzoi Books, and the colophon are registered trademarks of Random House, Inc.

A portion of this work has previously appeared in *The American Prospect.*

Library of Congress Cataloging-in-Publication Data
Reich, Robert B.
Reason : why liberals will win the battle for America / Robert B. Reich. — 1st ed.
p.   cm.
Includes bibliographical references and index.
ISBN 1-4000-4221-6 (alk. paper)
1. Liberalism—United States. 2. Political participation—United States.
3. United States—Politics and government—2001– 4. Political planning—United States.
I. Title: Why liberals will win the battle for America. II. Title.
JC574.2.U6R45 2004
320.51'3'0973—d22   2003069518

Manufactured in the United States of America
First Edition

To the memory of Paul and Sheila Wellstone

If we would guide by the light of reason, we must let our minds be bold.

—Justice Louis Dembitz Brandeis

We will not be driven by fear into an age of unreason.

—Edward R. Murrow

CONTENTS

REASON

INTRODUCTION

In my view, being a liberal is something to be proud of. Yet for more than twenty years, liberals have been on the defensive, and conservatives ascendant. I have watched and chronicled the nation's rightward drift, sometimes fretting and fulminating about it, twice participating in Democratic administrations that have tried to slow or co-opt it, every four years or so advising political candidates what they might do about it, often debating right-wingers on television and radio about whether it's good or harmful (it is, indubitably, harmful, as I will make clear), once running for office myself in a vain attempt to halt it in my home state, and rarely but occasionally—dare I admit it?— telling myself I should stop worrying about it and get a life (obviously, I haven't).

I write now with greater urgency. In recent years, the conservative agenda has become far more radicalized. Its latest incarnation is more threatening and potentially more destabilizing to America and the world than its previous forms. Barry Goldwater's "extremism in defense of liberty" was merely quirky and quixotic. Ronald Reagan's buoyant divisiveness was at least tempered by moderate Republicans, congressional Democrats, and two generations of Americans who had experienced the we're-in-this-together solidarity of the Great Depression and World War II.

Now, however, radical conservatives—Radcons, I call them—are taking over the public agenda, and they are meeting with woefully little resistance. Public debate has become grossly imbalanced. The Democratic Party has turned timid. The marketplace of ideas has retreated to a back-alley stall.

The administration of George W. Bush was more the result than the cause of this radical conservative ascendance, and its end will not mark the end of radical conservatism in America. Casting Bush as the villain of a dark conspiratorial drama may be emotionally satisfying to many liberals, but it doesn't illuminate the larger clash of ideas and principles. We need to look beyond any specific election in order to understand what is occurring and why, and consider the alternative choices facing America in the years ahead.

The Radcon agenda, undiluted and unopposed, is dramatically out of sync with the needs of America and the world. As such, it endangers our future.

Consider:

• When the integrity of our economic and political system is threatened by unbridled greed and abuses of power—fraud in corporate suites and on Wall Street, exorbitant payments to top executives, and unprecedented sums of money flowing to politicians in exchange for political favors—the nation needs tough laws backed by sturdy enforcement and uncompromising public indignation. But instead of a reinvigorated public morality, Radcons are focusing on private sexual morality, on personal sin and sex. They would rather police bedrooms than board rooms.

• When the differences in income and wealth separating rich Americans from everyone else have become wider than at any time since the Roaring Twenties (by some measures, wider than at any time since the Gilded Age), Radcons are cutting social services and school budgets, and showering the rich with tax breaks. When jobs and wages have grown especially precarious for the vast majority of Americans, Radcons are shredding social safety nets and privatizing social insurance.

• When international cooperation is most needed to guard against global terrorism, Radcons are turning their backs on the rest of the world, often treating it with contempt. They believe America has enough wealth and power to go it alone, so they launch preemptive wars and occupy nations they deem hostile. When we need to be especially vigilant to protect American freedoms at home, Radcons would prefer to stifle dissent and restrict civil liberties.

In all these respects, there is a clear alternative to radical conservatism. It is a bold new liberalism, properly defined. Such liberalism is more urgently needed than ever—to stop abuses of power and unconstrained greed at the highest reaches of America; to prevent this nation from becoming a two-tiered society comprising a few who are very rich and a majority who are barely making it; and to unite the world effectively against terrorism and hate.

We live in an era when "liberalism," a great and essential tradition, is mocked and its meaning grossly distorted. Radical conservatives have made a point of doing so, akin to demonizing an enemy during a war. They have depicted liberalism as a caricature of the sixties left. It is the equivalent, in their lexicon, to moral laxity and sexual permissiveness. It means taxes on the middle class in order to spend money on the undeserving poor. It is caricatured as the creed of "blame America first" pacifists who hate this country and don't want to use force against our murderous terrorist enemies. They call liberals effete and elite, traitors and scoundrels, and blame their naive, softhearted generosity and permissiveness for everything that's gone wrong with America. So the Radcons say—over and over again.

In fact, liberalism is not at all the cartoon version of the sixties left that the Radcons accuse it of being. The liberal tradition is directly relevant to the challenges America faces today. The classical liberal ideas that emerged in the seventeenth and eighteenth centuries and took root in American soil sought—for the first time in human history—to improve the well-being of *all* people, not just the rich and the privileged. Liberalism has stood for an economic system that betters the lives of average working people, and for a democracy that gives voice to the little guy. That liberal tradition animated American abolitionists of the nineteenth century who fought against slavery. It inspired suffragettes who demanded that women have the right to vote. And it motivated civil rights workers who put their lives on the line for equal rights.

American liberalism has also functioned like a balance wheel, saving capitalism from its worst excesses. It moved reformers at the turn of the last century to stand firm against monopolies and political corruption. It inspired progressives to battle for safety, health, and food and drug regulations. In the wake of the Great Crash of 1929, it led New Dealers to regulate banking and clean up Wall Street. As the Depression deepened, it prompted them to create Social Security, unemployment insurance, and a minimum wage, rather than resort to European-style socialism. The same liberal spirit aroused labor leaders to fight for better pay and working conditions for average working people. And it animated public-works spending to put millions of Americans back to work.

Those who see in liberalism a flaccid pacifism either don't know history or seek to distort it. Liberals have always stood in sharp opposition to fanaticism and violence, and against religious bigotry, totalitarianism, and nationalist zealotry. Liberal ideals inspired Americans to confront Hitler's fascism and Soviet totalitarianism, not only with our military might but also with our moral clarity about the sanctity of human life. In contrast to the "us" versus "them" swagger of Radcons, liberals understand our interdependence. They've held to the goal of an international community. After World War II they created the United Nations and international economic institutions. They relied on "collective security" against Soviet aggression. They pioneered a system of international law and human rights.

And it is liberals who again and again have championed decency and tolerance in civic life, in sharp opposition to demagogues who have demonized opponents and blamed the weak for what ails the nation.

These ideals—this profound insistence that Americans are all in it together, this search for practical reforms to make democracy and the economy work better for average people, this bulwark against bigotry and fanaticism, this smart internationalism, this demand for decency and tolerance—*this* is the true, robust liberalism, not the Radcons' paranoid delusion of the sixties left. And this is the liberalism that must be resurrected and adapted more effectively to our times because our times demand it.

I believe most Americans still share these mainstream liberal values. At the level of specific policies, polls show* a majority of Americans in favor of abortion rights, privacy to do whatever they want in their own bedrooms, civil liberties, and religion apart from the public schools. They want to ensure that top corporate and Wall Street executives act in the interests of small investors who have entrusted to them their savings for college and retirement. They want money out of politics. They support a progressive system of taxation, good public schools, and social insurance for those who slip and fall in a new economy that's inherently unstable. And they want a foreign

---

* For public opinion polls, see Appendix A. On public opinion generally, see Alan Wolfe, *One Nation, After All: What Middle-Class Americans Really Think About* (New York: Viking, 1998); John B. Judis and Ruy Teixeira, *The Emerging Democratic Majority* (New York: Scribner, 2002).

policy that effectively guards against terrorism by engaging and involving all our major and long-standing allies. They want an America that leads the world because of its moral authority, not one that aspires to control the world through military might.

But radical conservatism is setting the public agenda, and all of these items are "in play." Courts or legislatures are deliberating some of them; the executive branch has turned its back on others; or Radcons have created the false impression they are supporting them when in fact they are systematically undermining them. Right-wing views that were on the fringe of the Republican Party in the sixties and seventies—propounded then by a ragtag collection of Bible-thumpers, nativists, racists, anti–New Dealers, free-market fundamentalists, and rabid anti-communists—are now center stage.

Although Al Gore won the popular vote in 2000, for at least the past two decades radical conservatives have gained power steadily at all levels of government. They have risen to control Congress and the White House, most governorships, and the majority of state legislatures. Their views are represented in a steadily increasing proportion of the nation's school boards and a growing number of the nation's courtrooms.

I'm writing this book because I want to reach people, perhaps like you, who share liberal values even if you don't call yourself a "liberal"; people who are alarmed by the Radcon ascendance and the one-sidedness and shrillness of public debate in America, even if you're not a political partisan. I want you to understand the Radcon agenda for what it really is. And I want to give you the courage of your liberal convictions by helping explain them, and why they're so crucially important today.

Radcons have intense convictions; this is a part of their strength. They believe passionately in the righteousness of their cause. They are quite certain they represent the forces of good in a war against evil. And in making their case, they have cleverly and eagerly usurped the basic American values of morality, prosperity, and patriotism. In recent years liberals have had too little to say about these values. They have ceded the terrain to Radcons by default. In the following pages, I will try to correct this.

There is no "vast right-wing conspiracy." Radcons have risen by means of a highly efficient, self-reinforcing system designed to shape public opinion and politics. The system consists of a steady stream of money from corporate executives, wealthy ideologues, conservative family foundations, and Radcon media tycoons. It relies on a tight political alliance with the evangelical Christian right, and depends on a cadre of political operatives and southern and mountain-state legislators committed to winning at any cost. And it presents itself through a shock troop of radio and TV talk-show hosts and pundits spinning Radcon views into columns, books, web logs, and broadcast appearances.

All this would create a formidable political advantage for Radcons even if they faced a coherent opposition. But there is none. Liberals are in disarray and on the defensive, if not in hiding. The Democratic Party has ceased to provide viable alternatives apart from individual Democratic candidates or politicians who pop into public consciousness before elections and often vanish just as quickly. As a party, Democrats are undisciplined, intimidated, or just plain silent. The religious left is unorganized and disconnected from political struggle. There are almost no liberal radio or television personalities, few if any liberal pundits, an absence of expressed liberal ideas and ideals in the public arena. Many people who disagree with Radcons have grown disillusioned and demoralized with politics, and figure there's no point fighting back.

Hence, my final purpose in writing this book. If you're not already involved, I want to inspire you to get involved—not just in this or that election, but for the long term. The stakes are enormous, both here and abroad. As the last remaining superpower, America has an extraordinary capacity for good or ill in the world. That means that as citizens of the United States, each of us has enormous leverage.

Introduction

America can exemplify moral leadership or crass narrow-mindedness. We can grow the economy by widening the circle of prosperity, at home and elsewhere around the globe, or further widen the perilous gap between the rich and everyone else. We can unite much of the world against terrorism and hate or merely assert our bullying self-interest.

What we do as a nation depends to a large extent on what you and others like you decide to do in the months and years ahead. Politics is the applied form of democracy. If we fail to act, we not only cede democracy to the radical conservatives, but in doing so we give them control over the wealthiest and most powerful nation in the history of the world.

The radical conservative assault on America is well under way. Radcons must be met head-on by a bold and intelligent liberalism founded upon a love of America and grounded in public morality and common sense. We can—and will—win the battle for America because we better represent true American ideals. What's more, we have reason on our side, which is more than the Radcons can honestly claim. But idealism and reason bring us only halfway there. Winning back America will depend also on our organization, our passion, and our courage.

CHAPTER ONE

PRELUDE:
THE REVENGE OF THE RADCONS

WEALTH AND POWER

It might help you to know a few things about me so that you understand where I'm coming from. I was born in Scranton, Pennsylvania, and grew up in a rural part of New York State, near the Connecticut border. My father worked six days a week and my mother five days a week at their two clothing stores. We weren't poor, but I remember my father worrying a lot about paying the bills. Another thing you should know is I was very short for my age. I still am. Both my parents were normal size, so my short height was something of a puzzle. But being a very short boy, it was natural I got picked on at school.

There's no way of proving these things, but I suppose my early worries about paying the bills and being bullied had a few long-term effects. As an adult, I've been teaching and writing about the economy and government—that is, about wealth and power. I've also had the honor of serving under three presidents, most recently in Bill Clinton's cabinet. In these roles I've tried to help people without much money get better jobs, and also tried to stop some corporations from abusing their power.

The market is where wealth is accumulated; politics is where public power is exercised. In a democracy, they are supposed to be kept

11

separate. But in fact, people with a lot of wealth exert significant political power, and people with a lot of power can arrange things so that they end up with a lot of wealth. When wealth and power are concentrated in a relatively few hands, democracy can become a sham and a lot of bullying can occur. The great liberal Supreme Court justice Louis Brandeis put it best more than sixty years ago: "We can have democracy in this country or we can have great wealth concentrated in the hands of a few, but we cannot have both."[1] We are now losing our democracy, and we have to get it back.

I never used to think of myself as being a liberal. Compared to most students in the sixties, I was considered pretty conservative. I went to Dartmouth College, whose political epicenter in those days was about 25,000 miles to the right of Berkeley.

I rejected a lot of the values and politics of the student New Left of the sixties. Taking over college buildings and burning American flags seemed dumb to me. I viewed the Vietnam War as morally wrong but never drifted into the cynicism or anti-Americanism of some of my leftist friends, who started spelling America with a "k." I always believed it possible to reform the nation by working within the political system—and still do. I spent much of my senior year campaigning for Eugene McCarthy, by then the only presidential candidate who vowed to end the war. And I've spent a big portion of my life since then in public service. While I've never refrained from criticizing our political leaders when I thought they were wrong, I've always had a deep love for this country. To me, America is a great, noble, continuing experiment. We haven't achieved our ideals by a long shot. But the ideals are still worth working for: protecting the weak from the strong, overcoming prejudice, providing broad opportunity to everyone, creating a vibrant democracy.

My first full-time job after law school was working for Robert Bork at the Justice Department, in Gerald Ford's administration. Bork, you may remember, was the person who fired the special prosecutor, Archibald Cox, during the Watergate investigation. Cox had been trying to get the White House to hand over tape recordings of conversations that would show if Richard Nixon was involved in the Watergate break-ins. Nixon finally handed over the tapes anyway, on August 5, 1974. He knew their contents would condemn him. Four days later, Nixon resigned. A few weeks after that, I arrived in Washington and reported to Bork.

Bork had been one of my professors at law school. I didn't share his political views but I respected him. So when he asked me to come to Washington, I accepted. My job was to write briefs on behalf of the United States in cases that were to come before the Supreme Court. I stayed two years before moving to the Federal Trade Commission, after Jimmy Carter was elected president. Bork went on to become one of the most thoughtful radical conservatives in America. You may recall that in 1987 Ronald Reagan nominated him to the Supreme Court, setting off an intense battle over his confirmation. I quote Bork at some length in this book because his writing has been so influential among radical conservatives. I still disagree with him, but I still respect him.

It's possible to disagree and yet still be respectful. I strongly disagree with, but know and respect, several of the radical conservatives I quote in this book—not only Bork but also Bill Bennett, a former Reagan administration official who has become the Radcon voice of public morality; Bill Kristol, the editor of the *Weekly Standard*, who has articulated much of Radcon foreign policy; and Newt Gingrich, the former Speaker of the House. Their ideas deserve a fair hearing, and a clear case should be made for why they are dangerously wrong.

In the sixties (a period that in political and cultural terms actually ran from about 1964 to 1972), the New Left was the source of most of the political passion and intensity in America. Liberals were considered wimps—wishy-washy, bourgeois. The militant organizer Saul Alinsky adopted the definition of a liberal as someone "who leaves the room when a fight begins."

Now it's hard to find any sixties lefties, except maybe in the rarefied precincts of a few universities where aging radicals still debate Marxism and deconstruction. Most of the political passion and intensity these days are on the radical conservative right.

But the two extremes—what remains of the sixties left, and the Radcons—share much of the same sense of moral superiority, the same unwillingness to consider alternative points of view.* There's an important difference, though: The left never gained the power in America that the Radcons now have.

In my view, both extremes are wrong. Liberals, on the other hand, doubt that anyone has a monopoly on the truth. That's why liberals place such a high value on tolerance and democracy. That's why liberals have insisted on a clear separation between church and state. And it's also why liberals worry about wealth and power. When wealth and power become concentrated in the hands of a relatively few citizens, the strong become stronger; everyone else, more vulnerable.

The word "liberal" was used by George Washington to indicate a person of generosity or broad-mindedness, as opposed to those who wanted to deprive Catholics and Jews of their constitutional rights.[2] Franklin D. Roosevelt defined a "liberal" this way: "[S]ay that civilization is a tree which, as it grows, continually produces rot and dead wood. The radical says: 'Cut it down.' The conservative says: 'Don't touch it.' The liberal compromises: 'Let's prune, so that we lose neither the old trunk nor the new branches.' "[3] FDR himself expanded and altered the common understanding of liberalism. Before the New Deal, liberalism was mostly about protecting people's freedom.

---

* Even some of the individuals are the same: A few lefties from the sixties transported their moral absolutism to the radical right in the late seventies and eighties and became "neoconservatives." The term is generally applied to those who moved from far left to far right, but for the purposes of this discussion, I include them together with other Radcons.

But the Great Depression taught America that unemployment and bad luck could be just as harmful to personal freedom as tyranny. Protection against these required a larger role for government.

Henceforth, liberals were assumed to be in favor of a big government. But that's way too simple. The government's size or reach isn't the issue. It's what government does and whose interests it represents. Does it guard our civil liberties or intrude on our privacy? Does it protect the weak or promote the strong? I don't want a big government eavesdropping on my private telephone calls or e-mail, checking the books I've borrowed from the library, monitoring my movements, telling me what I can and can't say. I don't want a big government pouring billions of dollars into big companies—energy behemoths, agribusinesses, pharmaceutical giants, whatever—because they've made large political donations. And I don't like the idea of a giant military machine mounting "preemptive" wars without international backing. I don't want a big government that's the center of an intimidating, unaccountable empire.

Being a liberal isn't at all the same as being in favor of big government, despite what Radcons claim. Most liberals would prefer a small government that supported and protected the little guy over a big government that did the bidding of the wealthy and powerful. Frankly, people I know are more worried that our democracy is being corrupted by an increasing flow of campaign money from rich people and corporations to politicians. I also don't want a big government imposing any particular religious view on me or my kids, or on anyone else. In my view, government has no business telling people how to run their private lives or dictating personal morality. I don't want government giving or withholding funds to promote marriage, discouraging childbearing by welfare mothers, or pushing religion in our public schools.

Again: Government's size isn't the issue. It's what it does, and for whom.

RADCONS AREN'T REAL CONSERVATIVES

Here, briefly and in its most undiluted form, is the Radcon agenda for America:

- prevent sex before marriage

- ban abortion

- condemn homosexuality

- prohibit gay marriage

- require prayer in the public schools

- give large tax breaks mainly to the rich

- cut social services mainly for the poor

- "privatize" social insurance

- eliminate regulations on business

- allow pollution of the environment

- ban affirmative action

- impose long prison sentences and, for the most serious crimes, the death penalty

- make English the official national language

- invade and occupy countries that may harbor or help terrorists

- go it alone in foreign affairs, disregarding the United Nations and avoiding international treaties

- squelch dissent about foreign policy

- restrict civil liberties for the sake of national security.

Most open-minded Americans will grant that there are arguments for and against each of these positions. What defines a Radcon is not openness to the case for them but fervent certainty they're correct and necessary, and disdain for those who disagree.

This list, of course, doesn't cover all radical conservative goals. And not every radical conservative subscribes to every one of them. But most radical conservatives agree on most. The consensus among Radcons is strong because these goals are based on a common worldview—both about the forces America is battling at home and abroad, and about how these forces can best be overcome.

Most of this book is about why these views are wrong, what a vigorous liberalism stands for instead, and why our future depends on the latter. But it's important at the outset to understand the roots of radical conservatism. Radcons, it must be noted, are very different from real conservatives. A real conservative is somebody like the late Senator Robert A. Taft, of Ohio, or Senator John McCain, of Arizona—someone who wants to *conserve* many of the things that are great about America: the value we place on hard work, our dedication to family and community, our love of freedom, our storehouse of generosity and tolerance.

Real conservatives are cautious. They're skeptical of big ideas, grand plans, risky moves. When change is necessary, they prefer doing it gradually, carefully, methodically, step-by-step. And they're meticulous about laws and procedures: Means are as important to them as ends. They admire the great eighteenth-century British philosopher Edmund Burke, for whom the French Revolution offered a lesson in how easily radical change could get out of hand, how quickly the good could be destroyed along with the bad. "When the subject of demolition and construction is not brick and timber, but sentient beings," Burke wrote, "multitudes may be rendered miserable." Burke believed in going slowly. "Circumspection and caution are part of wisdom."[4] I believe that, too.

But radical conservatives are revolutionaries. For them, ends justify means. They'll do whatever it takes to win. Listen to Paul Weyrich, prominent Radcon founder of the Heritage Foundation and coiner of the term "Moral Majority": "We are no longer working to preserve the status quo. We are radicals, working to overturn the present power structure of the country."[5]

Radcons are intent on dramatic change and are willing to bet the ranch on unproven theories. For example, even if you believe that giving giant tax breaks to rich people who are already fabulously wealthy will cause them to invest the extra money in new factories and machines, and hence grow the economy, you've got to admit it's a big gamble. If the Radcons are wrong about this, a lot of things go wrong: The federal budget goes bust, long-term interest rates go sky-high, and baby boomers don't get the Social Security or Medicare they're counting on. Real conservatives wouldn't take this gamble. They're wary about public debt; they're fiscally prudent to a fault.

Even if you think it's smart to disregard the United Nations and international law, and unilaterally declare war on and then occupy nations capable of passing weapons of mass destruction to terrorists, surely you'll admit it's a giant roll of the dice. If the Radcons are wrong, we could end up stirring up *more* terrorism rather than less. We could find ourselves fighting guerilla wars all over the planet, and suffering a police state at home.

Real conservatives are concerned about civility. They have codes of honor and rules of conduct. They worry about the "coarsening" of American culture. And they're wary of demagogues who stir people up. Edmund Burke, again: "Rage and frenzy will pull down more in half an hour than prudence, deliberation, and foresight can build up in a hundred years."[6]

When I was about ten, I sat for hours at a time on the porch of an old codger who lived down the street. He told me Franklin D. Roosevelt was the worst thing ever to happen to this country and that communists were taking over America. Even at that young age I knew he was spouting nonsense. But I kept returning to his front porch for two reasons. First, he bribed me with lemonade and cookies. Second, he was one of the nicest people I'd ever met. He was a gentleman. I appreciated that. He taught me that traditional conservatives were polite. They were even willing to argue a point.

But radical conservatives are uncivil in the extreme. They fill the public airwaves and bookstores with nastiness. Listen to Radcon talk radio or cable TV news and what you mostly hear are venomous diatribes. Read the editorial pages of the *Wall Street Journal, Weekly Standard, Washington Times, New York Post, New York Sun,* or any other Radcon outlet, and you find vicious attacks. Open a Radcon political best-seller and you find more mean-spirited screeds. Radcons typically reduce political debate to nonsensical statements that seem to be making a point but are nothing but vague and angry assertions, unsupported by facts.

- America is "being overrun by psycho-lib Commu-Nazi organizations like the ACLU who defend child molesters and terrorists." This from Michael Savage, talk-show host.[7]

- "The liberal catechism includes a hatred of Christians, guns, the profit motive, and political speech and an infatuation with abortion, the environment, and race discrimination. . . . [T]hey hate 'flag-wavers,' they hate abortion opponents, they hate all religions except Islam (post 9/11)," writes Ann Coulter, author and pundit.[8]

- "The Democrats—far too many of them—are evil, pure and simple. They have no redeeming social value. They are outright traitors themselves or apologists for treasonous behavior. They are enemies of the American people and the American way of life," says Joseph Farah, web logger.[9]

- The American people reject what is "abnormal or perverted" including "commie libs," "feminazis," and "environmental wackos." This from Rush Limbaugh, talk-show host.[10]

• Why did 9/11 happen? "I really believe that the pagans, and the abortionists, and the feminists, and the gays and the lesbians who are actively trying to make that an alternative lifestyle, the ACLU, People for the American Way—all of them who have tried to secularize America—I point the finger in their face and say, 'You helped this happen.'" This from the Reverend Jerry Falwell. (Falwell subsequently backed away from this televised remark.)[11]

• Islam is a "very wicked and evil religion," says the Reverend Franklin Graham.[12]

•"A little nutty, a little slutty." This was how David Brock described law professor Anita Hill after she testified against Clarence Thomas; the description was used repeatedly by other radical conservatives.[13]

• "Head shots. Head shots." This is the way G. Gordon Liddy, a radio talk-show host, instructed his listeners on how to assassinate government agents from the Bureau of Alcohol, Tobacco, and Firearms.[14]

• "Barney Fag" is how Dick Armey, then House majority leader, referred to Representative Barney Frank, a gay member of Congress. (Armey subsequently apologized.)

By offering this sampling of quotes, I don't mean to tar all Radcons with the intemperate words of a few. Nor do I want to blame anyone for a slip of the tongue or a thoughtless gaffe later regretted. I want only to point out an incontrovertible pattern. I could have offered any number of quotations from the books, broadcasts, and political campaigns of radical conservatives. What unites them is their stridency and meanness.

Nasty politics is hardly new to America, of course. The two major slogans of the 1884 presidential campaign were "Blaine, Blaine,

James G. Blaine, the continental liar from the state of Maine," and "Ma, Ma, where's my pa? Gone to the White House, ha, ha, ha!" (the latter referring to Grover Cleveland's alleged illegitimate child). If you've entered the public arena, you've got to expect mud to be slung in your direction. I've run for office and let me tell you: If you don't already have a thick hide, you're in trouble.

Radcons aren't alone in their capacity for nastiness, either. Liberals and Democrats have also smeared opponents. They treated Robert Bork during his Supreme Court nomination fight as shabbily as anyone has been treated in public life.

But what we're now witnessing is something far more corrosive of civic life than the normal political vitriol: It's a viciousness directed toward anyone holding a view other than the prevailing radical conservatism. Insults are also calculated to belittle and ridicule entire groups who have relatively little power in our society—blacks, the poor, Hispanic-Americans, Arab-Americans, immigrants. Or who are judged to be "different"—gays, feminists, Muslims.

This kind of generalized venom closes off reasoned debate, chills dissent, and cuts people off from one another. It is especially dangerous to democracy when it's bankrolled by large amounts of money; when its perpetrators ally themselves ideologically with those who run our government; when it so dominates the media—talk radio, talk television, books, and the Internet—that the public hears and sees little else; and when it's repeated so often it becomes the accepted norm. Unfortunately, all of this is now the case.

The liberal tradition values free speech and debate. No one should be deterred from speaking his or her mind for fear of offending some group. I have little patience for "political correctness." But liberalism also values civility and a fair exchange of views. The mindless, mean-spirited trash talk that fills Radcon books and radio and television broadcasts panders to the worst in us and demeans us all. It may sell, but that's no defense; so does hard-core porn. Shame on those who poison our public life this way.

THE RADCON THEORY OF EVIL

I've asked myself repeatedly why Radcons are so often vicious and uncompromising, so willing to sacrifice means to ends. Marxists would say they're just shilling for the rich. Ordinary cynics would say they're motivated by the lure of great wealth or the headiness of power. But I think these interpretations are unfair. In my experience, most radical conservatives hold their beliefs sincerely. They're convinced they are speaking the truth—though often imprecisely or illogically—and are acting in the interest of the broad public.

To understand their radicalism, you need to understand their notion of evil.

To Radcons, the major threat to the security of our nation, the stability of our families, our future prosperity, and the capacity of our children to grow into responsible adults is a dark, satanic force. It exists within America in the form of moral deviance—out-of-wedlock births, homosexuality, abortion, crime. It potentially exists within every one of us in the form of sloth and devastating irresponsibility. It exists outside America in the form of "evil empires" or an "axis of evil."

There's no compromising with such evil. It has to be countered with everything we have. Religious faith and discipline are the means of redemption. Punishment and coercion are the only real deterrents. Fear is the essential motivator.

This overarching principle connects Radcon foreign policy and domestic policy with evangelical Christian fundamentalism. It forms a coherent system for thinking about and dealing with any problem. Sexual urges must be constrained, lest they cause the moral rot of America. Crime must be dealt with harshly or it will multiply. All of us must be subject to the discipline of the market, lest we succumb to lassitude and irresponsibility. American power must be asserted forcefully all over the world or foreign evil will overwhelm us.

Unless it is disciplined, the evil that lurks within all human beings will push civilization into chaos. "Every new generation constitutes a wave of savages who must be civilized," writes Robert Bork in his apocalyptic and influential 1996 best-seller, *Slouching Towards Gomorrah*. An undisciplined society "cannot summon the will to suppress public obscenity, punish crime, reform welfare, attach stigma to the bearing of illegitimate children, resist the demands of self-proclaimed victim groups for preferential treatment, or maintain standards of reason and scholarship. That is precisely and increasingly our situation today."[15]

To Radcons, unconstrained sex is evil. Sex outside marriage is evil. Homosexuality is evil. After the Supreme Court voted to strike down a Texas law criminalizing homosexual behavior in 2003, the Reverend Pat Robertson, the television evangelist, told his followers that the Court had "entered into the arena on the side of evil" (while praying that ill health would disable those responsible for the ruling).[16]

Radcons took the terrorist attacks of September 11, 2001, as confirmation of their moral mission to extirpate evil around the world. "A calculated, malignant, devastating evil has entered the world," explained Attorney General John Ashcroft.[17] "And we know God is not neutral," added George W. Bush.[18]

It's true, of course, that there are terrible people in the world who have done, or may yet do, abhorrent things to their fellow human beings. Hitler, Stalin, Osama bin Laden and others responsible for 9/11, Saddam Hussein, and Slobodan Milosevic all deserve to be called evil. So do those who presided and carried out genocide, or "ethnic cleansing," in Cambodia, Rwanda, Armenia, Kashmir, Burma, and elsewhere.

But there's a vast difference between calling someone or some group "evil" because of what they have done and using "evil" as an explanation for why they acted as they did and as a description of their goals. To think of "evil" as a satanic force that has "entered the world" suggests that our only alternative—and only hope for survival—is to expunge it. Evil cannot only be contained, reduced, negotiated with, offset, limited, impounded, constrained, or embargoed. If it is truly evil, it must be eliminated. You cannot be partly evil or potentially evil. You cannot, as someone who is not evil, occasionally side with evil, or think evil might have a point. You are either evil or you are good. If you are evil, or in league with evil, you must be eviscerated. If you have allowed yourself to be overtaken or tempted by evil, you must be cleansed, converted, and reborn. All or nothing. You are either with us or against us. For the Radcons, it's that simple.

Likewise, if you're good, you needn't bother yourself with second thoughts or subtle reasoning. You don't have to think through the consequences of your choices since there is no risk they will have evil effects.

The liberal tradition has never seen the world in such starkly Manichean terms. Where Radcons seek to expunge or destroy evil, liberals instinctively try to prevent or contain bad actions, even if the acts are abominable. The classic liberals of the seventeenth and eighteenth centuries rejected the medieval notion that satanic forces could take over human beings. They opposed religious persecution, the stoning of witches and wizards, and the common view that strangers and foreigners were contaminated. Modern liberals celebrate diversity and preach tolerance. They believe that what consenting adults do in private is no one else's business. They are willing to punish crime, but prefer to give young people a good education and job opportunities so that they don't fall into it. They accept the disciplinary force of the market, but think that people need to be protected against unforeseen risks or bad luck. They unambiguously oppose tyranny and brutality, but would rather find ways to prevent it through the spread of prosperity and democracy than by responding in every instance with military force.

These are more than differences of degree. They represent fundamentally different views about what threatens the human race and how best to deal with such threats.

In its moral absolutism, its faith in the redemptive power of discipline, its emphasis on punishment, and its theory of evil—in all these respects, radical conservatism sees itself as the counterforce to the sixties left. No matter that the sixties left has all but vanished. According to Radcons, it released an evil into the world that still imperils American civilization. Redeeming America requires that every trace of that sixties thinking and culture be erased—its sexual promiscuity, its radical egalitarianism, its godlessness, its disdain for authority, its humiliating defeat in Vietnam.

THE ABOMINABLE SIXTIES

The poet Philip Larkin writes:

> *Sexual intercourse began*
> *in nineteen sixty-three*
> *(Which was rather late for me)—*
> *Between the end of the Chatterley ban*
> *And the Beatles' first LP.*[19]

Dartmouth College is in Hanover, New Hampshire, about halfway up the border between New Hampshire and Vermont. I arrived in September 1964, before coeducation and before the interstate highway reached there. In other words, I went to school in Siberia. The college handbook warned that "fornication" was grounds for expulsion, but the college had little reason to worry. Girls (if you could find them) were allowed in dorm rooms only on weekends during daylight hours. Doors had to remain ajar and at least three of your feet had to remain on the floor, which resulted in some creative positioning. By the way, Dartmouth wasn't alone in its commitment to abstinence. I distinctly remember a sign in the lobby of one Wellesley dorm, solemnly instructing that "Men Will Withdraw By Ten."

All this changed in three years. The ground had shifted—not the granite under New Hampshire but entire tectonic plates underlying much of the Western world. The college handbook no longer banned fornication. Although Dartmouth hadn't yet gone co-ed, young women seemed to be all over the place at all hours. In fact, I began knowing some of them as people rather than the objects of my frustrated libido. And many of them started viewing themselves in a new light as well. They saw no reason they shouldn't become lawyers or doctors or business executives or anything else we young men aspired to be.

Marijuana also arrived on campus, in such quantity it must have been delivered daily in Mack trucks. Then, as if on cue, the Beatles turned hallucinogenic, the civil rights movement turned militant, hair lengthened considerably, Lyndon Johnson ordered up 50,000 more soldiers for Vietnam, and students began burning American flags. Sex, feminism, drugs, rock and roll, black power, flower power, power to the people, make love not war—the boomers came of age and America was never the same.

We boomers comprised the largest generation in American history. We began appearing in this world about nine months after my father, Ed Reich, and millions of other men from the "greatest generation" returned from war in 1945. By the spring and early summer of 1946, hospitals everywhere were jammed, diapers and cribs in short supply, baby clothes unavailable.

My mother gave birth to me on June 24, in Scranton, Pennsylvania. Twelve days later, on July 6, in New Haven, Connecticut, George W. was born. On July 21, Kenny Starr arrived. Kenny's future nemesis, Bill Clinton (born Billy Blythe III), came along a few weeks after. And on and on they emerged: George's future wife, Laura, that November; adorable Danny Quayle, the following February; Tom DeLay, later the fierce Republican majority leader, in April; Hillary Rodham, in October; Tom Daschle, December; sweet little Clarence Thomas, the next June; and within two years, several million other boomers, including cute Rush Limbaugh and cuddly little Bill O'Reilly.

Many of the boomers were raised according to the progressive dictums of Dr. Benjamin Spock, whose *Baby and Child Care* was first published that same boom year of 1946. Spock's book became the bible of post–World War II parenting, eventually selling more than fifty million copies. It told young parents that their children's needs were as legitimate as their own. Parents were to be rational and flexible with the little darlings, not arbitrary and absolute. They were to reason with and respect them, listen to their counterarguments and be prepared to be persuaded, and use approval rather than punishment as a way of motivating them.

Why did so many boomer parents accept Spock's advice? Perhaps they were reacting to the fresh scars of Nazi fascism and Soviet totalitarianism. Harsh, authoritarian discipline and punishment may have seemed uncomfortably close to the agonies the world had just endured. Maybe American society concluded, at some deep level of collective unconsciousness, that it had to reject the previous generation's model of strict fathering in favor of nurturing mothering.[20] Whatever prompted boomer parents to alter the older patterns of child rearing, emphasizing obedience to authority, the results were indisputable.

Taking these boomer adolescents out of their homes simultaneously in the 1960s, squeezing so many of them into holding bins called universities, letting their hormones rage, allowing their antiauthoritarianism free rein, and you had a formula for spontaneous combustion. Add in a civil rights movement that ignited the hopes of blacks until it got bogged down in northern inner-city poverty, and you had an explosion. Mix in a deeply unpopular war in Vietnam whose casualties were escalating, and a draft that threatened to force most young men to fight it, and you had a revolution.

The revolution occurred elsewhere around the world, too. A similarly giant wave of boomers hit Europe and parts of Asia, bringing America's anti-authoritarian boomer culture with them.

Of course, not all boomers were revolutionaries, by a long shot. Many of those who would become the advanced guard of the Radcon movement were also in college when the revolution occurred. Unlike most of the boomers, many of them were appalled by what they witnessed.

Some were intimidated by the wild goings-on. Others were college Republicans who had patiently worked the system and resented that it was now falling apart. Many southerners and westerners from churchgoing or military families were horrified at the decline of authority and at the casual anti-Americanism. There were also the children of Jewish intellectuals who fell under the spell of the University of Chicago's Leo Strauss, who taught that the goal of political life ought to be an objective sense of virtue and social order, not freedom and tolerance.

Many of them would eventually become counterrevolutionaries. As early as 1978, in his first successful race for Congress from Georgia, Newt Gingrich declared war on the sixties. "People like me are what stand between us and Auschwitz," he said. "I see evil around me every day. . . . We were promised all the multi-partner sex you wanted and penicillin would take care of it. We were promised all the recreational drugs you wanted and it wouldn't be dangerous, wouldn't be addictive. . . . The left-wing Democrats represent the party of total hedonism, total exhibitionism, total bizarreness, total weirdness, and the total right to cripple innocent people in the name of letting hooligans loose."[21]

A lot of America's traditional blue-collar families agreed. To them, the student radicals of the sixties represented the opposite of everything that was good about America—personal morality and the family, order, the value of hard work, and patriotism. Some of these white working-class families, especially in the South, had already been alienated by the civil rights movement; some in the North were turned off by forced busing and affirmative action. The hedonism of the student lefties was enough to send them careening toward the hellfire-and-brimstone of the radical conservatives.

Radcons continue to exploit the white working class's disgust. "What a mess the sixties were. A real nightmare. We almost lost the country," writes Radcon talk-show host Michael Savage in his 2003 best-seller, *The Savage Nation*. "The joy of America in the fifties was unmatched. . . . I loved the values of the fifties. . . . Everything was normal. Then, all of a sudden, the freaks popped up out of the woodwork and ruined America. . . . Tragically, we've never recovered from the sixties' madness."[22]

For Radcons, the sixties left was the source of America's subsequent moral decline. Historian Gertrude Himmelfarb blames it for "the collapse of ethical principles and habits, the loss of respect for authorities and institutions, the breakdown of the family, the decline of civility, the vulgarization of high culture, and the degradation of popular culture."[23]

Bill Bennett, the Radcon "morality czar" who was secretary of education under Reagan and in charge of the anti-drug campaign in the first Bush administration, finds in the sixties a "root cause" for the subsequent rise in divorce and out-of-wedlock births in America. The American family fractured because of "the massive shift in cultural, personal, and sexual values that began in the mid to late 1960s and took hold in the 1970s." In "the years of the New Left and the counterculture, of campus rioting and the spread of recreational drugs, Americans came to place a much higher premium on individualism, on unrestricted personal liberty, and on personal choice. Authority and traditional institutions were called into question."[24]

The editors of the *Wall Street Journal* are even able to assign a specific date for "when the U.S., or more precisely when many people within it, began to tip off the emotional tracks." It was "August 1968, when the Democratic National Convention found itself sharing Chicago with the street fighters of the anti-Vietnam War movement."

The *Journal* editors don't blame the protesters. They blame the "intellectuals—university professors, politicians and journalistic commentators—who said then that the *acts* committed by the protesters were justified or explainable." The editors continue: "That was the beginning. After Chicago, the justifications never really stopped. America had a new culture, for political action and personal living. . . . [The establishment] defended each succeeding act of defiance—against the war, against university presidents, against corporate practices, against behavior codes, against dress codes, against virtually all agents of established authority." Henceforth, the shapers of American opinion "would blow right past the broken rules to seek an understanding of the 'dissidents' (in the '6os and '7os) and 'activists' (in the '8os and now). Concurrently, the personal virtue known as self-restraint was devalued."[25]

This is nonsense, as I will show.

Radcons also link the disdain for established authority on the part of sixties rebels with America's defeat in Vietnam. To Radcons, Vietnam wasn't just a national humiliation; it represented the ultimate erosion of authority and discipline. "Something is still at stake in the argument over Vietnam," writes Bork. "The debate about that war is a contest between two opposed ways of viewing the world, whose current form is the war in the culture."[26]

The Vietnam War marked the epitome of leftist anti-Americanism, but the Radcons saw it as just the beginning. "The profound tremor that went through American society starting in about 1965 was not just about the Vietnam War," writes Mona Charen, Radcon columnist and author. "Some deep wellsprings of dissatisfaction, petulance, and irritability were tapped by the war. All at once, everything about American society—from its 'materialism' to its supposed 'militarism'—was decried and despised. . . . [I]n the mid-1960s, leftist anti-Americanism went mainstream. They condemned America for its poverty and at the same time for its consumerism. They demanded (and got) sexual license and grade inflation."[27]

In the Radcon worldview, the anti-war flag burnings, protest marches, and critiques of American values that emerged from the sixties also undermined America's military resolve. For liberals and Democrats, writes Charen, "the Vietnam War was immoral . . . and America as a nation was a depraved predator whose power represented a danger to the rest of the world."[28] Bill Bennett believes that "since Vietnam and especially since our defeat there, our culture has undergone a process that one observer has aptly termed *debellicization*. Military virtues have been devalued and shunned, and along with them the very idea that war solves anything or is ever justified."[29]

This presumed legacy explains, in part, why the Radcons have been so determined to reassert American power around the globe. Winning the Cold War wasn't enough; America won because the Soviet Union fell apart from the inside. To redeem America's greatness and to purge the nation of the anti-Americanism of the sixties, America must maintain preeminent military power. It must mount preemptive wars against potentially hostile nations. And it must disown any international organization or treaty that stands in the way of American hegemony.

This Radcon view emerged long before the terrorist attacks of 9/11. As early as 1992, a "Defense Planning Guidance" statement, drafted for then defense secretary Dick Cheney by Paul Wolfowitz (who became deputy defense secretary in the George W. Bush administration), called for "preemptive" attacks on nations that posed potential threats to the United States, and increases in military spending to the point where American power could not possibly be challenged.[30] In 1998, Donald Rumsfeld, among others, urged Bill Clinton to make removal of Saddam Hussein and his regime "the aim of American foreign policy."[31]

But the sixties occurred more than three decades ago, you might say. Why would radical conservatives continue to blame the sixties?

They do so because, in the Radcon worldview, the sixties are still with us. "[W]e see at work in today's culture the same attitudes, indeed many of the same people, that undermined America then," writes Bork. "Our division over the Vietnam conflict has been called America's second Civil War. 'Healing' will not happen until the people who remember have passed from this world."[32]

Surgeons have long known of a phenomenon called the "phantom limb." Someone who loses an arm or leg often continues to feel the limb despite its absence. The nerve endings haven't adjusted to the fact that the appendage is no longer there, and send signals back to the brain *as if* the arm or leg were still attached.

The Radcons' continuing obsession with the sixties left is roughly analogous. Radcons simply refuse to accept that the sixties are over and that the left of those days has disappeared. In point of fact, the limb is gone. Some of the student radicals of the sixties became aging hippies and moved to rural enclaves in Vermont, northern California, and other leftie preserves. A few drifted to university faculties. Some are still active in left-leaning politics. But most are middle-aged adults who do ordinary things like sell insurance or aluminum siding and bring up their families as best they can. They no longer burn draft cards or bras. Their politics is far more moderate than it was thirty years ago. Some, as I've said, have even become Radcons.

Yet to the Radcons, the student revolutionaries of the sixties are still poisoning America. "The Sixties may be seen in the universities as a mini–French Revolution that seemed to fail, but ultimately did not. . . . They and their ideology are all around us now," writes Bork. "It is important to understand what the Sixties turmoil was about, for the youth culture that became manifest then is the modern liberal culture of today."[33]

Herewith, the deep paranoia of America's radical right: They fear that sixties revolutionaries went underground after graduating, only to reappear in recent years as adults holding the same revolutionary values they did before. They're more dangerous now because they're disguised as normal, mild-mannered people. Some are in positions of leadership and their radicalism is secret. Here's Bork again:

> The temporary abeyance of the Sixties temper was due to the radicals graduating from the universities and becoming invisible until they reached positions of power and influence, as they now have, across the breadth of the culture. They no longer have need for violence or confrontation: since the radicals control the institutions they formerly attacked, the Sixties temper manifests itself in subtler but no less destructive ways. . . .

> [S]tudent radicals provided the McGovern cadres that took the party left in 1972. Later, as Capitol Hill staffers and elected congressmen, they moved the congressional Democrats well to the left of most Americans who consider themselves Democrats. . . . [T]he formulations of the Sixties are now deeply embedded in our opinion-forming institutions and our culture.[34]

This paranoia goes far to explain why Radcons hated Bill and Hillary Clinton from the moment the two arrived in Washington at the end of 1992. The first boomer inhabitants of the White House, they represented what the Radcons detested most about the sixties— its lack of discipline, its self-indulgence, its sexual permissiveness, its anti-war softness, and its in-your-face feminism. Rumors of Clinton's extramarital history had dogged his 1992 campaign; he famously avoided the draft; his first act as president was to issue an executive order allowing gays to serve in the military. Then he put his wife in charge of the most important initiative of his first term, health care.

"The spirit of the Sixties revived in the Eighties and brought us at last to Bill and Hillary Clinton, the very personifications of the Sixties generation arrived at early middle age with its ideological baggage intact," sniffs Bork, on the second page of his book.[35]

When I read Bork's words in 1996 my mind immediately flashed back to a quarter century before, when Bill, Hillary, and I listened obediently to Bork's law school lectures and eagerly answered the questions he put to us in class. Clarence Thomas sat in the same classrooms. None of us bore any resemblance to sixties revolutionaries. We were the very models of ambitious young people, seeking law school degrees so that perhaps one day we could, at most, help reform the system.

The Lewinsky scandal during Clinton's second term seemed to confirm for Radcons what they had suspected all along. Bill Bennett chided Americans who said they believed the charges against Clinton but didn't care about them. It was like "making a deal with the devil."[36] The challenge was not just removing Clinton from office but eradicating "decadence" in the country.[37]

Tom DeLay, then House majority whip, told a Baptist delegation in Texas that Clinton had to be impeached because he had "the wrong world view." DeLay told them God was using him to promote a "Biblical world view" in American politics instead.[38]

I don't excuse Clinton's behavior with Monica Lewinsky. His behavior was wrong; his lies about it even more so. Yet now, as I look back on the entire sordid business from a time when the nation is grappling with terrorism and war, it seems woefully trivial.

Like other puritanical upheavals in history, the Radcon movement is a counterrevolution against perceived moral lassitude. To Radcons, global terrorism and domestic degeneracy are symptoms of a deeper threat: an evil that exists around the world and also within each of us, an evil that was released in the sixties and never eradicated. The only sure remedies are coercion, self-discipline, punishment, and religious orthodoxy.

The counterrevolution against the sixties began when Ronald Reagan became president. It gathered momentum in the eighties and nineties, and is now in full force.

THE COUNTERREVOLUTION

By 1980, I was a low-level official in the Carter administration. But it didn't take long for the Reagan White House to find me. I left Washington just as I had begun there six years before—fired with enthusiasm. I got a job as a lecturer at Harvard's Kennedy School of Government, which is a kind of preserve for people who get fired by new presidents.

When I returned to Washington in the early nineties as Bill Clinton's secretary of labor, I discovered a different city from the one I'd left. Washington had been transformed into warring camps. In the intervening years, conservatives and liberals had gone to battle over two Supreme Court nominees—Bork and Clarence Thomas. The battles were intense because the Court was so closely divided on hot-button issues like abortion and prayer in the public schools, and either of these nominees might have tipped the scales. The tactics on both sides were shameful, with liberals demonizing both nominees and conservatives demonizing the liberal demonizers.

After Bork lost his nomination fight, Newt Gingrich announced that Radcons were declaring war: "The left at its core understands in a way Grant understood after Shiloh that this is a civil war, that only one side will prevail, and that the other side will be relegated to history. This war has to be fought with the scale and duration and savagery that is only true of civil wars. While we are lucky in this country that our civil wars are fought at the ballot box, not on the battlefields, nonetheless it is a civil war."[39]

Gingrich understood it would be necessary to resurrect the sixties left in order to inject the nascent radical conservative movement with vitality and purpose. But, in fact, the fights over Bork and Thomas represented the only significant times during the Reagan and elder Bush administrations when the remnants of the left stormed into battle. Most of the student left of the sixties had by then moved on into the Big Chill of careers and families. Most older liberals of the New Deal and Lyndon Johnson's Great Society were sliding into late middle age or retirement. Gingrich's upcoming savage "war" would be notable for the paucity of troops and weaponry on the other side.

Both sides became nastier, but radical conservatives marshaled more resources to promote their nastiness—more money, a more disciplined political organization, more media "shock troops" to back them up. Consider each, in turn:

1. *Money.* The first thing I noticed when I returned to Washington was its new wealth. Washington in the late seventies had still been somewhat tacky. There were far fewer lobbyists then, but whenever one of them wanted to take me out to lunch I'd suggest a small dive called Barney's, right across Pennsylvania Avenue from the Federal Trade Commission. The fanciest meal you could get at Barney's was ham and cheese on two-day-old rye. Barney's also had a fleet of cockroaches. I rarely saw the lobbyist again.

But now Barney's was gone. Pennsylvania Avenue glittered with the polished facades of refurbished hotels, restaurants, and bistros. The dazzle stretched from Georgetown to Capitol Hill—office complexes of glass, chrome, and polished wood; well-appointed condominiums with doormen who knew the names and needs of each inhabitant; hotels with marble-floored lobbies, thick rugs, soft music, and granite counters; restaurants with linen napkins, leather-bound menus, and heavy silverware.

Most of the money came from large corporations, now supporting an army of lobbyists, association executives, communications specialists, media advisers, political consultants, and, of course, political candidates. All were in hot pursuit of deregulation, privatization, and lower taxes—an agenda vigorously promoted by Ronald Reagan and radical conservatives. But Democratic legislators, some of them even liberals, had begun drinking from the same corporate trough. They assumed, correctly, that they held such an iron grip on the House

(Republicans hadn't been in control since 1954) that corporations would support them just to gain access. "Business has to deal with us whether they like it or not, because we're the majority," crowed Democratic Representative Tony Coelho, who became head of the Democratic Congressional Campaign Committee in 1981.[40] Democrats became so dependent on this funding that they would be disabled once they lost power. This dependence would also blur their message and limit their vision in future years, as became evident when many congressional Democrats voted against Bill Clinton's health care plan in 1994 and for George W. Bush's tax cuts in 2001 and 2003.

Money also started flowing into Washington from an avid group of right-wing billionaires and their family foundations, all with the goal of funding the counterrevolution. Out of their benevolence grew a wide assortment of Radcon think tanks, and also the Federalist Society, which became the center of Radcon judicial activism. This story has been well chronicled, and I will not repeat it here.*

2. *Political power.* The Radcon political revolution actually started two years after Reagan became president, when House Republicans lost twenty-six seats in the 1982 elections. Three members—Newt Gingrich, Trent Lott of Mississippi, and Dick Cheney of Wyoming— were spurred to create the Conservative Opportunity Society, dedicated to infusing the Republican Party with a new and more virile form of radical conservatism. Their strategy was to appeal to southern white voters wary of the Democrats' continuing support for racial integration and affirmative action, to working-class "Reagan Demo-

---

* According to a 1997 report by the National Committee for Responsive Philanthropy, between 1992 and 1994 alone, just twelve of these conservative family foundations awarded $120 million to organizations, institutes, and centers devoted to promoting the radical conservative cause. The comparable figure for a scattering of liberal groups was $18.6 million. National Committee for Responsive Philanthropy, "Moving a Public Policy Agenda," July 1997, p. 5 (www.ncrp.org/reports/moving.htm).

crats" whose earnings were dropping and who felt alienated from the remnants of the sixties left, and to the Christian right.

The strategy succeeded. Cheney became House minority whip. When the first President Bush named Cheney secretary of defense in 1989, Gingrich took his place. In 1994, when Republicans gained control of the House for the first time in forty years, Gingrich became Speaker, finally putting the Radcons in charge.

The emerging Radcon political organization, as well as its increasing stridency, was also fueled by evangelical Christian fundamentalists. By 1980, Protestant evangelicals constituted about 40 percent of southern white voters. They steadily shifted into the Republican camp. As many as 42 percent of the delegates to the 1992 Republican convention in Houston were connected with the Christian Coalition. It was there that the coalition's Pat Robertson warned that "unless America returns to her Christian roots . . . she will continue to legalize sodomy, slaughter innocent babies, destroy the minds of the children, squander her resources, and sink into oblivion."[41]

There was no effective counterbalance. By the mid-1980s, liberalism had gone into eclipse. Congressional Democrats were increasingly dependent on corporate donations; New Deal liberals were getting old; and the remnants of the sixties left—having rejected liberalism—had by now turned inward toward "personal development," the "identity politics" of race and gender, and academic theories about deconstruction. Democrats had nothing of any relevance to say to the vast number of working-class men and women whose incomes were growing increasingly precarious. Hence, American politics moved steadily rightward. Bill Clinton ran for office in 1992 as a middle-of-the road southern moderate with positions almost indistinguishable from those of moderate Republicans in the seventies.

I had seen Clinton occasionally since we were at law school together. I admired his efforts while governor of Arkansas to modernize the schools there, and was eager to lend a hand in his campaign. I contributed to his campaign plank, *Putting People First*, but the resulting document was hardly a liberal manifesto. "Our policies are neither liberal nor conservative, neither Democratic nor Republican," it read. It emphasized "the forgotten middle class" and spoke of "providing opportunity, taking responsibility, and rewarding work." Clinton pledged to sign the North American Free Trade Agreement, end welfare, and put more police on the streets and more criminals behind bars—positions that would have been barely recognizable to the Democratic Party of the seventies.

Yes, Clinton also promised to "guarantee every American affordable, quality health care," but this wasn't considered especially liberal at the time. Most Americans wanted affordable health care, and still do. Big corporations were also looking for ways to control the spiraling costs of employee health care. Medical costs had tripled between 1980 and 1992. The plan that emerged from the Clinton White House was way too complicated (I didn't even understand it and I was supposed to help sell it), but I doubt even a simpler plan would have succeeded. Republicans didn't want to give Clinton a legislative victory. They launched a multi-million-dollar campaign to kill it, featuring "Harry" and "Louise," two characters who appeared repeatedly on radio and TV in select media markets, warning that the plan would take away people's choice of family doctor and destroy many of the health benefits Americans already had. "Experts" from Radcon think tanks echoed the claims. Radcon talk-show hosts amplified them. These were trumped-up charges—the plan wouldn't limit choice of doctor and would expand most people's benefits—but they stuck. Republicans were united and steadfast; Democrats were disunited and unsure of themselves. Despite a Democratic Congress, the plan died.

After Gingrich's Republicans took over the House at the start of 1995, Washington turned even more bitterly partisan. I was secretary of labor then, and I remember the sharp change in barometric pressure, as if a hurricane had blown in. Almost overnight, the Labor

Department was deluged with demands from new Republican House chairmen for documents and information about all sorts of mundane things that went on in the department—meetings, telephone calls, expenditures. I knew they were fishing expeditions intended to find any small error or omission that might be used to catch me, and then fry me.

As Speaker, Gingrich was the Radcon commander in chief. I met him several times and each time went away with the impression he was a military general in an age where party politics had turned into warfare. He liked to describe himself as a revolutionary force, but he often behaved more like a naughty boy—grinning uncontrollably when I congratulated him on a particularly devious legislative ploy, or overly defensive when I gently chided him for misusing a certain historic fact. His office was adorned with figurines of dinosaurs, as you might find in the bedrooms of little boys who dream of one day being huge and powerful. To characterize him as "mean" missed this essential quality of naughtiness. It was the meanness of a nasty kid rather than a tyrant.

Gingrich's key lieutenants were southerners and westerners. Almost nine out of ten of his new committee chairs were from the South or West. This was no accident; these precincts were the sources of Radcon power. In many of these states, religious conservatives controlled the local Republican Party machinery. These new GOP leaders were virulently pro-life, anti-gay, pro-military, scornful of Democrats and liberals, especially repulsed by the legacy of the sixties left.

There is no need here to recount the subsequent events in detail—the shutdowns of the federal government; the charges against Clinton, culminating with impeachment; the bitterness and the brazenness of the 2000 presidential election. My point here is to place all of this in the larger context: the right-wing money that bankrolled the Radcon strategy; the political battle lines formed even before Clinton came to office; a Radcon legal establishment eager to pounce; and the Radcon media. Combine all this with a profound sense among Radcons that Bill and Hillary Clinton, and even Al Gore, personified the evil of the sixties left, and you begin to understand the intensity of the war. It continues today.

3. *Media "shock troops."* The third element of the counterrevolution has been an ever-growing cacophony of pundits and talk-show hosts who advance the Radcon agenda as they rage against immigrants, environmentalists, feminists, gays, the poor, the American Civil Liberties Union, the French, Arabs, Bill and Hillary, Democrats, and, especially, liberals. The media outlets for these "shock troops" were bankrolled by a new group of Radcon media tycoons such as Rupert Murdoch and the Reverend Sun Myung Moon; and they have been regularly echoed and supported by the formidable editorial pages of the *Wall Street Journal.*

Rush Limbaugh's radio show went national in 1988. By 2003, it was carried by more than six hundred stations, listened to by some twenty million people, and spawned imitators across the radio spectrum. Televised versions of Radcon talk shows began in the late nineties with Murdoch's Fox News Channel, commanded by Republican political strategist Roger Ailes. Fox News' slick brand of opinionated, right-wing talk began to attract a following that, by 2002, overtook CNN as the leader in cable news ratings. Its success also bred imitators. Soon, MSNBC television was featuring a similar right-wing formula.

I have often appeared on these programs as a token liberal. I do so because they present at least a chance to debate issues before the public—an opportunity that's becoming rarer and rarer. But unfortunately I've come to think that straightforward debate is the last thing on my hosts' minds. They only want the appearance of giving the "other side" a forum, not the reality. Typically, a booker for the program phones me in the late morning, asking my opinion about some issue in the news that the Radcon producer or host wants to highlight. If I say I strongly disagree with the prevailing Radcon position, the booker is pleased, and asks if I'm available that evening at a particular "hit time" (when the segment is tentatively scheduled to begin). Usually, I'm pitted against a Radcon analyst from the Heritage Foundation or some similar right wing–funded institution, or a Radcon politician. The five-minute exchange is intended to look like a balanced debate, although the host sides with my opponent and often interrupts me in mid-sentence.

It amazes me that Radcons continue to get away with charging America's news media with a "liberal bias." To support this accusation they rely on right-wing "media watchdog" groups bankrolled by wealthy Radcons. Even when Radcons admit to the right-wing bias of most radio and cable-television talk shows, they say it's necessary in order to balance the liberal bias of major newspapers, television networks, and public radio and television. This is utter nonsense. The argument equates right-wing political commentary with news reporting done according to well-established standards of journalism. The reality is this: To the extent that political opinions are offered in the media, they're overwhelmingly from the right. This has been well documented.*

As I've said, I first came to Washington right after the Watergate crisis of the early seventies. During that constitutional emergency, Republicans and Democrats alike distinguished themselves by their determination to preserve and protect the institutions of government, while forcing the resignation of a man who abused the power of the presidency. The system worked as it should.

After I returned to Washington in the nineties, a band of radical conservatives, intent on winning at any cost, undermined Bill Clinton's presidency, laid the groundwork for a new and risky foreign

* See Eric Alterman's *What Liberal Media?* (New York: Basic Books, 2003).

policy, abused the election process, and forced the Supreme Court to take sides in a presidential election. The system stopped working, and it hasn't worked since. Our public debate has become increasingly one-sided, and shrill; our political campaigns, engorged with money; our government, even including our courts, bitterly partisan. By the start of the twenty-first century, Newt Gingrich's notion of politics as a war "to be fought with the scale and duration and savagery that is only true of civil wars" has become a shameful reality. It is turning Americans against one another, and against much of the rest of the world. And it is undermining our democracy.

VALUES

The Radcons' dominance isn't due only to their money, discipline, and tactics. More fundamental has been the Radcons' capacity to shape the public debate around their idea of evil. Put simply, Radcons have offered America a set of ideas—about morality, prosperity, and patriotism—that celebrate "us" and condemn "them." We are virtuous; *they* are venal.

We are heterosexual, married, and clean-living. *They* are gay or lesbian, sexually active outside marriage, and in favor of abortion.

We are hardworking, white, and middle class. *They* are idle, poor, black, or Latino or Asian immigrants who don't speak English but benefit from our social services.

We are Americans. *They* are terrorists. They are also Muslims and Arabs. They are even French and Germans, or anyone else who is not with *us*.

Unless *our* values prevail, *they* will triumph.

This dangerously oversimplified way of looking at the world offers many Americans who feel angry and frustrated an easy explanation for what's gone wrong in their lives. And a lot has gone wrong.

Not the least, the rise of the Radcons has in fact corresponded with the widening drift of workers across America into two different worlds—one rich, the other economically anxious. Consider: The after-tax income of the top one percent of American earners has more than doubled since 1990, while the after-tax income of families in the middle has grown only slightly.[42] The richest one percent of Americans now have almost two-fifths of the nation's wealth. That's more than the combined wealth of the bottom 95 percent. The wages and benefits of America's blue-collar and low-level white-collar workers stopped rising in the late 1970s, and have barely budged since then. White men without four-year college degrees have actually experienced a decline in their pay. Meanwhile, the costs of staples of the middle class—education, health care, housing, and medicine—have risen faster than median family incomes.[43]

Naturally, many Americans have looked for someone or something to blame. Radcons conveniently offer "liberalism" and everything associated with it. And they manipulate the elemental passions of morality, family, and patriotism to explain why they're right and liberals are wrong.

You'd think America's large, anxious middle and lower-middle class would have the most to gain from a bold agenda focused on getting them good jobs, affordable health care, and excellent public schools, financed with progressive taxes. But there has been no such agenda. As I've noted, Democrats have fallen silent. The money pouring into Washington, coupled with the Radcons' highly disciplined political machine, and their media "shock troops," has blocked any such program. At the same time, the muted response of liberals and Democrats has allowed Radcons to exploit these economic anxieties for their own ends, diverting public attention and distorting public outrage.

As I'll show, the Radcon version of morality seeks to impose private religious norms about sex and the family on the entire nation, transforming matters of private morality into law. Radcons are looking in the wrong direction. America *is* facing a moral crisis, but it is abuses of authority at the highest levels of America that are stacking the deck against average working people and small investors, and undermining public trust in the entire economic and political system. They raise central questions of public morality.

The Radcon version of prosperity rewards the rich, gives almost nothing to the middle class, and penalizes the poor. Contrary to what Radcons say, this doesn't lead to economic growth. As I'll demonstrate, the real way to grow the economy is by widening the circle of prosperity to include Americans who have been falling behind. Shared prosperity isn't incompatible with growth; it's essential to it.

Finally, the Radcon version of patriotism is downright dangerous. I call it "negative patriotism" because it stifles dissent at home and insists that America be so much stronger militarily than any other nation that we can bully others into submission. In truth, both of these make America more vulnerable. If we're unable to hear criticism, we can't correct dangerous errors in our policies, and *all* governments make errors. If we appear to act like a bully, we can't get the cooperation we need from other nations—both in fighting terrorism and reducing the risk that nuclear weapons will fall into terrorist hands. As I'll discuss, we need a "positive patriotism" that recognizes that our security depends on our moral authority in the world, not simply on our brute strength. And that demands that all Americans—not just the middle class and the poor—accept their fair share of the burden of keeping America strong.

The Radcons' emphasis on exterminating evil—outside the nation as well as within it, and within each of us—is leading us down a treacherous path. It's turning us against one another and against much of the rest of the world at precisely the time when we have to stand together.

America needs a very different approach, based on reason and common sense. That's liberalism, properly understood.

ADDENDUM:
A GUIDE TO THE RADCON GLOSSARY

Many of the words and phrases used by Radcons have been crafted over the years by pollsters, wordsmiths, and media consultants seeking the most persuasive means of packaging Radcon values and demonizing their opponents. The results are widely disseminated by Radcon talk-show hosts, pundits, and politicians. Some have become such standard staples of American political discourse that they are almost taken for granted. A small sample:

Big government. Bill Clinton famously "triangulated" by saying that the era of "big government" was over, but the term continues to be used derisively by Radcons to distract the public's attention from the fact that Radcons epitomize big government. They have created the largest and most expensive military in the history of the world, given the Central Intelligence Agency and the Federal Bureau of Investigation broader powers to spy on Americans, and come up with some of the largest federal deficits in American history. In short, they've made government far bigger and more intrusive.

Blame-America-firsters. Anyone who expresses doubts that the United States is perfect in every way is assumed to be a member of this group—unless they're Radcons blaming America for its moral decadence. The phrase was first popularized by Jeane Kirkpatrick, columnist and U.N. ambassador under Reagan, at the Republican National Convention in 1984, when she attacked the Democrats. "When the Soviet Union walked out of arms control negotiations . . . Democrats did not blame Soviet intransigence. They blamed the

United States. But then, they always blame America first."[44] The phrase has since been used to criticize those who express even constructive criticism of American policies. During the Iraqi war of 1991, Bill Bennett wrote, "One reads the statements of the blame-America-firsters and listens to their chants, and one wonders if they have ever absorbed a single fact about the despicable character of Saddam Hussein. . . . There is a name for this attitude, and the name . . . is anti-Americanism."[45]

Class warfare. Liberals are accused of fomenting this if they even so much as point to the rapidly widening divergence of income and wealth in the United States. Or if they reveal that most of the tax breaks pushed by George W. Bush were meant to further enrich those at the top. The truth is that it's Radcons who have declared class warfare.

Death tax. This is used to refer to the tax on estates that applies almost exclusively to families in the top 2 percent. Republicans spent five years prodding their troops to use this term. Newt Gingrich made anyone who forgot and uttered "estate tax" put a dollar into a pizza fund.[46]

Environmental wackos, tree huggers, environazis. These are applied to anyone who expresses concern about the cleanliness of air and water, and a willingness to sacrifice some economic growth in order to improve their quality.

Family values (see also Traditional family). Liberals are accused of being opposed to these when they suggest that gays and lesbians should have the same legal rights as heterosexuals, that women and their doctors should decide whether an abortion is merited, or that government should help finance child care, health care, or family leave.

It's my money (sometimes phrased as "It's your money"). This is used by Radcons in anti-tax harangues to fool people into thinking that wage-earners should be allowed to keep all their income, ignoring the fact that their taxes pay for public schools, roads, water, clean air, bridges, national defense, seaports, police, fire departments, public health and safety, and other essential services. Imagine the nation without them.

Liberal establishment (also termed "liberal elite"). This phrase is meant to mask the reality that, by the start of 2004, Radcons were in control of the House of Representatives, the Senate, the presidency, a significant percentage of the federal courts, almost all political think tanks, most of the political-opinion media, and a large portion of the money pouring into Washington.

Liberal media. See pages 41–42.

Limousine liberal, liberal stooge, screaming liberal. These and similar sobriquets are self-reinforcing because Radcons have been successful in almost totally distorting what the word "liberal" means. As early as 1976, Representative Morris Udall said that although he continued to think of himself as a liberal, he used the term "progressive" to define himself in public because the word "liberal" was "associated with abortion, drugs, busing, and big-spending wasteful government."[47]

Operation Iraqi Freedom (see also War on terrorism). This term was repeated verbatim on all Radcon radio and television outlets to lull the public into believing that the purpose of the Iraqi war was to free the Iraqi people from Saddam Hussein, when the original purpose, as initially stated by the President, was to prevent "weapons of mass destruction" from getting into the hands of Al Qaeda's terrorist network, which might use the weapons against the United States.

Partial-birth abortion. This is an extremely rare medical procedure resorted to when the mother's life is in danger, but the term is used repeatedly by Radcons who want the public to think that abortion is the equivalent of killing a baby.

Political correctness, or PC. This term is still used by Radcons to describe liberal objections to forms of speech that are offensive and insensitive to certain groups. Radcons themselves consider it politically incorrect, however, to criticize America or American foreign policy.

Radical feminists, feminazis. These are applied to anyone who calls for equal opportunity for women.

Traditional family. This term is contrasted with single parents, gay couples, and unmarried couples, who are considered as "deviant" as bigamists or people who commit incest. According to Senator Rick Santorum of Pennsylvania, the Supreme Court's finding that homosexuals have a right to consensual sex is "antithetical to a healthy, stable, traditional family."[48]

War on terrorism. These words are meant to suggest that terrorism can be subdued through military actions staged against easily identifiable adversaries, involving bombs and troops, leading to decisive victories. The term "war" also creates the impression that suspensions of civil liberties, invocation of censorship, or the extraordinary powers vested in the president during such an emergency will be temporary measures until the "war" ends. In fact, fighting international terrorism is not like fighting a war. It's more like controlling crime, requiring continuous policing and cooperation among law enforcement personnel all over the world.

.   .   .

Words and phrases like these are powerful because they use emotion-laden images (birth, death, freedom, class, blame, family, warfare) to mask their political agenda. In this way, they serve as "conversation stoppers"—easy means of asserting Radcon conclusions without subjecting them to meaningful debate. Who, after all, could possibly be in favor of taxing people who die, killing partially born babies, or blaming America first? Why would we ever *not* want to uphold traditional family values or declare war on terrorism?

Through this deliberate campaign of distortion, Radcons have tried to stop America from examining the true Radcon agenda. It's a smart tactic, because on close inspection Radcon arguments fall apart. When the test is reason and common sense, liberals win—as I will now show.

CHAPTER TWO

PUBLIC MORALITY

WHAT'S PUBLICLY IMMORAL

My first direct experience with public morality occurred in September 1964. I was a member of Dartmouth's student court, which faced a perplexing case. The student handbook, remember, made fornication a capital offense, punishable by expulsion. A Dartmouth student had spent the previous spring break in Bermuda with his girlfriend. She had admitted it to her own college's dean, who promptly notified ours. The student court was to decide whether the Dartmouth student had committed the dirty deed during his Bermuda romp and, if so, whether its occurrence outside the school term and beyond the territorial boundaries of the United States mitigated the offense. As the only freshman on the court, it was up to me to ask the poor fellow the penetrating question. He admitted everything.

We excused him and began our deliberations. Three hours later, we decided to recommend to the dean that the young man be expelled.

I repressed this memory for years until one day about a decade later, when my wife, Clare, and I stopped in Hanover for a bit to eat on our way to Vermont. Into the restaurant walked the same young man, ten years older but unmistakable. The whole incident flooded back into my memory like an awful dream. I was so embarrassed I tried to hide my face in my plate. But he walked right up to me, extended his hand, and gave me a big hello. I asked him what had happened to him after he'd left Dartmouth. He told me he had been drafted and sent to Vietnam.

One of the most important distinctions a society draws is between private and public morality—which behavior should be left to a person's own conscience, and which to public law backed by social condemnation. In some respects, America has come a long way since young men and women were expelled from college for fornicating, and presidents sent young men to Vietnam to fight communists.

But Radcons are intent on making private behavior the subject of public morality, even so far as to try to legislate it. They think the following activities should be banned or discouraged by law, and condemned by society as a whole:

- sex outside marriage

- abortion

- children born out of wedlock

- divorce

- homosexuality

- gay marriage.

Radcons think these behaviors are destroying the American family. And here, again, Radcons blame sixties liberalism.

Radcons are correct in one respect: Public morality *is* important. By shying away from discussing it, liberals allow Radcons to define public morality the way they see it. But public morality shouldn't be about private sex. Liberals should be screaming from the rooftops about the real decline of public morality, about the real abuses:

- fraudulent accounting and stock manipulation

- insider trading

- tax evasion

- exorbitant pay of top executives

- financial conflicts of interest

- bribery of public officials.

Radcons dismiss *these* acts as essentially private, but they're not. People who abuse their power undermine the trust our society depends on. Radcons equate sexual permissiveness with the erosion of public morality because they're obsessed by the decline of discipline in society. They don't worry about the misuse of authority because they're focused on obedience to it, not its exercise. (Radcons become outraged by those in authority only when they are caught red-handed and have come to be seen by everyone as criminals, or when they succumb to sexual temptation and get caught.)

For more than two centuries, liberals have defended privacy and have stood for the proposition that matters of religious faith should be separated from public law. People can be truly free only if they're confident that they can go about their personal lives without being monitored or intruded upon by government, and that they can practice whatever faith (or lack of faith) they wish regardless of the religious beliefs of others. At the same time, liberals have stood firmly against abuses of power. In the eighteenth century, they opposed royal prerogatives and the unaccountable power of the British Crown. At the turn of the last century, they confronted the "robber barons" who monopolized American industry; and in the 1930s, they moved against "economic royalists" who abused their power to enrich themselves at the expense of average Americans struggling through the Depression.

There *is* moral rot in America, but it's not found in the private behavior of ordinary people. It's located in the public behavior of people at or near the top.

TAKING BACK MORALITY

Morality is sometimes hard for liberals to talk about. It seems too personal, too closely related to authoritarian religion, too easily used as a tool to justify or to condemn private behavior. Moralists often strike liberals as being intolerant. Hence, many liberals have adopted a kind of moral relativism; no single version of morality is superior to any other. By this view, abuses of power may violate legal or economic principles, but they don't raise moral issues.

This is a dangerous cop-out.

To their credit, Radcons have developed several useful ways to frame morality as a public issue. They go awry on the *application* of their ideas. Sex is the wrong target. But their willingness to introduce the concept of right and wrong into public discourse enables us to discuss why the abuses of authority that plague modern America are rightly matters of public concern.

Their first argument is that everyone has responsibilities to society. Our system can't function if everyone is only looking out for Number One. Yet selfish interest too often trumps the public interest. Bill Bennett rightly worries that Americans are "less willing than we once were to sacrifice or to keep commitments. We place higher value than ever before on 'personal growth,' self-expression, and self-discovery."[1] We have adopted "a deeply ingrained philosophy that glorifies . . . freedom from constraints."[2]

Bennett's target is sex, but his words would be better applied to the greed that has infected executive suites and Wall Street, and turned much of American politics into a financial slush pump. "[P]art of what it means to be a morally responsible human is to act in ways that are, sometimes, contrary to our 'natural' instincts," he

writes.[3] We struggle "against our biological impulses, against our emotional longings. We do not abjure the struggle because it is difficult or because we seem to be battling against something deep within us . . . even if it seems fundamental to who we are."[4]

In other words—using Bennett's logic, but applied to a different subject—unconstrained greed isn't to be excused just because it's part of human nature. People should be expected to rise above their base motives, particularly when entrusted with others' well-being. America has placed too high a value on selfishness, and now we're paying too high a price for it.

Radcons part with their fellow libertarians on this point. Libertarians argue that people should be able to do whatever they please as long as they don't directly harm anyone else. By contrast, Radcons believe in *virtuous* behavior. People should act in ways that promote the public good. Robert Bork warns of the "radical individualism" of those who "wish to be unhindered in the pursuit of pleasure."[5] Bork is right. But rather than worry about the unhindered pursuit of carnal pleasure, Bork and other Radcons should worry about the uninhibited pursuit of wealth and power.

Another useful point Radcons make: Tolerance isn't virtuous when the behavior that's being tolerated unravels the social fabric. This sort of tolerance invites more anti-social behavior. Political scientist (and frequent Radcon referent) James Q. Wilson provided a vivid example a few years ago. He noted that a broken window left unattended signals to a community that no one cares if windows are broken there. No one is sufficiently powerful or concerned to enforce the rule against breaking windows. Hence, the broken window is a kind of ongoing invitation to throw more stones. More windows break, and the social fabric of the community continues to unravel.

Wilson's analysis is surely relevant to the abuses of authority we've been witnessing. The corporate fraud, conflicts of interest, exorbitant pay of top executives, and surge of money into politics are like hundreds of broken windows. Although prosecutors have gone after certain highly visible "stone throwers," most of the fines and penalties are like slaps on their wrists. Meanwhile, America has disregarded the larger system that continues to produce too many stones and broken windows, at the cost of Americans' faith in our economic and political institutions. "Maintaining limits is a way of asserting community," says Wilson. "If the limits are asserted weakly, uncertainly, or apologetically, their effects must surely be weaker than if they are asserted boldly, confidently, and persuasively."[6]

Setting limits isn't just a matter of enforcing the law, say Radcons, and I agree. It's also about invoking public shame, expressing public outrage, and passing public judgment. We shouldn't be reluctant to condemn behavior that undermines society—and that condemnation should be active and noisy. Bill Bennett warns against "[t]he power of the religion of nonjudgmentalism that has permeated our culture, encouraging a paralysis of the moral faculty."[7] Our unwillingness to decry certain behavior "functions as an excuse for gross moral irresponsibility. Pretending to raise us above the 'common' view, it robs us of the ability to recognize and call things by their proper names."[8]

He's right. There is a proper place for public outrage. That Radcon moralists focus on sexual permissiveness rather than abuses of power doesn't make this broader point any less relevant. We, as individual citizens, have a moral responsibility *not* to tolerate behavior in others that undermines our society. As Bennett says, moral relativism is a "misguided conception of tolerance" that proclaims "we cannot know right and wrong, that rejects assertions based on inviolable principle, that believes truth is a mere social construction. But this is not tolerance; this is moral exhaustion and sloth."[9]

It is an act of gross immorality for Americans to conclude that the abuses of power and trust we have been witnessing are somehow inevitable; that the CEOs of the nation's largest corporations and the executives at the top of our most prominent professional firms can't be expected to place public values over private acquisitiveness; that there is no clear right and wrong with regard to looting companies, defrauding investors and employees, and bribing public officials with "contributions."

Finally, Radcons correctly worry about the consequences for society when standards of decency continue to erode. The late New York senator and former professor Daniel Patrick Moynihan termed it "defining deviancy down." As behavior deteriorates, a community may fall into the trap of lowering its standards. Conduct previously not tolerated comes to be seen as normal, and what passes for normal becomes acceptable. In this way, deviance is "normalized," and a society loses its sense of public morality by constantly lowering the bar.[10]

I remember visiting a school in a poor section of New York City with Senator Moynihan in the mid-1990s, while I was secretary of labor. The school had a good record of helping graduating seniors find jobs. Its principal proudly led us on a tour, along with a camera crew from a local TV station. We were ascending a staircase when Moynihan's attention was caught by a large "FUCK YOU" spray-painted on the wall.

"What's *this*?" asked the senator.

"Oh, just some . . . kids," stammered the principal, trying to shepherd us up the stairs. "This way, please."

Moynihan didn't budge. "Why are these words on this wall?" He pointed at them. The camera crew stopped and turned on their spotlight.

"It's nothing . . . really. . . . We clean these . . . things. Let's . . ." The principal was sweating. The tape was rolling. Moynihan was furious.

"You will clean this wall *immediately*," demanded the senator, still pointing.

The principal looked around helplessly. It seemed as if several hours passed. Finally, someone arrived with a bucket and a scouring brush. The tour resumed.

At the time, I thought Moynihan was grandstanding for the cameras, and maybe he was. But he was making a larger point, too: Antisocial behavior has to be addressed quickly and decisively. Otherwise, it's too easy for a community to embark on the downward slide of acceptance, until it barely notices anything wrong. Such is our current condition with regard to the greed and financial corruption that now infects America.

SEX AND EVIL

I made a recent Internet search that turned up 7,820 articles by Radcons condemning premarital, extramarital, and unmarried sex. They disapprove of certain sex acts even in privacy, including sodomy, cunnilingus, and masturbation. They don't want men to have sex with other men, or women with other women. They don't like men dressing up like women, or vice versa. They don't approve of sex toys, music with sexually explicit lyrics, or films or performances with sexually explicit scenes. Many disapprove of contraceptives. They don't want women to have abortions.

Radcons have blended Christian fundamentalism and right-wing moralism into their larger worldview. Unrestrained sex, they believe, unleashes an evil that hides inside human beings. It threatens the social order. Therefore it must be controlled. The evil sexual impulses inside us have to be disciplined, just as evil forces from outside have to be. The war on sexual "deviancy" is, in this respect, a lot like the war on terrorism: If we lose, Western civilization may fall into chaos.

"Throughout all time, societies have known that sex is not only the most powerful of human passions but an activity whose repercussions can be hugely destructive, wrecking human lives and inflicting wounds that can easily last a lifetime," writes Bill Bennett. "That is why all societies have undertaken to guide sexuality by means of ritual and law."[11]

The *Wall Street Journal* editorialized several years ago that the "weaker or more vulnerable" among us need social "guardrails." Elites may be able to handle indiscriminate sex, "but for a lot of other people it hasn't been such an easy life to sustain. Not exceedingly sophisticated, neither thinkers nor leaders, never interviewed for their views, they're held together by faith, friends, fun and, at the margins, fanaticism." Laws constraining sex are necessary in order to show them the way. While "most of the teenage girls in the Midwest who learn about the nuances of sex from magazines published by thirtysomething women in New York will more or less survive . . . some continue to end up as prostitutes on Eighth Avenue. . . . These weaker or more vulnerable people, who in different ways must try to live along life's margins, are among the reasons that society erects rules."[12]

These are the same *Wall Street Journal* editorial writers, incidentally, who don't seem to give a hoot if the "weaker or more vulnerable" can't find a job paying enough to keep their families fed and housed. These writers don't editorialize about why elites should pay taxes to help finance good schools and job-training programs so the "weaker or more vulnerable" can get the skills they need. They worry only that sexual permissiveness among elites may set a bad example. It's a form of trickle-down moral economics. "[T]olerance for bad behavior at the elite levels will inevitably trickle down to the Joe Lunchbucket crowd, with calamitous results."[13]

Pardon me, but this is paternalistic bull.

Behind it all is the same deep-seated anger about what happened in the sixties. According to Michael Savage, "[l]ittle by little, the pollutants of liberalism have been mixed into the cultural diet that we've been forced to consume since the sixties. . . . These lies of liberalism—the sexual free-for-all, the experimental drugs, the easy divorce, the banishment of Judeo-Christian anything from the schools . . . and the so-called abortion-rights movement—fall from the libs' lips so frequently we've come to accept the distinctively acidic taste."[14] Robert Bork traces "high rates of illegitimate births . . . and high rates of family dissolution" to "the infatuation of modern liberalism with the individual's right to self-gratification."[15]

With the sixties came the widespread availability of contraceptives, including the pill, and in 1973, legalized abortion. In the Radcon view, both led directly to the breakdown of the family. "Men and women today can have sex more promiscuously, more casually, and with much lower odds of pregnancy and childbirth," says Bennett. "For the first time, on a large scale, sex has been de-linked from both marriage and procreation." Before contraceptives and abortion, "sexual relations were conditioned on a promise of marriage if pregnancy resulted: hence, the phenomenon of the 'shotgun wedding.' " But after, "sex became commitment free" and "men, liberated from the consequence of their acts, drew further and further away from lasting attachment to family life."[16]

Radcons like Bennett want to go back to the norms of the 1950s to resurrect the family. That was "a period characterized by relatively strong, stable families and by a public ethic of marital commitment. . . . [The] '50s continue to have a great deal to teach us."[17]

Nonsense. I remember the fifties, and it was hardly idyllic. Shotgun weddings were not particularly joyous occasions. I also remember illegal abortions. A friend of mine accidentally impregnated his girlfriend. He had used a condom, but these things happen. The two of them found someone to perform an abortion for about $100. The girlfriend badly hemorrhaged but didn't become sterile or die. She did better than many.

Undoubtedly many husbands and wives were happy in the fifties. My parents had their ups and downs, but their relationship got better after Mom went to work in Dad's store. But I also remember a lot of unhappiness among my parents' friends. Several of Mom's women friends asked her about getting jobs, too. They were bored out of their minds stuck at home. No one talked about depression then, but in hindsight some of them were surely suffering from it. No one talked about domestic abuse in those days, either, but I remember hearing our next-door neighbor bellow at his wife and her crying. How many women were trapped in abusive marriages, unable to leave because they had no money and no job prospects?

There is no shortage of hypocrisy among Radcons who publicly condemn the moral lassitude of modern America while leading secret lives of debauchery. Yet it's not my purpose in this book to expose or denigrate the behavior of certain individuals. Regardless of what Radcons may do in private, their public arguments deserve to be taken seriously. Personally, I agree with them on some points. I abhor the ways corporations have packaged the excesses of the sexual revolution for commercial uses, turning women into sex objects in order to sell billions of dollars worth of films, music, magazines, clothing, and cosmetics. I hate how mega-media companies have found ways to cheapen and demean sexuality, and reach into our homes and influence our children with their trash. I also think marriage is a good idea. I've been lucky enough to be married to the same wonderful woman for over thirty years and we plan on staying married until the end of our days.

But Radcons think private sexual behavior should be a public issue, constrained by all sorts of laws. They want their views to be supported by strong public norms, the violation of which generates outrage and shame—not quite scarlet letters, but close. And they want to use the public schools to impose their views on our young. (I will return to this subject.)

It's perfectly fine for Radcons to declare strong personal convictions about sex and marriage—convictions often based on sincere religious beliefs. But it is quite another thing to insist that everyone else must share the same convictions. As I've said, the liberal tradition has wisely drawn a sharp boundary between religion and government. We've got to stop the Radcons before they impose their narrow-minded orthodoxy any further.

REPUBLICANS, DEMOCRATS, AND SEX

It turns out that how you come out in the sex wars is a better predictor of your party affiliation than almost anything else. During the 1996 presidential campaign, Clinton pollsters Dick Morris and Mark Penn came up with what proved to be a surefire way to tell if a voter was likely to choose Clinton or Dole. They asked likely voters the following five questions about sex, the last one indirectly on the subject:

1. Do you ever personally look at pornography?
2. Do you believe sex before marriage is morally wrong?
3. Would you look down on someone who had an affair while married?
4. Do you believe homosexuality is morally wrong?
5. Is religion very important in your life?

Anyone who gave "liberal" responses (yes, no, no, no, no) to three out of the five was twice as likely to vote for Clinton as for Dole. On the other hand, anyone giving "conservative" responses (no, yes, yes, yes, yes) to three out of five was twice as likely to vote for Dole. Answers to these questions predicted voting behavior more accurately than anything except race or party affiliation.[18] (Bear in mind, this little quiz was administered *before* Monica, and before Morris himself got caught sucking the toes of a prostitute.)

What are the sexual wars *really* about? I don't believe Democrats have a stronger libido than Republicans. In fact, I'd wager that Republicans have as much sex as Democrats, both inside and outside their marriages. They probably watch and listen to as much pornography as Democrats, too. Maybe Republicans feel a tad bit guiltier than

Democrats, but I've yet to see any surveys on this, one way or the other.

The truth is that so-called blue America (the states that tend to vote Democratic, usually East or West Coast, with large urban areas) took away one lesson from the sixties—the importance of tolerance, personal freedom, and individual autonomy. "Red" America (Republican, heartland, rural) took away a different lesson—the importance of self-control, marriage, and traditional "family values."

TRYING TO KEEP SEX INSIDE MARRIAGE

You can't stop teenagers from thinking about sex. I don't remember thinking about much else in ninth grade. While Miss Lee explained that China had gone communist, I daydreamed about doing it with Annette Funicello. I'm sure I wasn't alone. But can you stop teenagers from having sex? Radcons believe you can, and they also think America should adopt the goal as official public policy.

In 2003 the federal government spent $50 million urging teenagers not to have sex before marriage. That came to about $5 per teenager. Most of this money went into pamphlets, advertisements, and an "abstinence until marriage" lesson plan taught in over a third of America's public schools.[19] "Abstinence programs show real promise," said candidate George W. Bush, "because more and more teenagers understand that true love waits."[20]

Abstinence education might be worth the try (although I can't find the results of a single controlled experiment that shows it works). In any event, the $50 million could have been better spent on after-school sports programs, which high schools have been cutting because of budget problems. (Perhaps if we encouraged teenagers to exhaust themselves on the playing fields they'd be less likely to copulate in each other's homes after school.)

Radcons don't like to admit it, but almost no one's waiting until marriage. When it comes to abstinence, the counterrevolution isn't working. In the early sixties, roughly half of all twenty-five-year-old women had had sexual intercourse before they were married. By the late 1980s, five out of six had—and I doubt all of them were radical feminists. Moral judgments shifted in the same direction. In the early sixties, roughly three-quarters of American adults thought premarital sex wrong. By the 1980s, only a third thought premarital sex "always" or "almost always" wrong.[21] The trend has continued since then. The National Campaign to Prevent Teen Pregnancy recently reported that one in five kids under fifteen is not a virgin.[22] The rate is similar in most other post-industrial countries.

This trend may be morally troubling to certain people. It's also true that premarital sex can emotionally damage some young people who are not ready for it. But these facts alone don't make it a public problem.

Premarital sex would be a public problem if it inevitably led to a lot of young single mothers who couldn't support their kids. But premarital sex doesn't have to result in unwanted pregnancies if young women and men are educated about it, and if they have easy access to contraception (including RU-486, the "morning-after" pill) and abortion services either in school or through affordable health plans. But, of course, Radcons don't want them to have any of this.

To believe that the best and only way to prevent poor single women from having babies is to instruct young people not to have sex before marriage is like thinking the best way to prevent your house from leaking is to stop the rain. It would be a whole lot easier to fix the leak.

As a matter of fact, it turns out that the leak is slowing. The rate of teen pregnancies has been dropping. Among girls between the ages of fifteen and nineteen, it dropped by more than a quarter between 1970 and 2002. By 2002, the rate of teenage births had reached the lowest level since the government began tracking births, in 1906.[23]

Radcons want to attribute the decline to the legislation in 1996 that officially ended welfare, but the decline was well under way before then. The best explanation is that teenagers have had easier access to, and more information about, contraceptives and abortion. And much of the shame has been removed from both. Teenage girls have also had more opportunities for better-paying jobs, some as a part of a career trajectory. They no longer have to rely solely on having a baby to give their life meaning.

Teenage birthrates have been dropping for much the same reason overall birthrates have been dropping. In the mid-1970s, only about 10 percent of middle-aged women, mostly teachers or nurses—the major occupations open to women to who wanted careers—had never had a child. These days a decision not to have children isn't nearly as rare. Almost one out of every five women between the ages of forty and forty-five has never had a child. That's double the rate of 1970.[24] Some of these women are happily married. Contraception and abortion have allowed them to pursue interests other than raising children; new career paths open to women have given them the opportunity to do so. In addition, the cost of raising a child has risen so much since the seventies that some women (and men) have evidently decided it's not worth it. Home prices in safe neighborhoods with good schools have soared, as have college tuitions.[25]

Radcons assume child poverty can also be reduced if poor single mothers are coaxed into getting married. Recent welfare legislation requires recipients to work more hours and provides millions of dollars to promote marriage. In 2004, President George W. Bush called for spending $1.5 billion to promote marriage among the poor through "relationship counseling."[26]

Radcons have the logic backwards. It's not being single that causes women to be poor. It's being poor that makes it less likely they'll marry. Poor women generally don't have a bumper crop of marriage-worthy men to choose from. Most men available to them are either unemployed or employed part-time, and earn precious little when they do work.[27] It's entirely rational for a poor woman to hedge her bets and tell a male companion he's welcome to stay only so long as he pulls in enough money and behaves well.

Poor unmarried women who have babies often have men living with them. In nearly half of all out-of-wedlock births, the biological father is living in. But the woman has no reason to marry him unless he's a good breadwinner. Studies show that mothers are far more likely to marry the fathers of their children when the father is employed.[28]

There's no doubt that single-parent poverty is a major problem. But lack of marriage isn't the main culprit. The reason mothers are poor has to do with their lack of education and the lousy jobs they have to settle for. Jobs at the bottom of the income ladder don't pay enough to support a working woman and her children. They don't pay enough to support a working man and his family, either. So even if the mother is living and sharing expenses with a working man who's also at the bottom of the income ladder, they're still likely to be poor. If she's married to him and he doesn't have a job, they're often worse off financially than if the mother is living alone.

Government campaigns to promote marriage aren't the answer. The best way to improve the odds that children won't be impoverished is to help women—and men—get better-paying jobs. That means, at the least, access to good schools and job training. Liberals understand this. That's why liberals have been fighting for adequate school budgets, fewer kids per classroom, well-trained and well-paid teachers (talented women and men won't go into teaching solely for the personal satisfaction; they need to be adequately paid), and community colleges with enough resources to provide job skills to all who need them.

Yet school budgets all over America are being slashed, funds for job training are being cut, and community colleges are turning away many poor students. Over and over again I hear the same refrain from single mothers: "I can't find a job unless I get the right skills. But I can't afford to get them. Welfare won't cover the costs. And I have no time to take classes outside work, and no child care in the evenings."

Radcon moralists don't want to hear any of this. They'd rather promote abstinence before marriage, deny contraceptives, and prohibit abortions. They'd rather blame single mothers for their lack of self-discipline, push them into marriage, and fulminate against liberals for being too permissive.

Rubbish. Radcons have righteous indignation on their side, but not reason.

WHATEVER HAPPENED TO MARRIAGE?

The biggest obstacle for Radcons who don't want people to have sex outside marriage is that fewer adult Americans are getting married. We're less likely to be married now than at any time since statistics on marriage began to be tallied almost a century ago. The decline started in the 1970s. A snapshot in 1970 would have shown 68 percent of adults married, 15 percent never married, and the rest divorced, separated, or widowed. By 2000, only 56 percent of adults were married and 23 percent had never married.[29] The same trend away from marriage is occurring all over the Western world.

There's less stigma attached to not marrying. I'm old enough to remember when an unmarried woman was called a "spinster" or an "old maid," and was presumed to be sort of odd. Nowadays, it's perfectly acceptable for women—or for men—never to marry. "Abstinence until marriage" programs just don't work for this growing portion of our population. They're not going to dedicate their lives to chastity.

Radcons rail against the rising divorce rate and blame it on no-fault divorce laws, pushed by liberals. Bill Bennett asserts that "[n]othing has done more to undermine family life today than the 'divorce revolution,' which began roughly thirty-five years ago."[30] Radcons like Bennett want to repeal no-fault divorce "for the simple reason that it would make divorce harder to attain and less attractive to pursue."[31]

Undoubtedly, divorce can be painful for those who go through it, and can scar their children. But it's far from clear that forcing unhappy couples to remain together would be any less harmful to the kids. Here again, Radcons embrace a simple, facile solution to a problem—one size fits all, when of course it doesn't.

In any event, the divorce rate is no longer rising. It rose rapidly in the 1960s and 1970s, peaked around 1980 at about 23 percent of all women who had been married, and has fallen back slightly since then.[32] This is mainly because fewer people are getting married in the first place.

Why the decline in marriage? Radcons blame sexual permissiveness. They say there's less reason to get married when sex is readily available outside marriage. Liberals "bucked against the *Leave It to Beaver* family model, pushed 'open marriages' and, in turn, redefined the family."[33]

Wrong again. There's a much easier explanation. A lot of men no longer represent particularly good economic deals, and women no longer have to marry in order to have economic security. Thirty years ago, most men had stable jobs in a mass-production economy that earned them paychecks big enough to support families. And most women didn't have paid jobs, so they had to get married in order to have food on their tables and a roof over their heads.

Since then, stable mass-production jobs for men have dwindled, and their paychecks have shrunk.* Meanwhile, women have streamed into the workforce. They're making more money than ever (but sadly, still not as much as men doing the same job).

I'm not suggesting most unmarried women think about men and

---

* In 1970 the typical working man with no more than a high school degree earned $34,632 (all of these data are in 2001 dollars); in 1980 he earned $32,985; in 1990, $28,516; in 2001, $28,341. See U.S. Bureau of the Census, Historical Tables, P-16 and P-17. Census.gov/hhes/income/histinc/p16.html.

marriage in such a mercenary way. My point is only that in the new economy, such a calculation is entirely rational, and, consciously or unconsciously, a growing number of women seem to be making it.

The decline in marriage is no more a public issue than is the rise in premarital sex. Of course it's good for children to know their fathers. But kids aren't necessarily better off just because their parents are married. Research suggests that children do better with single parents who are stable and loving than with married parents who are angry and miserable with each other.[34]

Message to Radcons: Stop obsessing about sex outside marriage. Join with liberals, and help people get better-paying jobs. That's the best way to stabilize the family.

WHY GAY COUPLES
SHOULD BE ALLOWED TO MARRY

Radcons don't want couples of the same sex marrying. Personally, I don't see why two people who love each other, want to live together, perhaps want to raise children together, and who are committed to giving each other emotional and financial support for the rest of their lives, should be barred from having the legal benefits of marriage.

I'm not talking about *religion* now. Obviously, particular religions and congregations can decide whether they want to confer the religious meaning of "marriage" on a union of two people. I'm talking about the law. Again, we need to distinguish between church and state. Under the law, married couples enjoy many benefits (such as survivor's benefits under Social Security) that are denied to unmarried couples. Why should gay couples who want these benefits be treated any differently?

Part of the problem—and confusion—is that we give *marriage* both a religious and a legal meaning. But they really are distinct. The difference would be clearer if we used "marriage" in the religious sphere and employed different words, such as "domestic partnership," in all laws and regulations that now refer to "marriage." In this case, government would confer the same set of benefits—Social Security survivor's benefits, alimony, a fair distribution of assets if relationships end in divorce, and so on—on any two people who sought to make a lifelong commitment to each other, even if they were never "married" in the religious sense of the term. Under the law, a "domestic partnership" could be made as easy or as difficult to dissolve as a "marriage" is today.

The point is, everyone should be treated the same under the law regardless of sexual orientation. This is a logical extension of the same liberal tradition that fought for civil rights for blacks and women. Radical conservatives opposed these initiatives, too. They viewed them as threatening to an old order dominated by white men. They made every effort to block the Civil Rights Act, fight desegregation, and prevent the Equal Rights Amendment from becoming part of the Constitution. Now they want to block the civil rights of gay Americans.

When I ran for governor in Massachusetts, my advisers told me it would hurt my chances if I publicly supported gay marriage, but I did anyway. My support didn't drop; actually, the polls showed a slight gain. Many people, especially young adults, agree with me that the law shouldn't discriminate against gay people.[35]

But Radcons are apoplectic about gay marriage. In 1996, they successfully pushed Congress to define heterosexual union alone as the marriage standard for purposes of collecting federal benefits. In late 2003, after the Massachusetts supreme court declared gay marriage a constitutional right, Radcons began seeking a constitutional amendment to bar it.

Bill Bennett says "marriage is by definition the union of a man and a woman" and its purpose is "the quite specific end of procreation and the nurturance of the next generation."[36] But how exactly does Bennett know this? A Canadian court came to a different conclusion in 2003, reasoning that "[s]ame-sex couples are capable of forming long, lasting, loving and intimate relationships," thereby opening the way for Canadian legislation allowing same-sex marriage.

What, exactly, is wrong with two adults obtaining a legal paper that attests to their lifelong commitment to each other?

Radcons like Bennett worry that if gay marriage were allowed, gay couples would have equal claim to adopting children, "forcing us (in law at least) to deny what we know to be true: that it is far better for a child to be raised by a mother and a father than by two homosexuals."[37] But is this really true? The evidence is far from clear.[38]

Their real objection is that gay marriage is a slippery slope to something worse. "If same-sex marriage were to prevail, society would . . . have to accept that marriage is an arbitrary social construct that can be . . . redefined by anyone laying claim to it," argues Bennett. If accepted, there would be no principled grounds to "oppose the marriage of two consenting brothers . . . [or] deny a marriage license to three men who want to marry. Or to a man who wants a consensual polygamous arrangement. Or to a father and his adult daughter."[39]

Hence, the end of civilization as we know it. "[O]nce marriage has been detached from the natural, complementary teleology of the sexes, it becomes nothing more than what each of us makes of it. This way, chaos follows: social chaos no less than intellectual and moral chaos."[40]

The slippery slope is nonsense, of course; in effect, such arguments say people are not to be trusted to impose limits on how they want to live in society. I've never heard of an instance of two consenting brothers who want to get married, of three men seeking to marry one another, or of a father wanting to marry his biological daughter. And I doubt that if prevailing laws allowed same-sex couples to marry we'd witness a great stampede of people seeking these sorts of arrangements.

Slippery-slope arguments are always used by people who can't quite come up with a good reason for why a particular change is bad. It may not be bad in and of itself, they say, but it will inevitably *lead* to things that are bad. Radcons worry a lot about slippery slopes. If we allow people to do what they want to do in private, all hell will break loose.

This is what Pennsylvania senator Rick Santorum had in mind when he warned, in the spring of 2003, that if the Supreme Court overturned the Texas law against sodomy on the basis of a right to consensual sex within your home, "then you have the right to bigamy, you have the right to incest, you have the right to adultery. You have the right to anything. . . . That's not to pick on homosexuality. It's not, you know, man on child, man on dog, or whatever the case may be."[41] (It should be noted that Santorum was no mere senator when he voiced this opinion. He was the head of the Senate Republican Conference, making him the third-ranking Republican in the Senate.)

A majority of the Court, in fact, struck down the law, eliciting a preposterous dissent from radical conservative Justice Antonin Scalia, who went even further than Santorum in his list of potential sexual nightmares, predicting an "end of all morals legislation" banning "bigamy . . . adult incest, prostitution, masturbation, adultery, fornication, bestiality, and obscenity." Scalia admonished the Court for having "taken sides in the culture war" and "signed on to the so-called homosexual agenda."[42]

In other words, if homosexuals have a right to commit sodomy, it's only a matter of time before we're in Sodom and Gomorrah. Men on dogs. Goats on women. Polygamy. Ménages à trois. Quatre. Group sex. Orgies. Public masturbation. People copulating in the middle of your street. Civilization will turn into a frenzied explosion of sex.

Santorum and Scalia are advancing ludicrous arguments to avoid this simple truth: In a free society, a majority of legislators should not be able to prevent two consenting adults from doing what they want to do with each other in private, so long as they don't harm anyone else. Sodomy is their business. Adultery is their business, too, even though they may have to deal with the emotional distress it can cause to others. Incest is different, because of the public's valid interest in preventing adult relatives from sexually abusing children.

WHY THE SEPARATION OF CHURCH AND STATE IS A GOOD IDEA

Here is a real slippery slope that *does* concern me. Once we allow Radcons or anyone else to decide how we should conduct our private sex lives, where would it end? If we accept the idea that one religion's view about proper sexual behavior should be the law of the land, how do we decide whose religious views should count? The Judeo-Christian religion itself is not all that clear. Mormons once practiced polygamy and some Mormon fundamentalist sects still do. Under Orthodox Jewish law, it's okay for nieces to marry uncles but not for nephews to marry aunts. (Go figure.)

We are already slipping down this slope. Evangelical Christians are seeking to become a majority on many of our nation's school boards so they can impose their religious views on public school children. "When we get an active Christian Parents' Committee in all districts, we can take complete control of all local school boards," crowed Robert Simonds, president of the evangelical Citizens for Excellence in Education.[43]

Even Roderick Paige, the secretary of education in George W. Bush's administration, said he'd "prefer to have a child in a school that has a strong appreciation for values of the Christian community." He told the Baptist Press that "[t]he reason that Christian schools and Christian universities are growing is a result of a strong value system. . . . That's not the case in a public school where there are so many different kids with different kinds of values."[44]

Well excuse me, Mr. Secretary, but in my book, education is very much about grappling with different kinds of values.

Huge fights are occurring over sex education in school, as well as prayer. And fundamentalists are teaching many of our school kids that homosexuality is a sin. In early 2002, at Jacksonville Junior High School in Arkansas, fourteen-year-old Thomas McLaughlin refused to deny it when another boy called him gay. According to Thomas, his eighth-grade science teacher overheard the exchange. That afternoon, Thomas's guidance counselor called his mother at work to tell her Thomas was homosexual. Later, the science teacher wrote Thomas a four-page handwritten letter referencing the Bible's teachings on homosexuality, telling the boy he'd be condemned to Hell.[45]

People are entitled to have their own religious views about sex, of course. I just don't want to live in a country where everyone has to abide by the same religious views. For more than three hundred years, the liberal tradition has sought to free people from the tyranny of religious doctrines that have been imposed on them. Keeping church and state apart should remain sacrosanct.

Abortion is a hard case. Its opponents really do believe "personhood" begins when a human male sperm and human female egg combine to create an embryo. So they believe that putting an end to that embryo is equivalent to killing a person. Personally, I disagree. So does at least half the adult population of America. Where does that leave us?

Let's at least agree on three things. First, Americans are deeply split on the question of when life begins, or whether abortion constitutes the killing of a child. Second, how one comes down on this question is a matter of personal or religious conviction. Third, we don't want to live in a society where one set of religious views is imposed on a large number of citizens who disagree with them. That's not a democracy; it's a theocracy. One religion rules all.

Perhaps someday an overwhelming majority of Americans will come to believe that having an abortion is the equivalent of killing a baby. If so, opponents of abortion will be able to muster the large majority necessary for a constitutional amendment prohibiting it. But until then, the decision should be a personal one, up to the pregnant woman, in consultation with her doctor, and, where appropriate, the man who impregnated her. This is the liberal position. It also happens to be the position of most Americans. And here again, it's only reasonable.

DINS

Radcons who fret about sex outside marriage are missing what may be a bigger problem. Arguably, there's not enough sex *inside* marriage.

I'm talking about the modern stressed-out couples too tired to do anything in bed but sleep. I call them DINS—double income, no sex. I noticed the phenomenon several years ago, and whenever I speak about it publicly, I get a sympathetic reaction from most listeners. Many couples experience it, but they think their experience is unique. They're relieved to discover they have a lot of company.

For DINS couples, even trying to have a baby is a lot of work. As they try to coordinate their small slices of time together to maximum effect, they've created a boom in sales of home ovulation-predictor kits.

Once the little darling arrives, a third of today's working parents now divide up work and child care into shifts, with one partner working during the day while the other does parental duty, then switching roles for the evening.[46] They communicate with each other by notes, listing who called while the other was out, what happened in the baby's day, what's for dinner.

Few families synchronize their schedules sufficiently to dine together. The portion of married Americans who say "definitely" that "our whole family usually eats dinner together" has dropped by a third in the last twenty years, from 50 percent to 34 percent.[47] And more homes are effectively vacant for longer periods of time. Both partners are increasingly on the road, or if working in the vicinity, away for more of the day. In 1960, 70 percent of families had at least one parent who stayed at home. By 2000, 70 percent of families were headed by two working parents or by a working single parent.[48] Small children are trundled off to day care more often; elderly parents live alone or in nursing homes.

I don't know of any definitive survey about how often married people have sex. Presumably no one wants to admit to being a sexual loser. But take a look at the books being whisked off bookstore shelves — *The Sex-Starved Marriage, Rekindling Desire: A Step-by-Step Program to Help Low-Sex and No-Sex Marriages,* and *Resurrecting Sex* — and you get a sense of what's on people's minds. *Newsweek* reports booming sales of Avlimil, an herbal concoction that purports to help women put sex back into their marriages.[49]

Why the apparent increase in DINS? My guess is it's because the proportion of married women in the labor force who have children under six jumped from under 20 percent in 1960 to over 60 percent by the late 1990s, and continues to climb. And most people who are working for pay — men and women — are working steadily more hours than ever before. The result is very little time and energy left for nookie.

What's the answer? Radcons want more women to stay home and raise their kids. Bill Bennett feels "day care is no substitute for a parent's unqualified love and devotion."[50] Here, too, Radcons would like to rewind the clock and go back to the fifties. "One of the legacies of the social revolution of our time has been to stigmatize stay-at-home mothers as antiquated and unfulfilled. . . . [They've] had to apologize for the lives they had chosen — for, in effect, siding with their children instead of with the cause of women's liberation."[51] A false analogy if ever I've heard one. According to Radcons like Bennett, the solution is to change public attitudes. "Mothers who forgo a career . . . are worthy of praise."[52]

Radcons are way off base here. Most women and men are working because they have to. Women streamed into paid work in the late 1970s largely because men's wages started to drop, and families needed two incomes. There wasn't much choice. Most poor women have been working for pay all along. The poorest of them could stay home and raise kids because they had access to welfare. But Radcons fought against welfare, and now the poorest mothers have to work and send their kids to whatever day care they can afford. Even then, at the minimum wage, it's next to impossible for them to make ends meet.

Radcons also fought against Family and Medical Leave, which allows working parents time off to be with their children when the kids are sick or otherwise need them to be home. One of my first duties as secretary of labor was to put that act into effect. The final legislation allows only twelve weeks a year, without pay. Most working parents can't afford to go without pay, which is why so few take advantage of it. America is the only advanced nation that doesn't have paid family leave for many months. More than a third of working parents don't even get holidays or sick leave from their employers.[53]

If Radcons really want to keep sex inside marriage, the first step would be to help harried couples get sex back into marriage. Make it easier for women *and* men to have more flexibility on the job and attend to their families, especially when their children are young. Start by requiring employers to provide *paid* family leave. It's only common sense.

Helping women and men be better parents while they also earn their living is a worthy public issue. People's private sexual conduct is not.

PUBLIC MORALITY AND PUBLIC TRUST

As I've said, the real *public* moral breakdown is occurring at the top, where too many powerful and wealthy people—CEOs and other top executives of major companies, Wall Street bankers and analysts, and corporate lawyers and accountants—are abusing their authority. The biggest corporate scandals in history have left small investors and employees holding empty bags, often without retirement savings or jobs. Corporate books have been doctored, treasuries looted, big investors favored over the small. CEOs have been making off with the largest pay packages in history, even after the stock market fell far below where it was in 2000. And politics is awash in campaign money coming disproportionately from powerful people with enough clout to elicit "contributions" from their employees, suppliers, and partners.

The liberal tradition has always focused on abuses of power and authority at the highest levels of society. Liberal reformers have led the way to laws and rules that stopped those abuses. It's time to do so again.

Radcons dismiss these concerns. They say the problems at the top involve a few rotten apples, hardly a broad social problem. Predictably, the *Wall Street Journal's* editorial page refers to an "atmosphere of corporate vilification" that built "to a peak after the Enron implosion."[54]

This isn't about vilifying corporations or criticizing American capitalism. And it's not about a handful of people who have stepped over the line. The problem is large and endemic, and, unless checked, it threatens the future of American capitalism.

The recent (and, sad to say, ongoing) corporate frauds represent a larger violation of public trust than corporate transgressions of the past, such as the insider-trading scandals of the 1980s. Then, relatively few Americans invested in the stock market. But during the nineties, almost twenty-seven million new investors flooded in, an increase of about 50 percent over the decade. By 2001, about half of all American households had entrusted their savings to the CEOs of American corporations, or to the stockbrokers and mutual funds that, in turn, entrust them to those CEOs.[55]

These complicated scams have required the committed services of thousands of people who designed, promoted, and executed them, or made a point of looking the other way: junior executives, board members, armies of attorneys from major law firms; platoons of accountants and auditors from big accounting firms; squadrons of investment bankers, analysts, money managers, and brokers. Most of these people are still in place, and most are still doing (or failing to do) the same things that caused the abuses.

Where are the Radcons' pious declamations of irresponsibility and sin? Where are the right-wing evangelicals who are so quick to see signs of Gomorrah whenever anyone succumbs to temptation? Nowhere to be found. Apparently their gaze extends into the nation's bedrooms but not its executive suites. Could it be they don't want to offend their financial patrons?

Enron is the poster child, of course. In 2001, shortly after its former chairman, Kenneth Lay, sold about $100 million in Enron shares, and its chief executive, Jeffrey Skilling, cashed in about $67 million in corporate stock, the value of Enron shares went from the stratosphere into the cellar. Millions of investors lost money. Enron's employees' 401(k) retirement plan lost $1.2 billion, more than half its entire value, and ten thousand Enron workers lost their jobs.

It may be comforting to think of Enron as an exception, and suppose that its colossal fraud was the work of a handful of its topmost executives and their willing aides. But almost every major bank in New York helped Enron commit fraud, including Citigroup, J. P. Morgan Chase, Merrill Lynch, and dozens of others.[56] Robert Morgenthau, then the Manhattan district attorney, got J. P. Morgan Chase and Citigroup to agree to pay $300 million in fines and penalties, mere slaps on the wrists of these giants. Morgenthau explained that it would have been hard to show that any individual banker acted with intent to commit fraud, but the bankers "knew exactly what they were doing," he said, when they lent Enron large sums of cash that Enron used to defraud its investors and employees.[57] Enron's court-appointed trustee reported that the bankers didn't merely look the other way; they dreamed up and sold Enron financial schemes specifically designed to allow Enron to commit fraud.[58]

The partners at Arthur Andersen, the prestigious accounting firm that served as Enron's auditor, didn't just look the other way, either. Andersen was convicted of obstructing justice by shredding Enron documents. These days Andersen is only a memory and thousands of its employees have had to find new jobs. But most of the former Andersen partners who aided and abetted Enron, as well as all the other Andersen partners who made it their business not to know what was going on, are still very much at work, only now at other firms.

One of Enron's ploys was to remove poor investments from its balance sheet and put them into outside partnerships—complicated webs of special-purpose entities which were in fact under the control of Enron insiders. These deals were created by talented lawyers and accountants who were (and, in most cases, still are) partners at some of the most prestigious law and accounting firms in America. Despite $2 billion in reported earnings between 1996 and 1999, Enron didn't pay a cent in federal income taxes. Here again, it didn't dream up the tax dodges on its own. It relied on teams of outside lawyers and accountants who blessed the scams with "opinion letters" asserting they were entirely legal. One shelter used a "triad" of Cayman Islands entities to hide the money. Another allowed Enron to deduct the same dollars from its tax bill more than once. (Banker's Trust's presentation to Enron executives promoting this deal was headlined "Show Me the Money!")[59] The people who dreamed up or blessed these shelters are still hard at work, though presumably exercising more care to stay technically within the law, and still taking home fees of up to one-third of whatever tax payments they save their corporate clients.[60]

One study found that Enron manipulated the prices of wholesale electricity and natural gas during the energy crisis of 2000–2001, costing California taxpayers and consumers billions of dollars. But let's be clear that Enron was just one of many culprits. The same study identified more than thirty other major companies in the energy markets that participated in the scams. The authors of the study found an "epidemic" of price manipulation.[61] The whole system was rotten.

Enron went bankrupt and Andersen is gone, but elsewhere it's business as usual. Fraud continues to come to light at other big corporations and on Wall Street. Consider that when companies "restate" their earnings, they're basically acknowledging they misinformed investors. More than 200 companies restated earnings in 2003, triple the level of the early nineties.[62] And it's not just giant firms that have defrauded millions of ordinary investors. In late 2003, Eliot Spitzer, New York State's attorney general, found that many of the Street's biggest mutual funds had cut special deals with wealthy clients at the expense of small investors, in hopes of getting even more business from the wealthy. Such deals have cost ordinary investors an estimated $5 billion a year.[63]

The spotlight is on a few high-level executives who may have defauded investors—people such as Ken Lay and Jeffrey Skilling, Worldcom's Bernard Ebbers, Tyco's Dennis Kozlowski, and Global Crossing's Gary Winnick. The "perp walks," media circuses, and courtroom dramas may satisfy the public's thirst for villains, but they divert attention from the system that supported and encouraged these abuses and which is still in place. Prosecutors are nailing a few people on conventional crimes that are relatively easy to prove, such as trading on insider information, destroying evidence, and charging personal expenses to the business. But the truly large and systemic corruption is going unpunished because it's almost impossible to prove that any single person acted with intent to commit fraud. When hundreds of bankers, lawyers, and accountants are involved, when the deals are so complex as to defy the understanding of anyone other than people who specialize in them, and when they represent the aggressive application of techniques honed by some of the most talented professionals in their fields, the outcomes beg the question of what constitutes criminal intent.

Boards of directors who were supposed to be watching over these companies and funds turned a blind eye, not wanting to know what was going on. Many directors were placed on the boards solely because they were friends of the top executives. Most of these directors and their cozy networks are still there.

So are most of the investment bankers who pocketed huge fees and doled out coveted initial public offerings—essentially, first-in-line status to buy hot, new stock—to corporate chieftains who would shift business their way. So are most of the money managers who gave big investors lucrative trading privileges unavailable to small investors. So are most of the stock analysts who urged small investors to plunge into whatever companies the investment bankers were courting, even if the stocks were dogs. Merrill Lynch's Henry Blodget got caught because his e-mails were unusually explicit. He told a large institutional investor that there was "nuthin" interesting about Internet advertising firm GoTo.com, even though he and Merrill were publicly recommending it—prompting another Merrill analyst to worry in an e-mail that "john and mary smith are losing their retirement because we don't want [a GoTo executive] to be mad at us." But most others, more discreet and less flamboyant than Blodget—like the analyst from Lehman Brothers who assessed the same firm's stock ratings as "fairly meaningless" and noted "yes, the 'little guy' who isn't smart . . . may get misled"[64]—are still at their computers and on their phones.

It took a drain of the stock market to expose a lot of this, like the flotsam that appears when tides recede. Alan Greenspan, the chairman of the Federal Reserve, assured America that there was no increase in human greed during the 1990s, just an increase in the opportunities for greedy behavior. Perhaps. But most of those opportunities still exist.

New laws and regulations have been issued, but the reforms are full of holes. "I'm surprised at the day-in and day-out level of malfeasance that comes in under the radar," says William H. Donaldson, chairman of the Securities and Exchange Commission, after the reforms went into effect.[65]

Conflicts of interest are still endemic. In a late 2003 survey of professional money managers, more than two-thirds were skeptical that the new changes in corporate governance would prevent future accounting scams. Most thought the new anti-fraud regulations were ineffective.[66] In another survey, most said that trading abuses were "systemic."[67] Stephen Cutler, the SEC's head of enforcement, warned in late 2003 of a "conflicts of interest crisis" that continued to threaten small investors.[68] Despite new rules barring auditors from providing clients with management consulting advice, for example, auditing firms are still peddling lucrative tax shelters. At the "Big Four" accounting firms, revenues on such deals have been growing as fast as auditing revenues. Some of these schemes are blatantly illegal.[69] But anyone who believes that auditors are going to crack down on the tax shelters that their own firms designed for the same clients is not engaging in rational thought.

A few executives have been fined, but the fines are nothing compared to the money they ran off with. Blodget, for example, settled on a $4 million penalty for misleading small investors. Not a bad deal considering he made at least $20 million during his stardom at Merrill, and left with a buyout worth an estimated $5 million.[70] What kind of deterrence is that?

The Radcon editorial writers of the *Wall Street Journal*, you may remember, were quick to point out that the poor need strict social "guardrails." The Radcons cling to their belief that society's poor and weak need to be disciplined. No sex before marriage. No welfare payments unless they work forty hours a week. If they commit petty theft or are caught with drugs, lock them up. America's prisons are bursting.

But Radcons don't apply the same moral indignation to the Henry Blodgets of the world. The stronger and wealthier at the highest reaches of American economic power apparently don't need rules. They make their own. Now we know the consequences of this brazenly elitist assumption. And the people who have borne the brunt of it are millions of small investors and employees. Is the Radcon position reasonable? I think not.

Liberals believe that the CEOs of publicly held companies, Wall Street bankers, money managers, and publicly licensed lawyers and accountants hold positions of public trust. The old meaning of being a "professional" was to be anointed with a special obligation to the public. That's why professional schools of business and law were established, and why professionals take ethics courses and pass public examinations. But anyone looking at what's been happening has to ask: Whatever happened to professional responsibility? What is being taught in these graduate schools and ethics courses? What are the limits of acceptable behavior?

In reality, the only practical limit is the risk and cost of getting caught. The goal is to make more money and beat the competition *whatever it takes.* In the wake of the scandals, both the risks and costs of getting caught have ratcheted up somewhat. Hence, a spike in the costs of insuring corporate officers, directors, outside lawyers, and auditors.

Don't misunderstand me. Not many managers or professionals wake up in the morning and ask: What really bad things can I get away with today? The problem is that so few apparently ask: What bad things do I know about that I should try to stop? Even if it's technically legal, does it violate the spirit of the law? Does it hurt people who entrusted their savings and jobs to me? Does it contradict common sense about what's fair and right?

There are no guardrails at the top. And the Radcons don't seem terribly worried about it.

THE REAL SCANDAL OF EXECUTIVE PAY

In 1992, Bill Clinton campaigned against the exorbitant pay of corporate executives. He thought it unseemly for the average CEO to take home eighty-five times the pay of the average hourly worker. So Clinton proposed that companies be prohibited from deducting from their taxable earnings executive pay over $1 million year.

Things didn't work out exactly the way Clinton planned. By 2000, the average CEO was pocketing more than 500 times the pay of the average annual worker.[71] (By 2002, after the Wall Street bubble burst, and corporations lost about $7 trillion of investor value, the ratio settled down to a more modest 282 times.) To put this in perspective, consider that over the last twenty-some years, the pay of average rank-and-file workers, when adjusted for inflation, has risen by about 15 percent. Over the same interval, CEO pay has skyrocketed nearly 600 percent.[72]

Clinton's proposal quietly morphed into an innocuous Treasury Department rule requiring that executive pay be linked to company performance. When the irrational exuberance of the late nineties carried the public shares of almost all companies to dizzying heights, top executives took full credit and their compensation packages exploded, including generous options to buy the shares at their lower historic prices and cash in big time. Stock options were handed out like candy. Apple Computer's Steven Jobs and Oracle's Larry Ellison each got options on 20 million shares of their respective company's stock. CEOs had so many options that even slight upticks in company stock reaped them a bonanza. And because they could cash in as soon as a year after the options were granted, they had every incentive to pump up the share prices in the short term by exaggerating company earnings.

After the bubble burst and share prices plummeted, the same CEOs claimed it wasn't their doing. So their pay continued to rise. Their boards granted them more options at even cheaper prices. When Apple's stock tanked, Jobs got 7.5 million additional options priced even lower than the market value of Apple shares. After Apple's stock continued to fall, Jobs got the right to exchange his options for $70 million worth of stock outright.

At least basketball stars and baseball MVPs get pay packages that relate to their winning seasons (especially in arbitration). Not America's top executives.

The fiscal year ending in 2003 wasn't an especially good one for shareholders. Nor for employees: The paychecks of salaried employees grew an anemic 3.5 percent, and a lot of them got pink slips.[73] But according to a *Fortune* survey of a hundred of the nation's biggest companies, the typical CEO got a raise of 14 percent, bringing his total take-home pay to more than $13 million. Here's a sampling:

- William R. Johnson, chairman and CEO of H. J. Heinz, got a pay package valued at $8.8 million, a 47 percent raise over the previous year. Over the same year, Heinz stock dropped about 20 percent, or about twice the decline of the stock of other packaged food companies.[74]

- Jeffrey Barbakow, former chairman of Tenet Healthcare Corporation, cashed in stock options worth $111.1 million. In the aftermath of a federal probe of Tenet's finances, Tenet's share value plummeted nearly 60 percent.

- The disgraced Dennis Kozlowski of Tyco took home $71 million—not including the $2 million weeklong birthday party he threw for his wife on the island of Sardinia and other mammoth expenses he billed to the company—even as Tyco's shares tanked.[75]

- Richard Scrushy of beleaguered HealthSouth took in $142 million from selling stock.[76]

- Scott McNealy of Sun Microsystems hauled in $53.1 million over three years, mostly through exercising stock options. Meanwhile, the value of Sun shares plunged 92 percent.

- While the stocks of major airlines plummeted, CEO pay soared. Delta Air Lines rewarded Leo Mullin an estimated $13.8

million, up 104 percent from 2001. Meanwhile, returns to share-holders dropped 58 percent.[77]

• Michael Eisner of Disney took in $6 million, up 498 percent. Disney's shares were down 18 percent.

• David Komansky, chairman of Merrill Lynch, got $14.4 million, including a $7 million bonus, despite M-L's stock market plunge. CEO Stanley O'Neal took home $14.3 million.

• Jim Mulva, CEO of ConocoPhillips, the oil and gas giant, garnered $27.5 million, while its share price dropped 20 percent.

• Jack Welch of GE said he deserved the tens of millions he received annually during his tenure as CEO because GE's stock price soared. But did he deserve the $2.5 million a year he got in retirement perks after much of GE's paper value vanished? Those perks, incidentally, included a New York apartment, free flowers, wine, dry cleaning, vitamins, cars, aircraft, and security systems, as revealed in divorce papers filed by Welch's ex-wife, Jane.[78]

• David D'Alessandro, of John Hancock Financial Services, got a hefty $21.7 million, up 162 percent, while Hancock's share price dropped 32 percent.

Where's the shame? Radcon moralists blather on endlessly about shame and outrage. Bill Bennett has even written a book entitled *The Death of Outrage.* Almost every time I see Radcons on television or hear them on the radio it seems as if they're whining about some "shameful," "shameless," "disgraceful," "deplorable," "odious," "contemptible," "detestable," "depraved," "reprehensible," "heinous," "debased," or just plain "vile" behavior — usually attributed to someone who is poor, black, or Hispanic, or a feminist, environmentalist, or liberal. But I've never heard a Radcon apply any of these adjectives to

CEO pay. The only explanation I can come up with is that, here again, they don't want to alienate their friends and patrons.

These pay packages *are* shameful. There's absolutely no reason for them.

Corporate apologists try to justify them by saying CEOs will otherwise be lured somewhere else. Richard Syron, head of the compensation committee of John Hancock's board of directors, explained that "D'Alessandro . . . is a real major-league talent. He's not a guy who has to work in the insurance industry. He could go to work in a number of places and make big bucks." So D'Alessandro deserved $21.7 million, even though Hancock's shareholders took a bath.[79]

To believe this rationale you've also got to believe that (1) other companies are eager to hire top executives with such lousy track records, (2) top executives who ride the gravy train when the stock market is going up have no responsibility to ride it down, as most of their employees and shareholders must do, and (3) top executives can't be expected to be loyal to their firms. To put it another way, in order to justify these salaries, one has to engage in exactly the kind of "nonjudgmentalism" that Bill Bennett objects to. It's a tolerance, rooted in moral relativism, that refuses to distinguish between right and wrong.

The *Wall Street Journal* thinks these CEO pay packages are not only right, but good. "[L]ooking over the past 20 years," says *Journal* columnist Holman Jenkins, "we all benefit from the willingness of companies to wave big money carrots in front of their servants."[80] Come again? As Tonto asked the Lone Ranger, who's "we," kemosabe? Over the past twenty years, as executive pay moved into the stratosphere, the pay and benefits of average working Americans have gone essentially nowhere. In the 1990s, many of these same Americans invested their scant retirement savings in the stock market, only to discover—too late—that it was a bubble filled with hot air. Then they found out that a lot of reported corporate earnings had been pumped up with helium. CEOs, on the other hand, did just fine.

Their "big money carrots" were real. They cashed in their options early enough to beat the imploding market. How did they manage to do that? Because, contrary to Mr. Jenkins's glib assertion, CEOs are no one's servants. They're the ones who appoint the boards that give out the big money carrots.

This is bad for America, and bad for American business. When top executives get huge pay hikes at the same time as middle-level and hourly workers lose their jobs and retirement savings, or have to accept negligible pay raises and cuts in health and pension benefits, company morale plummets. I hear it all the time from employees: This company, they say, is being run only for the benefit of the people at the top. So why should *we* put in extra effort, commit extra hours, take on extra responsibilities? We'll do the minimum, even cut corners.

This is often the death knell of a company. Sometimes the loss of trust endangers the company immediately. Although the airline industry has one of the worst records of management-labor relations in America, most employees are still willing to accept pay cuts if their jobs depend on it. But in 2003, Don Carty, head of American Airlines, tested the limit. He asked employees to accept pay cuts in order to avoid bankruptcy but didn't tell them about $41 million he stashed away in a special trust fund to protect the pensions of forty-five top executives if the company went bust anyway. When the trust fund was revealed and employees balked at the deal, Carty was forced to resign.

Where's the shame? In 2002, Motorola contributed $38 million to a special pension trust fund with assets of $135 million for its top executives. Meanwhile, the company's pension plan for more than 70,000 employees and retirees was underfunded by $1.4 billion. Motorola's top management made no move to close the gap.[81]

Where's the outrage? No sooner do top executives receive their pay than they shelter it from taxes. In 2000, for example, William Esrey, then the chief executive of Sprint, earned $20 million in stock option profits. He promptly bought a tax shelter from Ernst and Young, the accounting firm, that enabled him to delay reporting the profits for tax purposes until 2030. I don't know how old Esrey is now, but I do hope he lives to a ripe old age.

What's the limit? Whatever it is, Richard Grasso exceeded it. In the midst of revelations about exorbitant pay packages at American corporations, Grasso, then chairman of the New York Stock Exchange—supposedly there to regulate American corporations—received $12 million for his services in 2002, about half the exchange's net income that year. In 2003 he got a compensation package totaling $139.5 million, including deferred pay from prior years. The news caused such a public firestorm that Grasso was forced to resign (taking his money with him).

The real scandal here was that the New York Stock Exchange, a nonprofit institution charged with maintaining investor and public confidence, allowed Grasso to be paid this much. How did this happen? Simple. Grasso had appointed the directors who decided on his pay. The head of the compensation committee was the lead director and co-founder of Home Depot, and Grasso simultaneously served on Home Depot's board. Talk about conflicts of interest.

The exchange's entire board should have resigned along with Grasso. But the Radcons at the *Wall Street Journal* came up with a rationale for their benevolence toward him. They editorialized that Grasso was worth every penny because he helped the Big Board's member firms prosper. "Now we know how much Mr. Grasso's efforts to preserve the [New York Stock Exchange] franchise are worth to those who benefit directly."[82] *"Those who benefit directly"?* The last time I looked, the New York Stock Exchange was supposed to regulate member firms on behalf of all investors, small as well as large. Given what happened to investors under Grasso's watch, he should have been sacked long ago, without pay. The Big Board was supposed to regulate; it obviously did no such thing.

Radcons can't have it both ways. They can't condemn the moral breakdown of American society and simultaneously celebrate all this flimflam in the highest realms of corporate America. Recall the stern admonition of political scientist James Q. Wilson, often quoted by Radcons: Maintaining limits is a way of preserving community. Without limits, there's no way to build the trust on which civilization depends. Remember Bill Bennett's warning: America has adopted "a deeply ingrained philosophy that glorifies . . . freedom from constraints."

Radcons don't apply their moral compass to people with inordinate wealth and power. They worry about alleged immorality among gays and the poor. But liberals understand that American society is endangered by the lack of moral scruple at the top—in many respects, more so.

The behavior of these executives and of the legions who help them is the moral equivalent of spray-painting FUCK YOU on the wall of a public school. It announces that there are no limits to anti-social behavior—that, essentially, anything goes. Moynihan was furious that the words had been left on the wall. We should be no less appalled.

We are defining deviancy down. Remember the public firestorm that erupted in 1996 when AT&T announced it was firing some 40,000 employees and then gave the boss stock options that raised his total compensation to $16 million from $6.7 million? Today, such behavior would be deemed normal. The only limit, it seems, comes when someone who's supposed to regulate Wall Street takes home more than $100 million.

Why did top executives go from earning 42 times what an average hourly worker took home in 1980, to 85 times as much in 1990, to more than 280 times as much now? As noted, their "market value" couldn't possibly have risen so much, especially in light of their company's poor performance in recent years. The answer is that there is no longer a norm that limits top compensation.

Years ago there were limits. Chief executives engaged in widely publicized rounds of bargaining with their labor unions. In wartime, they served on government boards and converted their factories to military production. In peacetime, they routinely responded to government requests to moderate price increases. If CEOs didn't exercise restraint, blue-collar production couldn't be expected to restrain their own demands for higher wages.

CEOs were also linked to certain cities where they built their headquarters and did most of their production—Kodak in Rochester, New York, Coca-Cola in Atlanta, Procter & Gamble in Cincinnati, and so on. They lived in proximity to their middle-level managers. They worked in the same communities as their blue-collar employees.

Under all these circumstances it would have been unseemly for them to take home wages and benefits wildly in excess of what other Americans earned.

But in more recent years, large corporations have morphed into global financial and technological networks. Their work is outsourced to an ever-growing number of contractors and suppliers all over the world, and many of their middle-level managers and hourly workers have disappeared. Corporations are less anchored to particular cities. Top executives now congregate in the rich suburbs of New York, around Washington and Los Angeles, and on tony spas and golf courses in the Southwest or the Caribbean.

In other words, the connections that once defined the corporation and linked its top executives to their employees and communities, and to the nation, have been disappearing. And with the disappearance of these connections, the social norms that constrained executives have also vanished.

Even in the early 1990s, before the stock market soared and then plunged, before the corporate scandals, CEO pay in America was "deviant" in the sense that it was far higher than the pay of the CEOs in other countries relative to their own workers, and far higher than at any other time in modern American history. Then it grew even more wildly out of line. But what had been disturbing came to be expected. Then, what became expected became acceptable. Finally, what became acceptable began to seem appropriate.

Radcons couldn't care less. If you're rich, you must somehow deserve it. If you're poor, you deserve that, too.

Liberals must sound the alarm.

LEGALIZED BRIBERY

Along with the meltdown of executive and professional ethics has come a flood of dollars into politics.

Follow the money: Elected officials need ever more of it for television ads. The costs grow with each election cycle, like escalating competition in nuclear armaments. Wealthy executives and professionals, flush with cash, provide the bulk of it. Their prime motivation isn't generosity or commitment to good government. Few would donate if the recipients had no idea—and could never discover—who the donors were.* They donate because they expect the candidate to reciprocate in some way, if elected. Some of that reciprocity enables the executives or professionals to avoid or skirt the law, and accumulate even more money.

In other words, most campaign donations—those that depend on the recipient knowing who gave what—amount to legalized bribery.

I say this with some remorse. Remember, I ran for governor of Massachusetts in 2002. Massachusetts limits campaign contributions to $500 per person per year, and I got started late. As a result, I spent

---

* One interesting proposal for campaign finance reform is to require that all contributions be passed through a kind of blind trust that would bar candidates from discovering who contributed what. Anyone could *claim* to have contributed vast amounts, but because the elected official would have no way of verifying such claims, no actual contributor would have disproportionate influence. See Bruce Ackerman et al., *Voting with Dollars: A New Paradigm for Campaign Finance* (New Haven, Conn.: Yale University Press, 2002).

about six hours a day on the phone, dialing for dollars, every day for ten months. Try this for several months and see if you don't have a new appreciation for campaign finance reform.

George W. Bush assumed he could raise nearly $200 million for his reelection coffers even before the general election got under way, another record. More and more of the really big dollars are coming from fewer wealthy people: Each of Bush's leading fundraising groups, the "Rangers" and the "Pioneers," was meant to be composed of only a few hundred members. To be a Ranger, one had to raise at least $200,000 in contributions of not more than $2,000 each (under current law); a Pioneer, $100,000.[83] Typically, the money was to come from friends and business associates. A prospective Ranger or Pioneer twists arms of junior executives, and pressures suppliers and contractors. Hence, the size of the bundle of donations he (almost always "he") is meant to accumulate perfectly represents the economic clout he wields.

Only a quarter of one percent of American voters ponied up $200 or more in the 2002 election. Yet their donations comprised half the total. About 40 percent of them had incomes in the top one percent.[84]

It's not just presidential campaigns whose costs are escalating. In 2002 mid-term races, Democrats and Republicans collected and spent more in direct contributions than in any mid-term election in history—43 percent more than in the 1998 mid-term.[85] Since 1980 the cost of running for an open House or Senate seat has roughly *quintupled*. The cost of gubernatorial races, as I painfully discovered, isn't far behind.

What's wrong with rich people influencing officials with campaign contributions? It leads to government action (or inaction) that further concentrates wealth and power, which leads to larger and more effective bribes the next time around. Talk about slippery slopes: Radcons see the sexual proclivities of relatively poor people leading to social disintegration. A far larger worry is the greedy proclivities of wealthy people undermining our democracy. America's rich are richer than ever; income and wealth are concentrated in fewer hands; the shadow bribes are getting larger.

Much of President Bush's financial support came from those who benefited most directly from the $1.7 trillion worth of tax cuts he engineered between 2001 and 2003. They're the people with incomes of over $1 million a year who received the biggest cuts—and who will avoid taxes on their giant estates as the estate tax is phased out. In 2003, Radcon Republican political strategist Grover Norquist advised prospective funders that "[t]he best way to 'lobby' to be in next year's tax cut is to cheerfully support the president's tax cut this year."[86]

The system is perfectly circular. The generous contributions allow top corporate executives and Wall Street financiers to enrich themselves at the expense of small investors and average workers. Why do you suppose Congress decided in 1994 that stock options should not be treated as liabilities on corporate balance sheets—and Congress still refuses to pass legislation recognizing them as such?[87] Why did Congress in 1995 decide to shield accounting firms from liability for inaccurate corporate reporting—and continues to shield them? Why, even after the corporate scandals, did the 2003 tax bill fail to close notorious tax shelters costing the government about $50 billion annually—loopholes serving no economic purpose other than reducing tax bills?* Why were proposals that would have required law firms to report clients that persistently broke the law so swiftly derailed? Why, on the heels of the government's supposed crackdown on corporate misbehavior, did the Securities and Exchange Commission kill, soften, or water down rules that would have imposed new obligations

---

* Despite the avowed purpose of reducing taxes on corporate dividends to avoid "double taxation" of corporate earnings (the first on corporate income, the second when that income is distributed as dividends), the 2003 tax bill didn't close loopholes and shelters. As a result, much corporate income won't even get taxed once. The Senate had proposed modest reforms, such as requiring that companies disclose transactions having large effects on their tax bills and barring transactions serving no economic purpose other than reducing taxes, but the House refused to go along after lobbyists applied pressure.

on lawyers and accountants? Why are conflicts of interest still rampant on Wall Street? Why are companies still allowed to distribute stock options without carrying them as expenses on their balance sheets? Why has Congress failed to require that fund boards be chaired by independent outsiders? Why are accounting firms that do company audits still allowed to sell their clients advice about how to avoid paying taxes?[88]

The answer to all these questions is the same: because lawyers, accountants, Wall Street investment bankers, money managers, and corporate executives insisted on it. And they got what they wanted because they're the ones pouring the most money into political campaigns. Radcons won't admit this, of course (and neither will Democrats who have sided with them). They will tell you that such measures would place an unwarranted burden on business and therefore retard economic growth. But, in fact, these reforms would improve investor confidence by preventing further outbreaks of fraud. They would thereby strengthen the economy, not weaken it.

In industry after industry, top executives are getting good returns on their campaign "investments." Pharmaceutical industry officials invested more than $50 million to help Republicans gain control of Congress in 2002. Just days after the election, the United States, alone among 144 members of the World Trade Organization, blocked a proposal to distribute patented drugs to developing nations at a fraction of their price. Even the *Wall Street Journal* noted the connection: "[T]he episode makes one fact of American political life undeniably clear: After spending millions of dollars on campaign help in recent years, the pharmaceutical industry has accumulated powerful friends it can turn to in a pinch."[89] The same could be said of oil and gas interests, which seem to have written the Bush administration's energy and environmental policies (Enron's errant Ken Lay has been one of the largest individual financial backers of George W. Bush's political career); military contractors, who reaped a bonanza from the defense buildup and occupation of Iraq; and agribusiness, which got a huge windfall when agricultural subsidies were hiked.

The brazenness of some bribes can only be described as astounding. As reported in the *Washington Post* in May 2002, Douglas Lawrence, then vice president of Westar Energy, sent an e-mail to Washington lobbyist Richard Bornemann, saying Westar wanted an exemption from a key federal energy regulation, and listing several Republican candidates and committees that should receive campaign contributions from Westar. In another e-mail, Lawrence told his colleagues that "[w]e have $11,500 in immediate needs for a group of candidates associated with [House majority leader] Tom DeLay, Billy Tauzin, Joe Barton, and Senator Richard Shelby." That same month, Westar made a $25,000 contribution to DeLay's political action committee. In September, DeLay met privately with Westar officials and Bornemann to address the amendment the company sought, and shortly thereafter Representative Barton added the provision to the House version of the energy bill. (The amendment was withdrawn a few weeks later only when it was disclosed that Westar was under federal investigation for alleged fraud and other matters.)[90]

When it came time for the Bush administration to award the major contracts for reconstructing Iraq after the 2003 war, bidding was restricted to four groups of U.S. companies, which had contributed a total of $2.8 million to political candidates between 1999 and 2002, mostly to Republicans. All told, the executives and PACs of the seventy individual companies that received government contracts for work in Iraq, as well as in Afghanistan, contributed more than $500,000 to Bush's 2000 campaign—more money than they contributed to any other politician in the previous twelve years.[91] The Bechtel Group was the largest single donor, having given $1.3 million. The largest single contract for reconstructing Iraq was awarded to Bechtel (more on Bechtel, later).[92]

Some of the contributions come from lobbyists for companies

that have played especially fast and loose with the law. The chief lobbyist for Freddie Mac, the home financing giant embroiled in an accounting scandal in 2003, staged at least fifty fundraisers for congressional Republicans in the two years before the scandal came to light, as well as a number of fundraisers for Democrats. During this interlude, the company—which depends on an implicit government guarantee to back up its debts—easily fought off attempts by some in Congress to bring it under increased federal regulation.[93] Likewise, legislators promise easy treatment to firms and industries that come through with cash. According to the *Washington Post*, in late 2002 Michael Oxley, chairman of the House Financial Services Committee, and his top aides pressured a consortium of mutual fund companies to replace their top Washington lobbyist with a Republican. Oxley's staff suggested to industry officials that a pending congressional probe of the mutual fund industry might ease up if they complied.[94]

Not only are campaign contributions dangled before members of Congress. Members also are eligible for lucrative lobbying jobs when they leave their public posts. More than one in five former members who left Congress in the 1990s turned to lobbying, up from a tiny fraction in the 1970s and 1980s.[95] The trend is similar for top officials of the executive branch. Sad to admit, more than half of the hundred top officials at the end of the Clinton administration turned within a year to lobbying or working for companies that do so, about the same record as the alumni of the first Bush administration.[96] What happened to Clinton's executive order barring his officials from lobbying for five years? In the final days of his administration, as lucrative lobbying jobs beckoned, Clinton was somehow moved to revoke it.

Understand that I'm not suggesting outright bribery, as commonly understood. Few wealthy corporate executives or top professionals contribute to political campaigns specifically to lower their tax bills or get a law or federal contract to their liking. Few members of Congress vote explicitly on the basis of who donated what to their campaigns, or of their own future job prospects. Usually, the corruption is more subtle. Those who give the money know they're supporting politicians who will accommodate their needs, be sensitive to their values, support their way of life. Politicians who take the money accept these conditions. On both sides, the increasing flood of campaign contributions is rationalized as "just the way the game is played."

But in fact we're witnessing a large-scale moral breakdown that threatens the capacity of our democratic system to meet the needs of our people. "The really damaging perception now is that many of these mega-incomes have been gained through the abuse of power—and that, in some cases, they are also being preserved by the use of that moneyed power in politics," intones the traditionally conservative *Economist* magazine, in assessing the state of American capitalism and democracy in 2003. "Worse still, the perception is largely correct."[97]

PERP WALKS ARE NOT ENOUGH

The problem isn't just a few "rotten apples." Footage of accused or convicted business leaders is nice for TV stations, but it doesn't touch a system that motivates tens of thousands of executives and professionals to do what's best for themselves even if it's bad for many other Americans.

Liberals should lead the charge. Laws must be strengthened to avoid conflicts of interest, and such conflicts must be better policed. All directors of corporations and mutual funds must be independent of management, and shareholders should be empowered to choose them. Politics must be better insulated from money. (One possibility: As a condition for keeping their broadcast licenses, require television and radio stations to run free campaign ads for all candidates meeting a certain threshold of eligibility.)

But the problem is deeper and more pervasive: It lies in a culture of unfettered greed at the top, which places personal gain above pub-lic responsibility. The toughest laws can always be circumvented by lawyers, financiers, and other lackeys clever enough to pry open tiny nuances and exploit possible ambiguities. To the well-trained attor-ney or accountant, laws are never black and white; they come only in shades of elastic gray. Hence, the existence of "aggressive" account-ing and lawyering in pursuit of ever more exotic ways to show profits, compensate executives, dodge taxes, and avoid campaign finance limits. As fast as the laws change, clever minds can invent new ways to skirt them. If all else fails, the global economy offers ever more entic-ing ways to conceal complex transactions.

Besides, wads of campaign cash can prevent tough laws from being enacted in the first place, or cause legislators to insert loopholes in them to render them toothless, or else blunt their enforcement. (One of the most effective and least visible ways to repeal tax and securities laws has been for Congress and the White House to starve the Internal Revenue Service and the Securities and Exchange Com-mission of staff to enforce them.)

There's no simple answer, but surely part of the solution is to take public morality seriously.

Enough of Radcon pieties about the moral deviance of gays, the moral weaknesses of poor single mothers, or the moral bankruptcy of liberalism. It's time for a vigorous liberalism that holds morally accountable those who abuse their authority. We need *moral* as well as legal limits on rapacious CEOs, accountants, lawyers, brokers, and investment bankers—people who are stewards of the economy but don't give a damn what happens to the millions of small investors, as well as employees, they're supposed to represent.

People with great wealth and power have a special responsibility to *refrain* from doing things their wealth and power might enable them to do, but at the same time will undermine the trust that our democratic capitalist system depends on. And we need to call them on it. Professionals must say *no* to lucrative business deals that may be technically legal but are wrong because they exploit the trust that investors or employees have placed in them. Executives must say *no* to pay packages that are ludicrously high compared with the pay of average workers. Politicians and their benefactors must say *no* to a system that rewards rich donors for showering money on people who are supposed to represent the public as a whole.

Absent this, those who abuse their authority often stand a good chance of dodging the consequences because the damage is inherently cumulative and systemic, resulting in a general reduction of trust by everyone—investors, employees, voters. Such abuses of power precipitate all manner of precautions. Red tape multiplies. Litigation escalates. The result can be a kind of social gridlock similar to what happens when a driver crowds into an intersection as the light turns red, blocking other drivers from going through on their green. As gridlock becomes the norm, the effect is to ensnarl everyone.

Cynicism about our economic and political system encourages everyone to act selfishly, even when widespread selfishness imperils the entire system. Without a shared sense of public morality, the individual feels powerless against the greedy behavior of others, and impelled to act selfishly in defense. "Why should *I* be a chump?" he asks. Hence, the employee engages in petty theft, the small businessman cuts shady deals, the small investor leaves and stays out of the market, the average citizen doesn't bother to vote. This is the real slippery slope, and we're already sliding down it.

Bill Bennett had it right when he said that "moral good and moral harm are very real things, and moral good or moral harm can come to a society by what it esteems and what it disdains."[98] Bennett had his sights on Bill Clinton and sex; he should have been talking about the increasingly rapacious behavior at the uppermost reaches of our economic and political system. A system that handsomely rewards platoons of high-powered professionals for circumventing laws and regulations, that enables top executives to accumulate unprecedented fortunes by manipulating company earnings and cashing in options before the company tanks, that allows rich and powerful people to influence politicians in order to maintain their lucrative dealmaking, and that imposes large costs on everyone else is not sustainable. Unrestrained greed is far more dangerous to the future of our republic than unconstrained sex.

Twice over the last century, liberals have saved capitalism from its own excesses. The first time was in the early 1900s. By then, captains of American industry had monopolized the economy into giant trusts, American politics had sunk into a swamp of patronage and corruption, and many factory jobs were unsafe—entailing long hours of work at meager pay, often exploiting children. In response, liberals championed anti-trust laws, civil service reforms, and labor protections.

The second save occurred in the 1930s, after the stock market collapsed and a large portion of the American workforce was unemployed. Then, liberals regulated banks and insured deposits, cleaned up the stock market, and provided social insurance to the destitute.

Both times, liberal reformers were accused of interfering in the free market. But in both instances, liberal reformers prevailed. They did so by appealing to public morality and common sense.

It is time, once again, for liberals to restore confidence in our system and save capitalism from itself.

CHAPTER THREE

REAL PROSPERITY

THE LIBERAL PROMISE OF PROSPERITY

Radcons insist on "privatizing" social insurance, cutting social services, and giving large tax breaks mainly to people who are rich. They say these measures encourage personal responsibility and spur economic growth. Liberals, to the extent they're heard at all, typically object that these steps are grossly unfair.

Looming as the backdrop to this lopsided debate is the fact that by 2004, the distribution of income and wealth in America was more unequal than at any time since the Gilded Age of the late nineteenth century. America had become the most economically stratified society in the advanced democratic world. The richest one percent of Americans earned about 17 percent of national income—and owned about 40 percent of the nation's wealth.[1] Over the coming decade, the Bush tax cuts will transfer more wealth to the richest one percent of the population than any fiscal policies in history.

Yet in a debate that seems to pit economic growth against fairness, liberals lose. Part of the reason lies in how liberals define "fairness." They make it seem like too squishy an idea—appropriate for soft hearts rather than hard heads. Besides, most of the people who are being hurt by Radcon cuts in social spending *appear* to be poor and black or brown—"them" rather than "us." And most of those who are getting tax breaks and accumulating fortunes are people whom a lot of Americans would like to emulate.

Liberals shouldn't abandon convictions about fairness. But to be persuasive to the rest of America, the ideal of fairness has to be embedded in a hardheaded program to promote prosperity for everyone. Rather than help wealthy people stay on top, we need to help all working people build their wealth. The truth is, fairness and growth aren't at odds; they complement each other. Prosperity is easier to achieve if it's widely shared. Let me explain.

THE FLOOD

In 1954, Hurricane Carol swelled the Naugatuck River and sent a ton of silt through my father's store, carrying away the whole stock of cheap cotton dresses and blouses. Dad decided to start over, going upscale this time. Mom convinced him there was more money to be made catering to rich women whose husbands worked in large paneled offices in the corporate headquarters that were sprouting all over the countryside.

"Sportswear," she told him with utter certainty. "Country casual."

But how to begin? Dad was broke and not a particularly good credit risk. Then he discovered he was eligible for government disaster assistance being made available to small businesses that were wiped out in the flood. With the money, he and Mom opened a new store. Luckily, it was a great success.

The episode has stuck in my mind because it's the closest my family came to going under. I'll never forget the fear that went directly from my father to the rest of us. The disaster relief saved us. By the way, a few years after the flood, Dad became a Democrat.

Disaster relief is a tiny sliver of government spending, of course. Yet in reality, most of the government is a big insurance agency. Other than the military, the biggest categories of government spending are Social Security and Medicare (insurance against poverty in old age), unemployment insurance (against loss of income from job loss), and Medicaid (against lack of health care if you are or become poor).

Many Radcons think government shouldn't be in the insurance business. They believe people should take responsibility for themselves and not expect government to bail them out. In the first year of the George W. Bush administration, his then blunt-speaking Treasury secretary, Paul O'Neill, told the *Financial Times:* "Able-bodied adults should save enough on a regular basis so they can provide for their own retirement and, for that matter, health and medical needs."[2] By the same logic, presumably, able-bodied people should put money aside in case they lose their jobs or their businesses.

I don't know what planet Mr. O'Neill lives on, but he doesn't know much about this one.

The idea of government as insurer was dreamed up more than a century ago by Germany's "Iron Chancellor," Otto von Bismarck, who came up with plans for old age, accidents, sickness, and unemployment. Franklin D. Roosevelt brought social insurance to America in 1935. "I see no reason why every child, from the day he is born, shouldn't be a member of the social security system," Roosevelt said.[3]

Some of this was less ambitious than it sounded. Social Security kicked in at age sixty-five, but when it was enacted the average person didn't live much beyond sixty-one. (Today's life expectancy is seventy-seven and still rising.) Still, these programs marked a whole new way of thinking about the role of government, and they were enormously popular.

They were created for Americans as a system of insurance, not welfare. The basic idea was that we are all in the same boat together. Misfortune can happen to *anyone.* The result was a giant system of redistribution—mostly from young to old (the typical retiree now takes out three times more Social Security and Medicare than he or she ever put into the system), but also from healthy to sick, employed to unemployed, people who didn't suffer a natural disaster to people who did. But it didn't *feel* like redistribution because the money didn't go from "us" to "them." It went from us to us.

These programs remained popular because they were based on "it could happen to me" thinking. Any one of us could fall out of the boat. Unless we promised to rescue one another, some of us would drown. And—here's the important part—there was no way to know in advance which of us might need the rescuing.

Over time, though, some programs became less popular because their beneficiaries started to look and seem different from the rest of us. One such program was part of the original Social Security Act, designed to help mothers whose husbands or partners died or abandoned them. Increasingly, the women who collected what came to be known as welfare checks were black or brown. "Why should *my* hard-earned tax dollars go to *them?*" became a common refrain among white working- and middle-class households.

Radical conservatives complained the most bitterly, and criticized welfare recipients the loudest. Welfare policies "have produced a large class of people, mostly female, who are dependent on welfare," wrote Robert Bork. ". . . [T]hese are mostly young women of substandard intelligence, self-discipline, and motivation; otherwise they would not be in the predicament they are."[4]

But those who complained about that "class of people" didn't seem to know the facts: By the mid-1990s, before welfare was essentially ended, most welfare recipients were white. Seventy percent of the people on welfare were off welfare and into work within two years. In large measure, welfare recipients were still *us*. But somehow welfare looked like a program exclusively for *them*, and *they* seemed blameworthy. Radcons emphasized their blameworthiness. Radcons in Congress handed Bill Clinton a punitive bill that essentially got rid of welfare, which Clinton signed.

I'm not defending the old welfare system. It wasn't working. Too many recipients became dependent on welfare checks and didn't do enough to help themselves. In his 1992 presidential campaign, Clinton had promised to "end welfare as we know it." But Clinton's original idea was to replace welfare with child care, health care, and job training—making it easier for poor people to get a job paying enough to lift themselves and their families out of poverty. The bill he signed contained none of this, and now there's a growing population who used to be on welfare but are working in lousy, dead-end jobs, and are still poor. (I'll return to this in a moment.)

In recent years, as Americans have started to split into two camps—the have-mores and the have-lesses—political support for other sorts of social insurance has begun to wane, too. The have-mores not only have more money but also, as noted, more political clout. And they've begun to notice they don't really need social insurance. Bad things are unlikely to happen to them or their children. If something bad does happen, they'll have enough money to take care of it themselves, or their company plan will cover the costs.*

The have-mores are also living farther away from the have-lesses. Often the have-mores reside in their own exclusive townships or gated communities, while poorer citizens occupy different parts of town or, increasingly, different towns altogether. Most of the have-mores don't know anyone on the other side of the widening divide, except perhaps for the person who tends their garden or cleans their house; most of the time they don't even *see* people on the other side. So not surprisingly, the have-mores no longer feel connected to them in the metaphorical sense of a boat they both inhabit.

When it comes to coping with risk, the have-mores can get private insurance at lower rates than the have-lesses. This is because richer

---

* The philosopher John Rawls argued that our idea of what's "fair" depends on viewing an action or policy as if we were behind a "veil of ignorance," incapable of determining how that act or policy would effect us in the real world. But as America splits between have-mores and have-lesses, the former may find it more and more difficult to do Rawls's mental experiment. See Rawls, *A Theory of Justice* (Cambridge, Mass.: Belknap/Harvard University Press, 1971).

Americans have a lower risk of all sorts of bad things happening to them. Among the biggest advantages of having a lot of money is you live more comfortably, you eat better, you have better medical attention, your work puts less strain on your muscles and bones, your life is safer, and you live longer.

Private employers are pushing more of the costs of health care on to their employees. As a result, premiums, co-payments, and deductibles are soaring.[5] The costs to poorer and higher-risk workers are rising the fastest of all; often, insurance is unavailable to them. At the same time, private insurers are going all out to sign up customers with the lowest possible risk of needing them. Why do you suppose private health insurers love upscale companies with a lot of young professionals?

So you see what's happening: The richer can get insurance at a lower rate because, increasingly, they inhabit insurance pools that exclude poorer people who have a higher risk of bad things happening to them. On the other hand, poorer Americans can't afford private insurance, partly because their "insurance pool" is filling up with people just like them—with a higher chance of becoming sick, dying early, or getting into an accident.

In much the same way, the richer can pool their abundant savings into private pension plans and get a nice return for their retirement. Plenty of financial brokers are eager to help. The richer don't really need Social Security. People who are poorer, on the other hand, often don't have any private savings. When they retire, Social Security is a necessity.

Enter the radical conservatives. FDR's safety net is in shreds. Welfare is mostly gone. Medicaid is being slashed. Companies are cutting employee health and pension benefits. And now the Radcons are talking about "privatizing" Social Security and Medicare. A new drug benefit is already partly privatized, given over to private insurance companies. Meanwhile, some forty-three million Americans, more than 16 percent of the total population, lack health insurance; over any given two-year period, nearly a third of all non-elderly Americans spend some time without it.[6]

In a more perfect world, Paul O'Neill and the Radcons would be correct: Adults would save enough to provide for their own retirement and for their health needs. They'd be smart enough to anticipate other risks and insure themselves against them in the private insurance market.

In the real world, privatization is a great idea if you're rich, but if you're not it can spell disaster. Radcons surely know that Americans are no longer in one boat. Some are in yachts, but many more are in dinghies that leak, and some are sinking fast. Many people don't earn enough to meet expenses, let alone accumulate savings. And even if they could manage some savings, they'd still face a market that discriminates ever more efficiently between high- and low-risk insurance pools. So if they're high-risk, they probably couldn't afford insurance anyway.

Liberals know what must be done. Most Americans face more economic risk today than at any time since the Great Depression. In the emerging economy, almost anyone can suddenly lose a job, and with it, their family's health insurance. (Even white-collar jobs are being outsourced to India, as I'll discuss in a moment.) So, in truth, the vast majority of Americans are in the same leaky boat. Most Americans need better and more affordable insurance, covering visits to the doctor, prescription drugs, and hospitalization, as well as sudden loss of earnings, and the costs of retraining and finding a new job.

This isn't for *them*; it's indubitably for *us*.

As I write this, Dad is eighty-nine, still collecting Social Security, and also living off money he saved after he restarted his business. He still believes we're all in it together, and a misfortune that hits one person can hit anyone, or everyone.

TOUGH LOVE

Radcons dislike social insurance not just because it bails out poor people whose boats are sinking but also because they dislike the whole concept of bailouts. And in that they offer an important insight about human nature that liberals often forget: When people know they'll be bailed out, they're less careful about the condition of their boat. When they bear the full consequences of their actions, they take better precautions to avoid harm's way.

Knowing there's a safety net to catch them, trapeze artists will more likely try wild aerial somersaults. Anticipating a flow of Social Security checks, people may save less for their retirement. Expecting government disaster relief, some may be encouraged to build houses on a floodplain. In the same way, unemployment insurance can invite more unemployment; welfare, more welfare; generous health insurance, more health care.

It needs to be pointed out as well that this principle is as true for executives of mega-corporations that get bailed out by the government as it is for everyone else. Washington lawmakers have been all too eager to bail out the savings and loan industry, airline companies, energy companies, steelmakers, big agribusiness, Long-Term Capital Management (the giant hedge fund whose 1998 collapse threatened a global financial panic), Chrysler, major military contractors, and insurance industry giants. If the executives of all these firms knew in advance that government wouldn't bail them out when they got into trouble, perhaps they'd be more vigilant about avoiding trouble in the first place.

But whatever the reason, some people need to be bailed out or they'll drown. So here's the basic question: How do we square the natural human tendency to be less careful when protected against the full consequences of one's actions with the genuine need for some protection? It isn't easy, but it can be done without eliminating all protection.

A man who had worked for me at the Labor Department died recently of a heart attack. His widow told me he had been laid off his job and was under enormous stress. But later in the conversation she said he was too heavy and she wished he had dieted and exercised more. I gently pressed the point: Why hadn't he taken better care of himself? Apparently he was taking pills to control his high blood pressure and he assumed they were enough. A conservative might conclude from this that he would have been better off without the pills (and the insurance that paid for them), which might have spurred him to exercise and go on a diet. A liberal might say he would have been better off had the government given him more generous unemployment insurance so he wouldn't have been so stressed about losing his job.

Liberals tend to emphasize the need for protection; conservatives, the need for responsibility. Both sides have a point. The best policy is usually a balance between the two: Cushion people against losses, but don't make the cushion so comfortable they fail to take reasonable precaution. (That's partly why insurance companies require people to pay the first portion of the cost of an accident or a prescription as a "co-payment," and why unemployment insurance is limited to a certain number of weeks at a fraction of one's previous salary.)

But radical conservatives take personal responsibility to an extreme and want to do away with protection altogether. Their approach is analogous to the parenting technique called "tough love" whose premise is that children learn to be responsible only if they bear the full consequences of their actions—even if it's not entirely their fault, and even if the consequences are dire.

A few years ago I was vacationing with my family on Cape Cod. One day when I was walking along the beach, I heard a boy about twelve years old pleading with his father to take a sailboat out into the bay. The father reluctantly agreed. About a half hour later I could see the boy, several hundred yards from shore, struggling to keep the boat from capsizing. The wind was up and he could barely manage. Meanwhile, the father sat passively on the beach, reading a book. Finally, the boat capsized and the boy called for help. The father continued to sit, seemingly oblivious to the calls. When I couldn't stand it any longer, I approached the father.

"Your son is having quite a time of it," I said, not wanting to sound critical of the father but feeling anxious about the son.

"Yup, I guess he is," said the father, impassively.

"There's a lifeguard just down the beach. Want me to alert him?"

"No," said the father. "Johnny will learn a lesson from this he'll never forget."

Sure, I thought, if Johnny doesn't drown first. I ran down the beach to tell the lifeguard anyway. Within a minute or two, the boy was saved.

Every parent struggles with the question of how to balance the need to shield a child from harm with the importance of allowing the child to learn from experience. Johnny's father's "tough love" is at one extreme. It's entirely consistent with how Radcons view human nature.

Here again, we find the Radcons' basic notion of evil, and the central importance of discipline as the way to conquer it. But here, the evil force isn't inside our loins and it's not outside the nation. The evil to be conquered is the presumed human tendency toward irresponsibility—laziness, torpor, idleness, foolishness, carelessness. Unless they fear (and experience) the full consequences of their actions, people won't take proper care of themselves.

In this view, government—whether lifeguards, welfare, Social Security, national health insurance, or other protection—insulates people from the consequences of their irresponsible behavior. Get rid of these buffers and people will be forced to become responsible.

If they don't drown first.

. . .

To Radcons, the ultimate disciplinary tool is the market. Its outcomes are sometimes harsh, but the harshness forces people to act responsibly, especially to work hard, to save, and to invest.

And once again, Radcons set themselves against the perceived excesses of the sixties. In this instance it's Lyndon Johnson's Great Society, when Social Security, unemployment insurance, and direct relief were all expanded, and Medicare, Medicaid, food stamps, public housing, and urban renewal were added. "The Great Society," says Robert Bork, amounted to "the most thorough-going redistribution of wealth and status in the name of equality that this country had ever experienced." To Bork, it exemplified the "antihierarchical, egalitarian sentiments" of the sixties.[7]

Milton Friedman, Nobel laureate and economic guru of the radical conservatives, was among the first to dub the Great Society a failure. That poverty actually fell in the late sixties and the income gap between rich and poor became smaller than at any time in the post–World War II era was apparently irrelevant to Friedman. "Their major evil," he writes, referring to programs started then, "is their effect on the fabric of our society. They weaken the family; reduce the incentive to work, save, and innovate; reduce the accumulation of capital; and limit our freedom. These are the fundamental standards by which they should be judged."[8]

Friedman might be called a market fundamentalist. To him and his followers, the free market has the same intoxicating quality that religion has to born-again Christians. Facts aren't especially relevant. The perfection of the market has to be accepted as a matter of faith. And like religious fundamentalism, market fundamentalism offers the promise of redemption to those who adhere to its gospel. Allow the market free rein and civilization will be saved.

But, of course, the free market is an oxymoron. Markets don't exist without laws and rules. Markets are human artifacts, the shifting sum of a set of judgments about how we should live together. What is mine, what is yours, and what is ours? Which mishaps are my responsibility, which are yours, and which are everyone's? Answers aren't found in logic or analysis alone. Different cultures, at different times, have answered these questions in different ways.

Market fundamentalists ignore this social reality and insist that government shouldn't "intrude" on the market. As early as 1980, Friedman was advocating an end to Social Security. He argued that unimpeded market forces would give people adequate incentive to save during their working years. "The winding down of Social Security would eliminate its present effect of discouraging employment . . . [and] would add to personal saving and so lead to a higher rate of capital formation and a more rapid rate of growth of income."[9]

At the time, few people took Friedman's proposal seriously. Now that Radcons are in charge, the proposal has moved into the mainstream. Yet it begs an important question: Once Social Security is "privatized," and elderly people are on their own to invest as best they can, what happens to those who made bad investments and lost their savings in the casino that's known as the stock market?

In a similar fashion, market fundamentalists have long argued that poor mothers should be exposed to the discipline of the market. "Had welfare not seduced [young single mothers] into the lives they lead," writes Bork, "they probably would have entered the job market much earlier in life and by now would have learned the habits and attitudes that employers require."[10]

Now that welfare is no longer generally available, we know what happens to undereducated mothers who try to enter the job market: Even with habits and attitudes employers require, most of them still have trouble finding a job. And the jobs open to them don't pay much more than the minimum wage. Since welfare ended, most of these women have shifted from being poor and on welfare to being poor and working. One major study that traced former welfare mothers into the job market found that most were working for around $12,000 a year.[11] The major difference is now they have the added expense and stress of trying to find someone else to care for their young kids.* Another study showed that one in seven women who left welfare between 2000 and 2002 had no work, no spousal support, and no government benefits. Census Bureau data for 2002 showed a marked increase in the number of children living in poverty.[12]

I'm not saying we should go back to the old welfare system and do nothing to reform Social Security and Medicare. Liberals need to acknowledge that people must take responsibility for themselves, and if they're too coddled, they won't. Reforms should give people an incentive to be prudent. There's a good argument for charging Medicare beneficiaries a small sum every time they see a doctor, for example, or encouraging low-wage workers to save more for their retirement by matching every dollar they save with, say, twenty-five cents in federal contributions. And it's reasonable to expect the unemployed to be actively looking for a job or enrolled in job training. But let's be clear—bad things do happen, regardless of how careful people are. Fate is too fickle alone to support a decent society.

In the second Bush administration, social services were slashed across the nation. Radcons squeezed them at the federal level, cutting everything from after-school programs to low-income housing. State cuts were even larger, because most state governments were deep in the hole. Rather than help them—a logical way to stimulate the economy—the White House decided to let the states fend for themselves. Tax breaks to the wealthy were deemed more important.

Who gets hurt as a result? Take a guess. The cuts disproportionately hit working families and the poor. States pay up to half the costs of Medicaid; most of the costs of health care for lower-income people who don't qualify for Medicaid; more than half the costs of special

---

* In 2003, Congress proposed to further tighten requirements for workers receiving temporary welfare aid; they would have to be working forty hours a week rather than thirty, as had previously been required. As a result, they would need more help with child care, although little or none was being provided.

education; most of the costs of prisons and law enforcement, as well as homeless shelters, youth services, elderly services, mental-health services, K–12 education, community colleges, and state colleges.

All these were on the chopping block. Not surprisingly, the most populous states with the largest cities and biggest concentrations of working poor—New York, California, Massachusetts, Illinois, Ohio—had to cut these critical services the most.

Much of the burden has been shifting to cities and towns. The pain is most apparent at this level but nearly invisible to the national media. As Americans are becoming ever more segregated by income, wealthy suburban townships can get by relatively unscathed. They're less reliant on social services, and can raise property taxes to fill the funding gap for their schools and police officers. But poorer towns and cities, with growing needs and tiny tax bases, are getting clobbered.

Tough love indeed. In a time of peace and widespread prosperity, further tax breaks for the very wealthy (whose after-tax incomes have skyrocketed) would be grossly unfair, and cuts in social services simply cruel. In a time of terrorism, war, and continued economic hardship for many households, these policies are shameful. Radcons preach we're-all-in-this-together patriotism but practice what is in fact scathing divisiveness. The cruel irony of our time is that they're getting away with this by diverting the nation's attention to external threats.

SOCIAL DARWINISM REVIVED

Radcons do offer a moral justification for all this, however. To them, wealth is a badge of virtue; poverty, a sign of vice.

There's a young man who lives a few streets over from me in one of the largest and well-appointed houses within miles. He seems to do nothing all day except tinker with his sports convertible. One early summer evening I walked past his driveway (where he was tinkering, as usual) and introduced myself, and we engaged in small talk. Finally, I asked him what he did. For a moment he seemed stumped by the question. "I don't work for a living, if that's what you mean," he said with a smile, and without a hint of embarrassment. "My great-grandfather invented cellophane tape."

The inventor had long since been laid to rest and his accomplishments amply rewarded. And now here in the driveway of this mansion was his heir, perhaps giving money to charity but adding no more to the productive capacity of the nation than someone collecting welfare checks. When it comes to passing money down to one's idle grandchildren, apparently there's no such thing as tough love.

Abolishing the tax on inheritance, as Radcons are on the way to doing, will allow millions more of these privileged princes and princesses to while away their lives in self-indulgent bliss, without ever learning the habits and attitudes employers require.

This is illogical. How can Radcons argue that people born poor should be forced to confront the harsh realities of the market while people born rich should be able to relax and enjoy the money coming their way, tax free?

Radcons see no inconsistency. Cellophane Great-Grandpa contributed mightily to civilization, they'd say, and the market rewarded him for it. He may be dead now, but part of what drove him to inventing when he was alive was the expectation he could pass on the resulting wealth to his heirs. If he couldn't, he might not have been sufficiently motivated to invent. If people like him can pass on even more of their wealth, they'll be motivated to even greater deeds.

Here we come to the moral heart of Radcon economics. In this view it's perfectly appropriate that the poor should get less money and the rich more because the poor have no inherent virtue. The money they received came as welfare checks, not paychecks. The rich have great virtue. Their money came (at least originally) from satisfying others through the market. If it's thereafter handed down through their families in perpetuity, that's a just reward for original virtue.

To Radcons, the market decisions of millions of individual consumers about what they want to buy and how much they're willing to pay create a vast and elegant system of rewards and punishments. Consumers bestow the largest rewards on those who give them the most satisfaction. By this calculus, a person's net worth equals his or her net worth to society. If the virtuous are allowed to keep more of their earnings—that is, pay less in taxes—they'll have even greater incentive to be virtuous. They'll invent more splendid products, invest in more factories and machinery, and create more jobs.

This is the argument of the so-called supply-siders, who during the Reagan administration slashed the top income tax rate from 70 to 28 percent. It's also given as justification for many of George W. Bush's tax cuts on capital gains, dividends, and even the estate tax.

Radcons believe that if you're rich you must be smart, and if you're smart you must be benefiting society. "If you're real smart in the United States today," says Radcon sociologist Charles Murray, "you'll probably end up going to a real good school, you'll probably end up in a profession that pays good money, and your salary's going to continue to go up."[13]

"In America," says Robert Bork, " 'the rich' are overwhelmingly people—entrepreneurs, small businessmen, corporate executives, doctors, lawyers, etc.—who have gained their higher incomes through intelligence, imagination, and hard work."[14]

This glowing attribution of virtue to the rich is the great creed of market fundamentalists. But it's fatuous, based on nothing but faith. The true believer entertains no suspicion that the rich may have got that way because they inherited their wealth. In 2003 a quarter of all estate taxes came from just 467 families, each of which was worth more than $20 million. The only thing their heirs did to merit this windfall was being born to rich parents.

Nor does the market fundamentalist dwell on the possibility that the rich were lucky to be born into families that gave them access to excellent primary and secondary schools, talented teachers and tutors, summer "enrichment" programs, prestigious universities, and all the contacts and connections that come from wealthy parents and classmates and membership in exclusive clubs. (One of the most powerful predictors of people's incomes as adults is their parents' incomes when they were growing up.)[15] Or the possibility that they became rich by defrauding investors or customers, bribing politicians in return for special favors, stacking their boards with lackeys who voted them exorbitant salaries, or receiving inside stock tips.

Nor, finally, do market fundamentalists seem to care about the long-term consequences. As taxes are cut on great wealth, it won't be long before a relatively small group of exceedingly rich but not necessarily talented children control vast segments of the American economy. My neighbor seems like a nice fellow, but all he does is tinker with his sportscar. Isn't it a bit reckless for us to entrust a growing portion of the economy to the investment decisions of such people?

To find out where this market fundamentalist faith comes from you have to look back into American history. An almost identical faith was in vogue during the last period of radical conservatism in America, the Gilded Age. Robber barons controlled much of American industry, the gap between rich and poor had turned into a chasm, urban slums festered, immigrants poured into our cities, politicians were bought off by the rich, and the nation turned much of the hemisphere into a vast imperial project. Sound familiar?

The dominant economic doctrine then was laissez-faire, and its philosophical root came to be known as social Darwinism.

Few Americans living today have read any of Herbert Spencer's writings, but they had an electrifying effect on America during the last three decades of the nineteenth century—a greater effect than in Spencer's native England. To Spencer and his followers, the marketplace was a field for the development of personal character. Work provided people with moral discipline, which was critical to survival.

Life was a competitive struggle in which only those with the strongest moral fiber could survive. It was through this struggle that societies became stronger over time. Only the fittest were able to prosper, because only they were able to muster the necessary resources to sustain themselves and their offspring. It was Spencer, not Charles Darwin, who coined the phrase "survival of the fittest."

A correlate of this principle was that government should do little or nothing to eliminate poverty. If the "fittest" wanted to bestow charitable gifts on some of the less fit, that was okay. But government intervention to improve the lot of the poor would interfere with natural selection. Spencer's avid follower, William Graham Sumner, a professor of political and social science at Yale, put the case succinctly. The rich simply *deserve* to survive and prosper, he asserted, while the poor do not. "Let it be understood that we cannot go outside of this alternative," Sumner thundered. Civilization has a simple choice: "liberty, inequality, survival of the fittest; not-liberty, equality, survival of the unfittest. The former carries society forward and favors all its best members; the latter carries society downwards and favors all its worst members."

It's almost startling to find how exactly Spencer's and Sumner's views are echoed by today's Radcons. To Sumner, the economy should offer great rewards to men of good character, while punishing those who are "negligent, shiftless, inefficient, silly, and imprudent." The progress of civilization depended on it. "Millionaires are the product of natural selection, acting on the whole body of men to pick out those who can meet the requirement of certain work to be done. . . . It is because they are thus selected that wealth aggregates under their hands—both their own and that intrusted to them. . . . They may fairly be regarded as the naturally selected agents of society. . . . They get high wages and live in luxury, but the bargain is a good one for society."[16]

Social Darwinism perfectly fit the Gilded Age, offering a precise moral justification for its excesses. It allowed John D. Rockefeller to claim that the fortune he accumulated through the giant Standard Oil Trust was "merely a survival of the fittest . . . the working out of a law of nature and a law of God."[17] The market fundamentalism wielded today by radical conservatives offers much the same justification, under remarkably similar circumstances.

Both doctrines conveniently ignore large shifts in the economies of their respective eras—shifts that individuals have no ability to control on their own. In the late nineteenth century, America went through a technological revolution. Railroads, electricity, and large-scale manufacturing ripped through the social fabric of the nation, creating vast fortunes for a few men who were lucky, ruthless, devious, or clever enough to take advantage of the upheaval, but also creating large unmet social needs. Factories were unsafe and unsanitary, young children labored long hours, tenements lacked adequate light and ventilation, food and drugs too often contained bacteria and transmitted disease, widowed mothers and children often went begging.

Today's social problems differ in many ways but the upheaval caused by today's technological revolution is no less dramatic, and the unmet needs of many Americans no less urgent.

THE END OF ROUTINE JOBS

By the late 1950s, when my father stopped selling cotton dresses and started selling silk scarves and cashmere sweaters, the factories that extended eastward from the Hudson Valley through western Connecticut were just beginning to disappear. Textile and shoe manufacturers found workers in the Carolinas and Georgia who would tend the machines for a fraction of the wages of workers up north. At the same time, national chain stores were starting to replace small retailers on Main Streets throughout the Northeast. Dad had been swimming against both these currents before the Naugatuck flood beached him.

But a fresh current was moving in: Large corporations were fleeing New York City for the country, bringing with them squads of white-collar employees and their wives. Farms were being bought up and sliced into fancy subdivisions with long, low-slung houses behind manicured shrubs and wide green lawns. Mom was right; country casual was coming into its own. Dad going upmarket caught the wave.

No one knew then that this was the beginning of an epochal change in America. The factory jobs that disappeared in New England in the fifties started to disappear all over America in the seventies and eighties. By the start of the twenty-first century, manufacturing workers were a vanishing species in America. The proportion of the American workforce employed in manufacturing had dropped to 11 percent, down from 30 percent in the mid-1960s. Unions were disappearing, too. In the 1950s, over a third of all workers were unionized. By the time I became secretary of labor in 1993, fewer than 10 percent of private-sector workers were in unions. The decline continues.

It's hard to exaggerate the significance of this change. The giant American middle class of the fifties was largely the product of an American economic loop based on mass production. The weekly paychecks of mass-production workers fueled the mass consumption that the production system depended on.

I remember Saturdays at Dad's store because Friday was payday, and on Saturdays many of the wives of blue-collar workers binged on shopping. On Main Streets all over America, Saturday was the most important day of the week. How he did on Saturday determined the condition of Dad's stomach for the following six days.

Factory jobs paid well. They were typically unionized. Large manufacturers were confident they could pass on the rising wages and benefits to consumers. Big companies didn't worry much about price competition in those days. Most industries were oligopolies: Only three major automakers dominated the market, three major steel producers, two giant appliance makers, three major chemical producers, five big food processors, and so on. Despite rising wages and minimum competition, prices stayed moderate because of the huge efficiencies of high-volume production.

But these days, relatively fewer jobs pay middle-class wages and benefits. As I've noted, men without four-year-college degrees (this still describes most men in the labor force) have been hardest hit. They have the fewest opportunities for advancement. They've had to take relatively low-paid retail jobs, or drive cabs, or become custodians or attendants or security guards. Often they work two or three jobs.

They've endured other degradations: Not only do their wives have to work, but some of their wives' jobs pay better than their own. And many workplaces are now filled with professional women who earn a lot more, and have a lot more power than they do. Sadly, in our culture, men feel humiliated rather than relieved by this. In the movie *The Full Monty* a few displaced blue-collar men end up stripping for money and enjoying it. In the real world, such men feel stripped of their dignity, and many are angry.

As secretary of labor I traveled all over America, talking with men who had turned in their blue collars and overalls for lousy jobs.

"Hi, I'm Robert Reich, secretary of labor!" I said, bounding toward them with my right hand extended.

"Congratulations. What have you done for me?"

"This administration has created millions of new jobs!"

"Yeah, and I've got three."

As we've seen, Radcons have exploited these workers' anger and channeled it toward those familiar targets they want to blame: poor blacks and Latinos, welfare recipients, affirmative action, immigrants, women, Washington bureaucrats, Hillary and Bill, and, of course, liberals. Anger is a potent political force. Radcons have been remarkably, and tragically, effective at their scapegoating. That is not something to be proud of. Meanwhile, some on the left, including organized labor, want to blame free trade.

Few changes in American life have invited as much nonsense and demagoguery as the eclipse of blue-collar America.

Let's be clear about the facts: Every task that's repetitive — anything that can be done more cheaply by automated machinery or computer software or by a person laboring in a poor country — is no longer going to be done by Americans at American wages. Period. I'm not referring here to entire industries or even entire products or services. I'm just talking about any routine task involved — say, in making a car.

During the time I was labor secretary, the transmission in my car wore out. It was an old car and I decided it was time to buy a new one. I searched for the best deal in my price range and settled on a Toyota. I was just about to check it out at the nearest Toyota dealer when Clare reminded me I was secretary of labor of the *United States*. Maybe it would be a better idea, she said sweetly, to limit my search to an American automaker. So I found a Ford that looked promising. But before I bought it, I asked the dealer whether the car was actually made in America by American workers.

The dealer looked at me for a long instant, trying to decide why I asked. Then he smiled. "Which answer would you prefer?"

Most cars sold in the United States, whatever their brand, are made partly overseas. Many of the standard components (those involving routine work) come from abroad. That's true of more and more products. The phrase "Made in America" doesn't mean much any longer.

Companies are becoming global networks. We used to have the "Big Three" U.S. automakers. Now one of them is DaimlerChrysler, headquartered in Frankfurt, Germany. Dr Pepper is British, as was Burger King until a group of Texans bought it in 2002. Bridgestone is Japanese, as is Columbia Pictures. Zenith is South Korean. The German publishing giant Bertelsmann published this book.

Regardless of where the pieces come from or where they're put together, fewer and fewer people are required. Have you visited an

American factory lately? I toured one recently containing four employees and two hundred computerized robots. The four live people sat in front of computer screens and their keystrokes instructed the robots. I bet in a few years the factory won't have a single employee on site, except for an occasional visiting technician who repairs and upgrades the robots, like the gas man changing your meter.

Factory jobs are vanishing all over the world. Between 1995 and 2002 the United States lost about two million manufacturing jobs, an 11 percent drop. During the same interval Brazil lost 20 percent of its manufacturing jobs, Japan lost 16 percent, and China lost 15 percent. Wherever you go, it's the same story: Robots and numerical machine tools can do factory work more efficiently than people. Even as manufacturing employment dropped around the globe since the mid-nineties, industrial output rose more than 30 percent.[18]

We should stop pining for "manufacturing" jobs and the days when a lot of people were paid good money to stand along an assembly line and continuously bolt, fit, solder, or clamp what went by. Those days are over. Don't blame poor blacks, Latinos, or all the other usual suspects.

And don't blame poorer nations whose workers get very low wages. Of course their wages are low; these nations are poor. Poor nations can become more prosperous only by exporting to rich nations. When we block their exports by erecting tariffs or subsidizing our industries, we prevent them from doing better. As I'll show in the next chapter, helping poorer nations become more prosperous is not only in the interest of humanity but also politically wise because it lessens global instability.

Hence, it makes no sense for the left to demand that our trade treaties with poor nations include "labor and environmental standards," unless such standards are pegged to what poorer nations can afford. As poorer nations become wealthier, their workers' wages and their environmental standards should be expected to improve.

You want to blame something, blame *knowledge*. Knowledge created the electronic gadgets and software that now do almost any routine task. And this goes well beyond factory work. America also used to have a lot of elevator operators, telephone operators, bank tellers, and service station attendants. Almost all of them are gone now, replaced by software and gadgets. Supermarket checkout clerks are being replaced by automatic scanners; airline ticket personnel by computerized ticket kiosks.

The Internet has taken over the routine tasks of travel agents, real-estate brokers, stockbrokers, and accountants. Meanwhile, back-office work is being shipped out over satellite dishes. With digitization, high-speed data networks, and improved global bandwidth, an Indian office park can seem right next door. The nice man on the phone who advised me on how to fix my computer glitch told me he was sitting in Bangalore, India.

In 2003 companies headquartered in the United States paid workers in India, China, and the Philippines almost $10 billion to handle their data entry, billing, customer service, payrolls, insurance claims, taxes, accounts receivable, and even routine software development and computer coding. India already has over a half million such workers. Forrester Research estimates that by 2015, more than three million more American white-collar jobs will move from the United States to low-cost countries, mostly to India.[19]

Got it? Everything is coming from everywhere. And any job that's even slightly routine is disappearing from America.

THE TWO JOBS OF THE FUTURE

This doesn't mean there are fewer jobs overall. It simply means there are fewer *routine* jobs.

A decade ago I had my two hips replaced. The old hips were breaking down. It was a genetic problem, somehow related to my short height. The operation went fine and I've been walking without pain ever since. I love my new hips. But recently I started to wonder about them. Where were they made? Who made them?

I called the hospital where I had the operation. Their records and invoices didn't show for sure, but they thought my new hips were fabricated in Germany. A machine tool in Germany shaped a piece of metal to exactly the right dimension, and a computerized injection-molding machine created a disc of specialized plastic that was then attached to the top of the metal. A few German technicians guided these machines. The machines themselves were also made in Germany.

Where were my new hips designed? Most likely by a French engineering firm that specializes in prosthetic devices. I have French designer hips.

Were any Americans involved in my new hips? Turns out that most of the research and development for them—new metal alloys and plastics with just the right blend of minimal weight and high strength—was probably done in a laboratory in New Jersey. Marketing and sales of my new line of hips was done by a group of medical-supply specialists headquartered in Atlanta. A lot of the legal and financial work took place in New York and Washington. Installation occurred in Boston by a skilled surgeon who trained in Texas and his team, along with attendants who emptied my bedpan (made in China) and nurses who fed me what passed for food (harvested from uniquely tasteless crops grown in Indiana). Although the hospital's billing system is run out of Bangalore, India, the physical therapist who helped me learn to walk with my new hips lives in Somerville, Massachusetts.

The total cost for all this was about $50,000. My group health insurance plan covered most of it. The $50,000 was divided among people all over the world, in proportion to the value they added along the way.

There is no question that technology and globalization confer huge benefits. Our standard of living is infinitely better because of them. Technophobes, neo-Luddites, and anti-globalists be warned: You're on the wrong side of history. You see only the downsides, especially the loss of jobs. You're overlooking the huge upsides. And you're not seeing all the *new* jobs.

Look closely at the American economy today and you find two growing categories of work. The first involves identifying and solving new problems. People in this category do research and development, design, and engineering. They're responsible for high-level sales, marketing, and advertising. They're filmmakers, performers, composers, writers, and producers. They're lawyers, bankers, financiers, journalists, choreographers, insurance executives, doctors, and management consultants.

I call this "symbolic analytic" work because most of it has to do with analyzing, manipulating, and communicating through abstract symbols—numbers, shapes, words, ideas. Computer technology gives symbolic analysts even more tools for thinking, creating, and communicating.

Most symbolic analysts work alone or in small teams. If they work with others they often have partners and associates rather than bosses or supervisors. Their yearly income varies, depending on how much value they add to their business. Their work environments tend to be quiet and tastefully decorated, often within office parks or tall steel-and-glass buildings. They rarely come in direct contact with the ultimate beneficiaries of their work. When they aren't analyzing, designing, performing, or strategizing, they're in meetings or doing e-mail or on the telephone—giving advice or making deals. Many spend lots of time in jet planes and hotels. They use cellphones constantly. They're articulate, well groomed, and well educated. Symbolic analytic work now constitutes more than 20 percent of the jobs in America.

The second growing category of work involves personal services, such as the nursing and physical therapy I got when my new hips were installed. Also included in this group are retail sales personnel, restaurant and fast-food workers, hotel workers, barbers and hair stylists, personal trainers, cab and limo drivers, household domestics, repairers, plumbers, electricians, custodians, security guards, child-care workers, elder-care workers, and hospital attendants and orderlies.

Computers and robots can't do these jobs because they require human beings; their value comes from human touch, care, or attentiveness. Workers in other nations can't do them because they have to be done *in person.*

Personal service workers are usually paid by the hour, are carefully supervised, and rarely require much more than a high school education. They're usually in direct contact with the ultimate beneficiaries of their work. Women, minorities, and new immigrants make up a large proportion of these workers. Personal service workers now constitute more than 30 percent of the jobs in America.

The number of jobs in both these categories is growing while routine production work is shrinking. Today more Americans work for Wal-Mart than for the entire U.S. auto industry; more work in laundries and dry cleaners than in steel mills.

But these two categories of jobs aren't equal by any means. And that's a growing problem.

Symbolic analytic jobs pay well. Credit supply and demand: The supply of people who do them is limited because the jobs require special training. Most symbolic analysts have four-year college degrees; many have professional degrees.

Meanwhile, the demand for symbolic analysts keeps growing because they add significant value to products and services. Companies can no longer depend just on economies of scale to keep them competitive. For businesses to grow, they need a steady flow of good judgments, insights, and new ideas. Advances in communications technologies have brought the potential demand worldwide: Europeans hire American management consultants, business strategists, and investment bankers. Developing nations hire our civil and design engineers. Almost everyone is buying the output of our pop musicians, television and film stars, and their producers. The headquarters of global corporations are filled with symbolic analysts who manipulate information and then export their insights. IBM, for example, doesn't make much in America any longer; however, it exports strategic planning and related management services.

Most personal service jobs, on the other hand, pay low wages. The reason goes back to supply and demand: Few of these jobs require special qualifications, so many people can do them. And at the same time, the demand for these services is comparatively weak. That's because the market for them is small and local.

The wealth and economic vitality of any city or region is coming to depend on its collection of symbolic analysts. Without them— without the bankers, lawyers, financiers, architects, designers, engineers, creative artists, and others who sell their knowledge and insights far and wide—money wouldn't stream into a city from outside its borders. Local retailers, restaurants, hotels, nursing homes, taxi companies, and health spas wouldn't be able to sell their services, because there'd be no money to buy them with.

A retail sales worker in Boston isn't that much more productive than a retail sales worker in Bangladesh. The Boston worker earns a lot more money because his *customers* are far wealthier. They're wealthier, in large part, because Boston's symbolic analysts are adding a lot more value to the global economy than are Bangladesh's symbolic analysts. Money flows into Boston from New England, America, and the rest of the world.

This disparity, by the way, gives symbolic analysts lots of political clout. If they decide to move—say, because they think their property taxes are too high—a local economy can dry up. Mayors and governors scramble to keep or attract symbolic analysts. The state of Iowa suffers because a large portion of its college grads leave the state soon after graduating. In the emerging economy, such "brain drains" are direct threats to prosperity.

All this means that the big issue shouldn't be the number of jobs. During an economic downturn that may seem like the biggest issue. But after the economy turns up again almost everyone who wants one can find some sort of job.

The big issue is the quality of jobs. Over the long term, most symbolic analysts will do just fine, as long as they stay at the cutting edge. It's true that symbolic analysts are popping up all over the world, and companies are outsourcing ever more sophisticated tasks. India graduates two million college students a year. General Motors and General Electric both have R&D labs in Bangalore.[20] Hyderabad is becoming a center for software development. But demand for symbolic analysts in the United States continues to grow faster than supply. No other country does a better job preparing its citizens for symbolic analysis than does the United States. And none has surpassed America in providing experience and training, often within entire regions specializing in one or another kind of symbolic analysis (New York and Chicago for finance, Los Angeles for music and film, Silicon Valley and greater Boston for science and bio-medical engineering).

Besides, there's no necessary limit to the number of symbolic analytic jobs around the world because there's no finite limit to ingenuity of the human mind or to human needs that can be satisfied. Hence, even as the supply of workers around the world capable of doing symbolic analytic work increases, the demand for such people is increasing at an even faster pace. Recessions temporarily slow such demand, of course, but the long-term trend is toward greater rewards to people who are at or near the frontiers of new knowledge—as well as the professionals (lawyers, bankers, venture capitalists, advertisers, marketers, and managers) who support innovative enterprises.

But personal service workers are in trouble. The supply of them is growing quickly, as more and more people who'd otherwise have factory jobs join their ranks. Legal and undocumented immigrants are also pouring into this sector. And because personal service workers tend to be unskilled and dispersed among smaller businesses, they rarely have unions or powerful lobbies to stand up for them.

Hence, the pay gap between them and symbolic analysts continues to widen, and America divides ever more sharply between have-mores and have-lesses. The account I've given you doesn't explain the stratospheric pay packages of top corporate executives and Wall Street bankers. Their lofty positions are due less to supply and demand than to power and influence, as I showed in the last section. But the distinction between symbolic analysts and personal service workers—and the steady decline of routine jobs that once paid middle-class wages and benefits—goes far to explain why most people in the top 20 percent are doing better, while so many other Americans are not.

FEEDING THE SPARROWS
BY FEEDING THE HORSES

What should we do about this? We can't bridge the widening gap just by transferring wealth from the have-mores to the have-lesses. Direct redistributions are politically treacherous. With wealth comes power, and the wealthy won't happily shell out money to the poor. There is also the valid Radcon concern about personal responsibility; a system of ongoing redistributions would render poorer citizens permanently dependent.

A large part of the answer lies in economic growth. This is hard for some liberals to accept. They assume growth means more pollution, bigger gas-guzzling cars, suburban sprawl, strip malls, big-box retailers surrounded by asphalt, and piles of electronic gizmos. But growth doesn't have to mean any of this. A growing economy has more capacity to do all sorts of things, including making the air and water cleaner, putting aside more open space, and finding more efficient ways to use energy. The poorest nations in the world are also among the most polluted, with the ugliest scars of industrialization.

More growth also creates more opportunities for more people to enjoy a better life—health care that's affordable, Social Security and Medicare for boomers when they retire, more leisure time.

How we spend our additional wealth is a political choice, and we should be careful not to measure growth solely in terms of what's bought and sold. I'll come back to this.

But the Radcons are dead wrong about *how* to grow the economy. Their solution is to raise the level of savings and reduce consumption in order to create more capital. You know the drill: Cut the highest income-tax rates; reduce or eliminate taxes on savings, investment income, and wealth; and phase out the estate tax. Meanwhile, cut spending on social services; privatize public insurance; and relax government regulations on health, safety, and the environment.

These measures widen the wealth and income gap even further. Income-tax cuts mostly benefit upper-income groups whose earnings have been rising and who thus pay the most income taxes. Tax schemes that make it more costly to spend earnings than to save them inevitably hurt lower-income people (who have no choice but to spend a high proportion of their earnings) more than higher-income people (who can afford to defer consumption). The $1.3 trillion tax cut of 2001 was a windfall for people earning over $500,000 a year, who got about 40 percent of its benefits. The tax cut of 2003 was even better for high rollers. Those with net incomes of about $1 million got an average tax cut of $90,000 a year. Taxes on the typical middle-income family dropped just $217. Many lower-income families, who still pay payroll taxes, got nothing back.[21]

Meanwhile, when the objects of regulation—clean air, clean water, safe products, and safe working conditions—become less available to the population in general, they become private commodities available only to those who can afford to have them. People with higher incomes buy bottled water, move to higher elevations and pristine environments where the air is cleaner, purchase products they know to be safe, pay a bundle for homes in safe neighborhoods with good schools, and take office jobs where the possibility of injury is remote.

At a time when the mega-forces of globalization and technology are already cleaving Americans into have-mores and have-lesses, it seems mindlessly cruel to compound the damage by cutting taxes on the rich, squeezing social services for the poor, and reducing regulatory protections for those who need them. By 2000, America's four hundred wealthiest taxpayers accounted for more than one percent of all the income in the United States—more than double their share in 1992, according to the Internal Revenue Service.[22] Why concentrate wealth even further?

Radcons try to justify this further leap toward inequality by saying it will spur growth, and that growth will help everyone in the long run. Even the poorest will eventually see the benefits as the additional capital works its way through the economic system. "The key to growth," says George Gilder, an early supply-side enthusiast, "is quite simple: creative men with money. The cause of stagnation is similarly clear: depriving creative individuals of financial power."[23]

It's called "trickle-down" economics. Feed the sparrows by feeding the horses.

Radcons use lots of misleading figures to justify their claims. Among their biggest whoppers: After supply-side tax cuts, "average" wages rise and "average" taxes fall. But "average" doesn't mean much when people at the top enjoy such stratospheric gains they pull the average way up. The basketball player Shaquille O'Neal and I have an "average" height of about six feet. Get it? In a world where a few giant fortunes are being amassed, talk about "averages" doesn't tell you what's happening to most people, especially the little guys.

A better measure of prosperity is found by looking at the person or family smack in the middle of the income ladder. By this measure, trickle-down economics fails. We tried it in the 1980s and almost nothing trickled down. It still hasn't. The American economy is now much larger than it was in 1980, but a worker smack in the middle is only slightly better off today than he or she was then. What happened to all the extra prosperity? It went mostly to the richest 20 percent of the population. And most of *that* sum went to the top 5 percent.

By the way, don't believe the Radcon propaganda about how easy it is for people at the lower rungs to climb the ladder. By most accounts, there's less upward mobility now than twenty years ago.[24] That's because it's a much harder climb. First, the economic ladder is longer—the rich are far richer, the poor are poorer, and all of the rungs in between are wider apart. Second, several rungs that used to be in the middle—representing good-paying middle-class jobs that don't require much formal education—are now gone. Third, it's harder for poor families to afford college—even though a college education is more important than ever to economic success. Almost three-quarters of students at the nation's most selective colleges are from affluent families; just 3 percent are from poor ones.[25] Americans still cling to the old myth that anyone can make it with enough hard work, guts, and gumption, but that's less likely than it used to be.*

But suppose we give Radcons every benefit of the doubt. Assume they're correct that trickle-down growth will benefit everyone. Say the American economy grows 20 percent over the next five years because we do everything the Radcons propose. Although most of that growth goes to people at the top, people at the bottom gain a little bit, and those in the middle do fairly well. In other words, the economy grows 20 percent and everyone is better off than before. Yet the discrepancy is even wider than before. Would you say the country is more prosperous?

If you're not sure, try this experiment on two people. Here, I'll call them Mike and Ike. In the presence of both, offer Mike $10 but only on condition he divides it with Ike, and Ike agrees to the division. Ask

---

* A Gallup poll taken in the spring of 2003 found that 31 percent of Americans expected to become "rich" someday, including more than one in every five people earning less than $30,000 a year. Sadly, this belief, reflecting the eternal optimism of Americans, is based more on hope and history than on present-day reality.

Mike to write down on a piece of paper how much of the $10 he'll part with and hand the paper to Ike. If Ike doesn't agree to the amount on the paper, neither of them gets a penny. (They're not allowed to negotiate, and they have to assume they don't know each other so friendship plays no part.)

Presumably Ike should be content with $1, or a nickel, or even a penny. After all, Ike is better off getting even a tiny bit of the $10 than nothing at all—which would be the outcome if Ike doesn't agree to accept what Mike has written on the piece of paper. It would be irrational for Ike to refuse whatever Mike's offer if it's more than zero. Right?

For years, I've done this experiment with my university students. Students pair up, and one acts as the recipient of my largesse. What's the outcome? Interestingly, very few of the Ikes agree to any amount under $4. Quite a few won't agree to anything under $5. When I ask them why they were willing to forgo any lower amount (remember, their non-agreement means no money for either of them) they say something like "it just didn't seem fair," or "it made me angry to be offered only $2."

Is this reaction irrational? It is only if you define "rational" to mean a willingness to accept any improvement in your situation regardless of how others do by comparison. But it is perhaps not so irrational if you figure that well-being is a subjective feeling based in part on how others are doing. Radcons dismiss such sentiments as "envy" but they actually reflect a deep-seated human desire to be treated fairly. (Experiments suggest that the desire may extend even to monkeys.)*

Relative position matters. We once used the word "deprived" to

---

* In one experiment, brown capuchin monkeys were taught to swap plastic tokens for bits of cucumber. But the monkeys got angry if they saw another monkey get a grape instead. In about half such trials, the shortchanged monkeys either stopped handing over their tokens or rejected the cucumbers; some threw the tokens or cucumbers out of the cage. They became even angrier if the other monkey got a grape for nothing. See S. F. Brosnan and Frans de Waal, "Monkeys Reject Unequal Pay," Nature 425 (September 2003): 297–99.

describe the poor in America. Compared to the poor in sub-Saharan Africa, poor Americans are well off. But because they're deprived of many of the benefits of middle-class American life, they're poor by comparison. Most other countries define poverty as a percentage of their nation's median income (in Britain, for example, it's 70 percent). Yet America's official definition of "poverty" relies on an absolute rather than a relative measure—the "poverty line" is three times what it costs a typical family to buy food.

So when Radcons say it's just fine for America to grow 20 percent, even if most of the extra wealth goes to people at the top, they don't understand human nature. Or maybe they do and just don't want to admit it because it gets in the way of their simplistic thinking. Under these circumstances, the nation may technically be more prosperous. But widening inequality can make people at the lower end of the economic spectrum *feel* poorer, more disenfranchised.

BUBBLE-UP ECONOMICS

The Radcons' whole growth premise is wrong. They make a totem out of savings and investment. Cut taxes on savings and investment so that we'll have more capital! Allow the rich to keep more of their money so that they'll create more jobs!

Baloney.

In the new global economy, financial capital is as likely to trickle out as to trickle down. It's going wherever in the world it can get the highest return. If there's more money to be earned in Mexico or the Philippines, that's where the extra non-taxed dollars of wealthy Americans will head. The idea that there's a kind of giant piggy bank of "American" capital separate and distinct from the savings of the rest of the world is obsolete. American savings, European savings, Saudi savings, Russian savings—almost everyone's savings now end up in mega–investment pools that slosh around the planet in search of the best returns.

Recently a colleague at another university complained to me about "American jobs" going overseas. "American companies should only be investing in *America*," he said indignantly.

Then I asked him about his university pension plan and where he thought his pension savings were being invested. He said he didn't know. But I did. As faculty members he and I both have our savings in a giant pension fund called TIAA-CREF. This multi-billion-dollar pot of money is invested all over the world.

"*You're* not limiting your investments to America," I said. "Why should American companies?"

He stared blankly. I pushed my point: "How much of your future retirement earnings would you be willing to sacrifice in order to invest only in America?"

He walked off, muttering.

It makes perfect economic sense for Americans to invest all over the world. When we save and invest more, we add to the pool of global capital. That's good for American investors. It's also good for people in other nations. People all over the world invest in America, too.

The real question is how do we attract some of this large pool of global capital to America to create *good* jobs?

Mayors, governors, and even heads of state are openly competing for global capital. They're giving tax breaks and doling out subsidies to businesses that promise to come. At best, these efforts are irrelevant. At worst, they're counterproductive. When DaimlerChrysler recently decided to replace its big Jeep assembly plant in Toledo, Ohio, it got the city and state to cough up $300 million to keep the replacement plant there. All together, these corporate giveaways are costing cities and states an estimated $50 billion a year. These are dollars that might otherwise have gone to schools, roads, and other public investments that are more important for sustained growth.[26]

Basically there are only two ways to attract global capital. The first is to make labor, materials, and other costs of doing business so inexpensive that global capital automatically gets a high return on its investments. A lot of global capital heads to China, Southeast Asia, and Latin America because the cost of making or creating things there is relatively cheap.

The second is to offer high productivity. A lot of global capital goes to America and Europe, *despite* relatively high salaries and strict environmental and safety regulations, because many workers in these nations generate a lot of value—hence, a high return on investment. Most of the best symbolic analysts in the world are found in these regions, linked together by efficient systems of communications and transportation, under the most stable governments and reliable legal systems in the world.

When Radcon economists (typically paid by businesses or on the payrolls of right-wing think tanks) warn that America has to reduce the costs of doing business here—slash corporate taxes, bust unions, rescind environmental and safety regulations, and reduce spending on schools and universities, and health care—what they really mean is we have to compete for world capital by being cheaper. They have it backwards.

There's no way America can be among the world's cheapest places to do business without sacrificing our standard of living. We can't hold on to low-cost production. No matter how cheap we tried to be, there will always be somewhere else in the world that can do it cheaper. Many of the shoe and textile factories that moved from New England to the Carolinas and Georgia in the 1950s are now in Southeast Asia. Manufacturing plants that moved from the Midwest to Mexico in the 1980s are now shifting to China.

The only way to attract global capital and also improve our living standards is to increase the productivity of Americans.

America's basic strategy for economic growth must be to equip a larger portion of our people to add more value to the world economy. And the way to do this is to increase our investments in our people: We need to ensure that a good-quality public education is available to every child from the age of three all the way through at least two years of college, so that any talented American kid can become a symbolic analyst regardless of family income or race. We need to help personal service workers be more productive by giving them access to better training, and career ladders linking increased expertise to higher pay scales. We need to provide better health care and improve the environment, so that Americans can lead fuller and more productive lives, and both feel and be more prosperous.

This approach to economic growth is the exact opposite of trickle-down economics. Rather than cut taxes on the rich in order to generate more financial capital, we need to use those tax revenues instead to improve the productivity of all Americans. Think about it: In a world where financial capital moves across borders at the speed of an electronic impulse, our *people*—our *human* capital—are the one asset that's uniquely American, on which our future prosperity uniquely depends.

Call it "bubble-up" economics. It's the only growth strategy that will pay off in a lot of good jobs. Of course, private investment is still necessary. But we get the private investment we need to create good jobs only if we have the public investment that attracts it. By growing the economy from the ground up rather than from the top down, this strategy also broadens the circle of prosperity. It gives more Americans a direct stake in the future.

In the George W. Bush administration, the Radcon trickle-down agenda was introduced with a vengeance. While taxes were slashed on the very rich, more kids were crowded into classrooms, textbooks became obsolete, and after-school programs were cut. Public higher education was also put in jeopardy, as states were forced to slash funding. Rising tuitions made it impossible for many children of working families to attend.

Many Democrats have obsessed about the effects of the Bush tax cuts on the federal budget. Some Democrats have even called for a balanced budget, and I wish they wouldn't. They're missing the point.

Whether deficits are good or bad depends on whether the nation is in a recession (in which case, deficits may be necessary to kick-start the economy). They also depend on what the borrowing is used for. A family that borrows to go on a world cruise may be irresponsible; one that borrows so that the kids can attend college is acting wisely. Government borrowing is no different. If the government goes deeper into debt so that a lot of wealthy people can buy bigger yachts or Middle Eastern oil rigs, that's cause for concern — *not* because the government is going into deeper debt, but because it's going into deeper debt for the wrong reason.

The shame of the Radcon policy is that tax cuts for the wealthy strip the government of revenues needed for education, health care, and other vital investments in the future productivity of Americans.

THE WORSHIP OF THE GDP

As I've said, economic growth is good. Liberals should embrace it. But be careful how you measure it. Economists typically measure it in terms of something called the gross domestic product, or GDP. The GDP is essentially the total value of all the nation's goods and services in a given year. A growing GDP means the economy is growing. But it doesn't necessarily mean we're more prosperous.

Before she went to work in my father's store, my mother was at home. But she was never idle. She vacuumed our living room carpet so intensely she wore down the pile. She washed the clothes so often we ran out of hot water. She taught me to read when I was four. And when a birthday came around, she spent hours baking. She made my birthday cake from scratch with flour, sugar, and cocoa. If wheat, sugarcane, and cocoa could have been grown in our backyard, she would have sown and harvested them.

Once Mom started working at the store, she had to compromise. She did as much as she could around the house, but every few weeks she paid a cleaning woman to help. And on my birthday she started using cake mix. She felt bad about that.

By the time Clare and I had kids, we handled things differently. We were lucky. Both of us had satisfying work that compensated us appropriately. We had someone in to clean once a week. (Between times, the house was a wreck.) When our children, Adam and Sam, had birthdays, we ordered ready-made cakes with customized messages on top. It was more expensive than cake mix, but who had the time?

These days it's not unusual for hardworking parents to "outsource" even more. For many families, takeout meals are the norm. And when it comes to the kids' birthdays, whole parties are contracted to specialized restaurants that supply not only the cake but also balloons, party favors, and games—plus supervision and cleanup. You can pay extra and get a clown, or even someone to take the video. Meanwhile, Mom and Dad can duck out to check for messages.

When my mother baked my birthday cake, her labors contributed only indirectly to the GDP, showing up as a minuscule addition to agricultural production and retail sales of the ingredients she bought. When she started using cake mix, the "processed foods" category of the national product grew a tad. By the time Clare and I gave birthday parties to Adam and Sam, the ready-made cakes we bought added a bit more to the GDP. The modern subcontracted party adds still more, including the personal services of party planners, waiters, clowns, and attendants with video cameras. Each stage reflects greater prosperity, although the cakes have not improved noticeably.

Today, most children under the age of five—more than ten million of them—need to be looked after while mothers and fathers go out to work. Some of these children (mostly the children of personal service workers) are cared for by relatives or neighbors. Most of the rest are cared for by the staff at day-care centers or nursery schools, by nannies, or by paid babysitters. Families are also subcontracting the care of elderly parents—another job traditionally performed by women at home—to nursing homes, residential long-term-care facilities, and personal home attendants. Some families even subcontract the sort of personal care and attention one spouse or partner might have given the other when they had more time and emotional energy: Now they rely on massage therapists, coaches, counselors, spiritual guides, and personal trainers.

When all this caring, cleaning, and birthday-partying was done inside the home, usually by stay-at-home moms, it wasn't included in the GDP because it wasn't purchased. Now that families are subcontracting more of what they used to do themselves, these tasks have emerged as growth industries, and the GDP is that much larger. In fact, there's a multiplier effect: Many of the people—mostly women—who get paid to do these subcontracted tasks devote a portion of what *they're* paid to paying someone else to take on some of the tasks they no longer have time or energy to do within their own families. So the GDP grows larger still.

Consider, too, the modern consumer who buys gallons of bottled water at the supermarket because the tap water at home tastes bad or can't be relied on. On days when the air quality outside is hazardous, he breathes purified air from his home air-filtering system. He feels secure against crime because he has purchased a home security system and pays for private security guards to patrol his gated community. On weekends he takes the kids not to a public park but a franchised "pay-per-use" playground or private play center in the shopping mall. At night, he falls asleep despite the pressures of his job thanks to anti-anxiety medication. Perhaps he dreams about all the wondrous ways he's raised the GDP.

The privatization and commodification of all facets of life may spur the GDP to new heights, but it doesn't necessarily mean that all these products and services have improved our quality of life. We would be better off with regulations that give us cleaner water and air to begin with, so we don't need to buy bottled water or install air-filtering systems; community policing and after-school programs that reduce crime, so we don't need to spend as much on security; and more pleasant public parks, so we don't have to purchase private sanctuaries. And we'd probably feel less stressed at work and less dependent on anti-anxiety medications if employers were required to provide at least four weeks paid vacation each year and give paid family and medical leave, and if, when we lost a job, unemployment benefits were more generous and lasted longer.

Radcons are quick to claim that government spending and regulations retard the growth of the GDP. But the ultimate goal isn't to raise the GDP. It's to improve the quality of life for most Americans. If measures such as these improve our quality of life without requiring all that private spending, we come out ahead.

A society is different from an economy. People aren't just buyers and sellers in a market. They're also citizens engaged in a joint project of improving the well-being of current and future generations.

Radcons are imposing on America a crimped and narrow definition of prosperity. They've given us policies premised on the hypothetical power of human greed and fear. A society that simultaneously offers the possibility of princely private wealth and the threat of severe poverty will surely inspire great feats of personal daring and cutthroat ambition. But it just as surely will reduce the capacity of its members to work together toward common ends.

This Radcon promise of prosperity is an illusion. Perhaps it was well suited to a frontier economy, but it's shamefully inappropriate to a post-industrial society that depends on what we achieve together. With the economy undergoing radical change and jobs and incomes so unsteady, social insurance is crucially important, and progressive taxes the only fair way of financing our needs. But Radcons, relying on social Darwinism, would rather reward the rich and penalize the poor. With financial capital moving around the world at electronic speed, the nation's "human capital" is more important to our future prosperity. Hence, the need for more and better public investments in education and training. But Radcons think prosperity will "trickle down" from the wealthy—despite evidence to the contrary—rather than "bubble up" from millions of people who are better equipped to be productive. With the environment, public safety, and work stresses such widespread concerns, we need carefully crafted business regulations and high-quality public services. But Radcons reflexively condemn any regulations or spending that may retard the growth of the gross domestic product.

Our real prosperity depends on what we achieve together. This has been a central tenet of American liberalism for over a century, and it's more relevant than ever. In America in the twenty-first century, real prosperity is shared prosperity. That's what we are losing rapidly, and that's why Radcons are wrong and their thinking is dangerously obsolete.

CHAPTER FOUR

POSITIVE PATRIOTISM

HOW TO TAKE PATRIOTISM BACK

What is the role of patriotism in an age of terror? Radcons emphasize pledging allegiance, showing the American flag, and singing the national anthem. They label as "traitors" anyone who criticizes the President or questions any detail of America's "war on terrorism." Their goal is to keep America the most powerful nation on earth, and force into submission any other nation that might threaten us. Their patriotism is all about expunging "evil" outside our borders. Terrorism is another evil that must be eliminated through discipline and force. And the war on terrorism is another example of us against them—if you're not with us, you're against us.

The Radcon version of patriotism requires no real sacrifice by most Americans. And it asks nothing of the more fortunate members of our society. Radcons don't link patriotism to a citizen's duty to pay his fair share of taxes to support the nation. And they don't think patriotism requires that all citizens serve the nation. Theirs is a shallow patriotism that derives its emotional force from disdaining foreign cultures and confronting foreign opponents. As such, it imperils the future security of America and the world, for reasons I will outline in a moment.

Yet many liberals have been silent about patriotism. They seem wary of it or, at best, embarrassed by it. Perhaps that's because, in recent decades, patriotism has so easily morphed into crass "America First" chauvinism. But that's not the only form patriotism can take.

Liberals should embrace patriotism—not the negative and imperialistic version the Radcons are peddling, but a positive patriotism that's better suited to our time: a patriotism that's based on love of America, but not on contempt for what's not American; that cherishes our civil liberties and our democratic right to dissent; that understands that our national security depends as much on America's leadership and moral authority in the world as it does on our military might; and that emphasizes what we owe one another as members of the same society.

This hopeful and reformist version of patriotism has deep roots in American liberalism. Unlike the Radcon's chest-thumping pride—exhibited by all great powers in history, from Rome to imperial England—the liberal version flows from an awareness that America is defined by its ideals. As John Adams, Thomas Jefferson, and James Madison well understood, American power is not an end in itself; it is a means of preserving and advancing those ideals.

WHY IT'S NATURAL AND EVEN HEALTHY TO LOVE AMERICA FIRST

Think of yourself standing at the center of a set of concentric rings spreading outward in every direction, reflecting how connected and responsible you feel toward those within them. Inside the closest ring is your immediate family. Inside the next are your close friends. Within the next is your community—neighbors, other friends and acquaintances, colleagues at work. Eventually you reach the nation as a whole. Beyond that national ring may lie another one, which includes all the people of the world. Most of us feel vaguely connected to other people on the planet simply by virtue of our common humanity—73 percent of Americans agree with the statement that "I regard myself as a citizen of the world as well as a citizen of the United States"[1]—but the closer the ring, the stronger the feelings of affinity.

Some on the left—the remnants of sixties activism—don't love America first. They consider themselves citizens of the world rather than of any particular nation. By the same token, there are conservatives who don't seem to love America first, either. At a recent college reunion I came across a former classmate (I'll call him Jim) who's now a top executive at a large global corporation. Jim told me proudly that his company has customers, investors, and employees from all over the world, and that he himself owns homes in Connecticut, the Bahamas, and southern France. Politically, Jim described himself as a "staunch free-market Republican conservative." But when I brought up the subject of American patriotism, he winced. He said he felt no more connection to Americans than to the citizens of other nations where he does business or resides. Jim isn't the first global executive I've met who feels no special moral allegiance to any particular country.

Thankfully, for most of us, there *is* a moral difference. We're connected to other Americans in ways we aren't connected to people living outside our borders. We may have a general moral obligation to every human being on the planet, but we feel a special bond with other Americans. We also feel a particular responsibility. As citizens, we have entered into a compact with one another.

Every nation and culture possesses such a compact—sometimes implicit, sometimes spelled out in detail; usually a mix of both. In fact, a nation is *defined* by its social compact. It is found within the pronouns "we," "our," and "us." *We* hold these truths to be self-evident; *our* peace and freedom are at stake; the problem affects all of *us*. These pronouns are powerful because they reflect feelings of affinity and connection, not because they draw upon hate or contempt for "them" outside the compact.

Patriotism that springs from feelings of affinity and responsibility is different from patriotism that glorifies our nation and denigrates others. Both kinds of patriotism give priority to "us" over "them." But the two kinds draw on different emotions, and have different consequences.

The first kind—call it "positive patriotism"—involves a special concern about the well-being of other Americans, but not necessarily to the exclusion of others around the world, and not at their expense. The second kind—negative patriotism—wants Americans to do better and be better than anyone else. Negative patriots also want to keep careful control over our borders, lest American culture and language become "diluted" by what's outside.

Negative patriotism is just about all we hear from Radcons. Talk-show host Michael Savage's harangues are typical: "[O]ur future as a nation depends on reawakening to the American identity that made us the greatest nation on the Earth. What is that identity? Borders, language, and culture."[2]

Robert Bork fears for the unity of the nation. "It was still possible to think of the United States as more or less culturally unified in the 1950s," he writes. "But now we are reversing direction and becoming a chaos of cultures that cannot, or more accurately will not, be unified. . . . [M]ulticulturalism is essentially an attack on America, the European-American culture, and the white race, with special emphasis on white males."[3]

These sentiments are poor substitutes for thought. Savage and Bork long for a cultural purity America never had. They echo tirades of the late nineteenth and early twentieth centuries, during the country's previous great wave of immigration. Xenophobic rants are as unwarranted now as they were then. Our unique strength as a culture has always been our pluralism, diversity, and tolerance. Most of us are descended from people who crossed our borders from somewhere else, with a different language and culture. Eventually they and their descendants merged into America. And they also changed it.

Negative patriots want Americans to believe in the "superior goodness of the American way of life," as Bill Bennett puts it. Patriotism, to him, requires that we tell ourselves and our children that America has provided more freedom, equality, justice, and prosperity, and spread it more widely "than any nation in the history of mankind" and that "our open, tolerant, prosperous, peaceable society is the marvel and envy of the ages."[4]

This is pure drivel. First of all, Bennett should get his facts straight. As I've said, income and wealth are distributed less equally in the United States than in any other major advanced economy. When it comes to life expectancy, the percentage of children in poverty, or health insurance coverage, America still lags behind Canada, France, Germany, Britain, and Japan. We rank forty-second in the world in infant mortality, behind all of Europe as well as Hong Kong and Taiwan. And "peaceable" isn't one of the adjectives that immediately comes to mind when comparing the United States to other major nations in rates of murders and assaults.

But facts aside, why, exactly, is it so important to think we're better than everyone else? It's entirely possible to love America more than any other country without believing it's the best in all respects. In fact, thinking we're the best may lead to smugness that stands in the way of our becoming better or learning from others.

Radcons celebrate American preeminence itself. But being "superior" is nothing new in history; the world has known many great powers that rise and subsequently fall. America's uniqueness is found not in our bravado but in our ideals. America was invented as an aspiration — "conceived in liberty and dedicated to the proposition that all men [that is, all people] are created equal." This was the great liberal insight of our Founding Fathers, and it became America's gift to history. It's a goal still worth fighting for.

National security is important to both kinds of patriots — positive and negative. But they have very different views about the best way to achieve it. Positive patriots see security as the by-product of strong alliances with allies who share our basic values, of international cooperation backed by military strength when necessary, and of America's moral leadership in the world. They also understand that a nation whose citizens have a well-developed sense of mutual responsibility will be stronger than one whose citizens feel disconnected, because the former are more likely to support and serve their country.

Negative patriots, on the other hand, tend to think national security comes from being the most powerful nation on earth—with the biggest armaments, best military technology, and strongest fighting force. They want America to be free to assert its power anywhere, unconstrained by treaties. (A "core" principle of conservatism, says columnist George Will, is "to preserve U.S. sovereignty and freedom of action by marginalizing the United Nations.")[5] They emphasize the superiority of America rather than the mutual responsibilities of Americans.

Positive patriots have to stand ready to stop aggression and genocide, of course. But positive patriotism doesn't need a foreign enemy to define itself or in order for it to flourish. At its best, the American tradition of liberal internationalism has reflected our drive to expand our founding ideals of liberty, equality, and democracy.

Negative patriotism, by contrast, automatically sets nation against nation, culture against culture. When well-being and security are assumed to depend on having more wealth and power than anyone else, there can be only one winner. Negative patriotism is fueled by the threat of evil foreigners "out there" eager to destroy us or to poison our culture. Without that threat, negative patriots wouldn't have much to talk about. Guided by negative patriotism, American activism in the world is the bullying typical of every great power in history.

My paternal grandfather, Alexander Reich, was born in New York in 1891. His future wife, Minnie Gottlieb, was born there a few years later. Both families were Jewish. Al and Minnie met each other when they were still in their teens and married in 1913. But their parents wouldn't attend their wedding. Why? Because Alexander's had come to America from Austria, and Minnie's had come from Hungary. The Austrians looked down on the Hungarians; the Hungarians resented the Austrians. Al and Minnie weren't trying to marry outside their Jewish religion or even, for that matter, outside their same five-block section of New York City. Austria and Hungary had even been part of the same empire. Nonetheless, the two families were so blinded by negative patriotism, they missed the wedding.

If missed weddings were the worst consequence of negative patriotism, it wouldn't be so dangerous. But negative patriotism linked to nation or tribe causes bloodbaths. In recent years it has led to slaughter in Kosovo, Bosnia, Rwanda, Iraq, Kashmir, Liberia, Afghanistan, Sri Lanka, Indonesia, and Israel, to name some of the killing fields. It has fostered anti-Semitism and anti-immigrant violence in Europe. And it nurtures terrorist hate.

Certainly, America must be on guard against terrorists and other evil aggressors "out there." But a patriotism based on the combination of fear of certain outside groups and unquestioning glorification of America will only harm us. If America, as the remaining superpower, is to lead the world—guide, not try to dominate or control—we have to respect other nations and cultures.

After college, I went to England for graduate study. Bill Bennett may disagree, but the English way of life isn't so bad. Though I don't much care for English cooking, their gardens are spectacular, and they do have a way with words. Oxford University, where I studied philosophy and economics, is still one of the best institutions of higher learning in the world, some four hundred years after its founding. Moreover, as the world's oldest democracy, England has done more than its share to spread freedom, justice, and tolerance—although its record is far from perfect.

I was a bit lonely when I arrived. I figured the best way to meet English students was to get involved in a dramatic production. Even if they don't recite Shakespeare in their sleep, most Brits love the theater. When I went to read for a play, I met a young Englishwoman who was also auditioning. We began talking, and within minutes I was smitten. Not wanting to appear an overly aggressive American, I didn't ask for her name and address—a terrible mistake. There were ten thousand students at Oxford, and there was little chance that either of us would get parts. What to do? My ingenious American mind came up with a plan. I decided to direct my own play, and put posters up all over Oxford announcing my auditions a few days later. Sure enough, she appeared, and I cast her in the female lead. That was thirty-five years ago and she's still my leading lady. To this day, Clare thinks she got the part on the basis of her acting ability.

Okay, I confess it: I married an Englishwoman. I could have married American, but I chose English. Sorry, Bill Bennett and Michael Savage. But I still love America.

WHY RADCON POLITICAL
CORRECTNESS IS DANGEROUS

All you have to do is tell them they are being attacked, and denounce the pacifists for their lack of patriotism and exposing the country to danger. It works the same in every country.

—Hermann Göring[6]

Radcons charge liberals who look for ways to improve this country with "blaming America first." It's an old debater's trick: Impugn the motives of someone who levels a criticism, and shift the conversation away from the content of the criticism to the person making it. The maneuver silences those who might be tempted to criticize and gives the public an excuse to ignore those who do. It tags anyone who questions American policy as unpatriotic. Bill Bennett says liberals have "turned a simple and noble impulse, love of country, into a suspect category—or, just as corrosively, an unfashionable one."[7]

It's a ludicrous accusation. Being critical of the nation is a far cry from being unpatriotic or anti-American. In fact, most social criticism—Bennett's included—is based on a love of America's ideals and a concern we're not living up to them. If our nation's social critics didn't care so much, they wouldn't bother.

Suffragettes didn't "blame America first" when they demanded that women have the right to vote. They were patriots who rested their entire case on the ideal of American democracy. Muckraking journalists such as Ida Tarbell and Lincoln Steffens didn't blame America first when they discovered corruption in high places. Labor leaders who demanded a minimum wage, a forty-hour workweek, and safe working conditions rested their case on America's founding ideals. So did civil rights leaders who pointed out the wide gulf between America's promise of equal opportunity and the reality that black Americans experienced every day.

Among my earliest memories is my father telling me what a wonderful place America was and what a privilege it was to live here. Even though he worried about making enough money to support our family, he always thought of America as a land of wondrous opportunity.

Dad was a member of what's now called the "greatest generation." He lived through the Great Depression and served in World War II, although he wasn't exactly a war hero. He spent most of his time during the war taking urine specimens. One day a country boy approached his desk. "What am I supposed to do?" the boy asked.

"Pee into one of those jars," my father answered, pointing to the row of small containers on the wall.

The boy looked surprised. "From *here?*"

Dad told this story at least a thousand times.

My father was a patriot, but that didn't stop him from being critical of America or of the people who lead it. He thought Senator

Joseph McCarthy was a villain, and, years later, that Lyndon Johnson deceived the nation about Vietnam. He was the first person I heard say Nixon was a crook.

Dad's patriotism was grounded in American ideals. He got upset when he noticed a wide gap between those ideals and what actually occurred. And in these moments he was participating in the very essence of Americanism.

That gap is still with us and always will be. The ideals are just that—*ideals*. They're goals and aspirations. But unless we acknowledge the gap, we can't even begin to close it. If we accept the Radcon view that good citizens should keep their criticisms to themselves, we won't ever be able to mobilize the political will to do better.

A childhood friend of mine, Michael Schwerner, went to Mississippi during the summer of 1964 to register black people to vote. Mickey was in his twenties, brimming with optimism and courage. He was murdered by racist thugs, along with two other civil rights workers, Andrew Goodman and James Chaney. What motivated the three of them to participate in "Freedom Summer" was that they loved America enough to risk their lives for it, and they were determined to help close the gap between American ideals and American practices. Schwerner, Goodman, and Chaney were true patriots.

Radcons label anyone who criticizes their unilateral militarism as "anti-war," and assume anyone who's "anti-war" must hold the same critical view of America that many of the young people who opposed the Vietnam War more than thirty years ago did. "The liberal tendency to dismiss or underestimate threats to the United States seems to be a permanent condition," says columnist Mona Charen.[8] According to Bill Bennett, "where armed conflict is concerned, the arguments of today's 'peace party' are basically rooted in the period of the Vietnam war and its aftermath. It was then that the critique of the United States as an imperialist or 'colonialist' power, wreaking its evil will on the hapless peoples of the third world, became a kind of slogan on the Left."[9]

This is political correctness at its worst. Radcons consider any criticism of the "war against terrorism" so offensive that they ignore the content of the criticism and attack the motives of the critic. Just as attacking liberals for fomenting "class warfare" or advocating "partial-birth abortion" subverts discussion of what's really at stake in these debates, accusing those who oppose the Radcons' methods of countering terrorism of being anti-war zealots from the sixties is a debater's ploy to shut down discussion about the validity of those methods.

Whatever hostility young people felt toward America more than thirty years ago is irrelevant to the debate we ought to be having now over how best to deal with terrorism. But, for some, Vietnam just won't go away. Radcons are even rewriting history. "Liberals were horribly, catastrophically wrong about Vietnam," insists Charen. "Liberal views, forged in Vietnam and tempered in Central America and beyond, got the world all wrong."[10]

Charen never states precisely how liberals were wrong about Vietnam except to note that after the fall of Saigon, the North Vietnamese executed many South Vietnamese and sent thousands of others to concentration camps. Charen and other Radcon revisionists apparently want us to believe that America's continuation of the Vietnam War, even with the cost of many more lives, would have been preferable to ending it when we did.

I was one of millions who opposed the Vietnam War because I didn't believe America's national interest was at stake. I still think that the death and destruction America inflicted on Vietnam, and the casualties we endured, were unnecessary. The Vietnam War was a civil war between North and South Vietnam, not a front line in America's cold war with Soviet communism. The so-called domino effect that the Johnson administration used to justify the war supposed that the fall of South Vietnam would set off a chain reaction of nations falling to communism across Southeast Asia and then elsewhere around the world. But the fall of Saigon didn't presage the triumph of Soviet or Chinese communism in Southeast Asia. In fact, by 2004, Vietnam was well on the way to becoming a capitalist nation. Even China is a rapidly growing capitalist force, although still far from being a democratic one.

What Radcon revisionists don't say is that by the time we finally left Vietnam, most Americans—not just those on the left—were deeply opposed to the war. They were not anti-American, nor lacking in patriotism. To the contrary, they were—and, presumably, still are—committed to the American ideals of liberty and democracy. America's role in the Vietnam War violated those ideals. The anti-war movement of the sixties deserves great credit for helping to bring an end to one of the sorriest chapters of American foreign policy.

When Radcons accuse those who disagree with a president's foreign policy of being "anti-American," they discourage debate about issues the public needs to explore and understand. This is especially dangerous during wartime, when patriotic feelings run high and when a president, as commander in chief, has wide latitude to decide what's in the nation's interest. Considering that the "war" against terrorism is unlikely to reach a point where the United States can declare total victory—at least for a generation—the Radcon effort to suppress debate reduces our capacity to discuss our future. As such, it imperils the effort to control terrorism by discouraging an honest airing of facts and judgments that could help correct errors. Worse yet, it strikes at the heart of our democracy.

Attorney General John Ashcroft even questioned the patriotism of people who said the administration went too far in compromising civil liberties for the sake of homeland security. "To those who scare peace-loving people with phantoms of lost liberty, my message is this: Your tactics only aid terrorists, for they erode our national unity and diminish our resolve. They give ammunition to America's enemies, and pause to America's friends."[11] *Phantoms* of lost liberty? When anyone the administration chooses to label as an "enemy combatant," including Americans, can be held indefinitely and denied access to lawyers and family members; when hundreds of detainees in Guantánamo can be held indefinitely, with no chance to contest their captivity; when the government can do secret searches of private homes and obtain records of anyone's book purchases or borrowings from bookstores and libraries—when all of this is allowed, we are not dealing with phantoms. Liberty has been lost, plain and simple. And unless Americans can openly debate whether these lost liberties are justified by a wartime emergency, we are also in the process of losing our democracy.

No, Mr. Attorney General. You, too, have got it backwards. It's your tactic of condemning critics of the administration that bolsters our enemies and worries our friends.

HOW AMERICA PLUNGED FROM EDWARD R. MURROW TO BILL O'REILLY

Prior to 1987, when Reagan-appointed commissioners on the Federal Communications Commission overturned the Fairness Doctrine, broadcasters had to air opposing views on controversial issues if they wanted to keep their broadcast licenses. Now, it's almost the opposite. Opinionated hosts of talk radio and talk television—almost all, Radcons—are interested in only one view: their own. And their view is relentlessly one-sided. Radcon media moguls reinforce the same right-wing messages.

In March 2003, as America moved closer toward an attack on Iraq, Natalie Maines, the lead singer for a country music group called the Dixie Chicks, told her fans during a London concert that "[w]e're ashamed that the president of the United States is from Texas."[12] In response, a number of Clear Channel Communications Company's 1,200 radio stations stopped playing the Dixie Chicks. Clear Channel stations also sponsored a series of pro-military rallies around the country. At about the same time, Cumulus Media, owner of 262 stations, instructed all its country stations to stop playing the Dixie Chicks. "We pulled the plug out of deference to our listeners," explained Cumulus's chief executive. At a pro-war rally promoted by a Cumulus station in Shreveport, Louisiana, a bulldozer crushed a collection of Dixie Chicks albums. The Cumulus executive described it as "an event that was precipitated by listener demand."

Nonsense. "Listener demand" couldn't have been the reason Clear Channel and Cumulus "pulled the plug." The Dixie Chicks' albums continued to sell well. Nor was the group blackballed because their albums or song lyrics were allegedly subversive. The censorship here was more insidious and more dangerous. It was because their lead singer had the temerity to express a particular political view.

Both Clear Channel and Cumulus are among America's largest media companies. As such, they're particularly dependent on the Federal Communications Commission, whose then chairman was Michael Powell, son of Colin Powell, President Bush's secretary of state. At the time, the FCC was considering whether to expand the number of radio stations a single company could own. (In June 2003 the FCC did expand the number.) Moreover, one of the more prominent members on the board of Clear Channel (which also syndicated Rush Limbaugh's shows) was Thomas O. Hicks, a wealthy investor with close ties to President Bush. Hicks bought the Texas Rangers from him, thereby helping make George W. Bush a multi-millionaire.

But what if it *was* listener demand? Suppose that, across the nation, tens of millions of radio listeners and television viewers decide they don't want to hear or see anyone who makes a negative comment about the President. Suppose they don't want to tune in to anyone who might say something even vaguely critical about the administration or its foreign policy.

Even this wouldn't justify banning dissenters from the airwaves.

Imagine the consequences if broadcasters routinely responded to "listener demand" by blackballing anyone who had voiced an unpopular political view. Careers could be ruined with an offhand comment that struck some major broadcaster as politically incorrect. The Dixie Chicks already had a large and loyal following. But knowing the consequences of the remark of their lead singer, how many up-and-coming artists, writers, or even pundits will now dare to criticize a U.S. president? More broadly, how many mid-level executives, young entrepreneurs, rising editors or producers, even presidents of universities seeking donations, will publicly express concern about administration policies? Freedom of speech is a fragile right. If its public exercise depends on "listener demand," it doesn't amount to much.

With escalating vituperation since 9/11, Radcons have been stifling any alternative views about the war on terrorism. Referring to people who protested against the war in Iraq, talk-show host Michael Savage said on MSNBC, "[t]hey are absolutely committing sedition, or treason."[13] Added Joe Scarborough, a former Republican congressman who hosts a show on MSNBC, "[t]hese leftist stooges for anti-American causes are always given a free pass."[14] One Fox News correspondent referred to war protesters as "the great unwashed."[15] Neil Cavuto, a Fox News host, told "those who opposed the liberation of Iraq" that "you were sickening then; you are sickening now."[16]

Bill O'Reilly of Fox News instructed his millions of viewers that "we expect every American to support our military, and if they can't do that, to shut up. Americans and, indeed, our allies who actively work against our military once the war is underway will be considered enemies of the state by me. Just fair warning to you, Barbra Streisand, and others who see the world as you do."[17]

Even after the fall of Baghdad, the mere suggestion by an O'Reilly guest that Bush's war against terrorism should be more fully examined summoned angry responses from viewers conditioned to O'Reilly's rants.

To: Reich@brandeis.edu
From: abl87rct@attbi.com
Subject: you
Robert,
I just want to remind you that because America has gone to war, you exist. And freely at that!!! Would you talk like you do before the true Founding Fathers? They put peoples heads and wrists in racks for just spitting on the sidewalk. What would they do to people like you? Stop using their first amendment as your right to talk against America.
Anonymous

Stop using their First Amendment as your right to talk against America. Pardon me, but I thought it was mine, too. And I thought it existed to protect dissenting views.

I remember sitting next to Dad on our family's maroon Castro convertible in 1954, squinting at a box with a small picture tube, our first television. I was seven years old. By then I'd taken on a few school bullies and held my own, at least to the point where I no longer felt threatened. Now America was being threatened and bullied. We had every reason to fear Soviet communism; five years before, the Soviets had detonated their first atomic bomb. No one knew whether or not they'd try to attack the United States.

Dad was as concerned as anyone else, but he also worried about another bully named Joseph McCarthy, a senator from Wisconsin. McCarthy had been searching for subversives—communist "fellow travelers" in government. His search had extended to the media, to Hollywood, to writers and artists all over America. Careers had been ruined for no good reason, and criticism of America frozen.

We watched the small screen as McCarthy accused the U.S. Army of shielding communists, and even browbeat a young lawyer not involved in the hearings. That finally prompted Joseph Welch, counsel for the army, to ask, "Have you no sense of decency, sir?"

Most of all, I remember watching Edward R. Murrow, a correspondent for CBS News, on a popular program called *See It Now*. On one particular evening in March 1954, Murrow devoted his entire program to the senator from Wisconsin. Murrow played tapes, read from transcripts, and allowed McCarthy's own words to reveal his techniques for smearing people with baseless accusations. I remember Murrow's summation at the end of that broadcast. It caused Dad to applaud. Since I couldn't remember it word for word, I looked it up. This is what Murrow said:

> We must not confuse dissent with disloyalty. . . . We will not be driven by fear into an age of unreason, if we dig deep in our history and our doctrine and remember that we are not descended from fearful men—not from men who feared to write, to speak, to associate and to defend causes that were, for the moment, unpopular. This is no time for men who oppose Senator McCarthy's methods to keep silent. . . . We proclaim ourselves, as indeed we are, the defenders of freedom, wherever it continues to exist in the world, but we cannot defend freedom abroad by deserting it at home.[18]

Terrorism is at least as frightening as the specter of communism—more so, since the terrorists have already attacked America and so far claimed more than three thousand lives on American soil. We are justifiably afraid. Fortunately, America hasn't yet re-created the McCarthy era, but we're in imminent danger of confusing dissent with disloyalty.

At its core, terrorism is intended to *terrorize* a nation's people, to inhibit their freedoms—not only freedom to travel, assemble, and engage in commerce, but also their freedom from searches without warrants, freedom from being held indefinitely without trial and without access to lawyers, and their freedom to speak their minds, which includes the freedom of dissent. To this extent, we are already its victims.

In the era of Bill O'Reilly, where can we find Edward R. Murrow?

WHY WE CAN'T FIGHT
TERRORISM WITH IMPERIALISM

Though I'm against the way the Radcons are waging the war against terrorism, I'm not "anti-war" and I'm certainly not "soft" on terrorism. I'm all for using military force when necessary. But the Radcons are using it irresponsibly. As a result, they're increasing, rather than decreasing, the likelihood of further terrorist attacks.

The Radcons' main strategy for fighting terrorism is to use bombs and troops to take over unfriendly nations. And if our traditional allies won't help us do this, we'll do most of it ourselves. While we're at it, we'll create a giant shield to protect ourselves from enemy missiles. *Weekly Standard* editor William Kristol and foreign policy specialist Robert Kagan put the Radcon case bluntly: "The United States *can* 'go it alone,' and it is hardly surprising that the American superpower should wish to preserve its ability to do so."[19]

This is a naked assertion posing as an argument. Who wouldn't want to control all the marbles if you could do it freely and effortlessly? It's what you have to pay for them and what you must give up in order to keep control that determine whether the effort is worth it. The mere fact that America *can* go it alone doesn't mean we should. Here again, Radcons confuse means and ends. The goal is not to remain the world's only superpower; it is for all of us to have secure and prosperous lives. If the price of remaining the only superpower entails sacrificing our security and prosperity, it is not worth the candle.

You have only to consider recent history. Our major reason for invading Iraq in the spring of 2003 wasn't to end Saddam's brutality, despite all the hoopla about "liberating Iraq" and the White House's slogan OPERATION IRAQI FREEDOM emblazoned across Fox News and MSNBC broadcasts. Yes, Saddam was brutal, and the Iraqi people are better off without him. But America often turns a blind eye to brutal tyrants. During the Cold War we helped despicably brutal regimes—the Shah, Mobutu, Somoza, Greek colonels, Korean generals, Pinochet, Marcos, the mujahideen. We advised them, trained their death squads, schooled and equipped their torture specialists, and helped them squirrel away their vast wealth. Not so many years ago we helped the Taliban in its war with the Soviet Union. We funneled aid to Saddam Hussein himself when he was battling Iran. Even now, as we fight against terrorism, we ignore repression in nations whose cooperation we need—Russia, Uzbekistan, Saudi Arabia, Egypt, Indonesia, the Philippines, and China.

Cynics would say the real reason for invading and occupying Iraq was to secure Iraq's oil fields against the possibility that the House of Saud wouldn't be able to keep the lid on Islamic revolutionaries in Saudi Arabia. If this was the rationale, the invasion and occupation could backfire by inciting Islamic revolution all over the Middle East, including Saudi Arabia.

But give the Bush administration the benefit of the doubt and assume that the basic reason for the invasion was exactly what the White House originally said it was—to advance America's "war against terrorism," and reduce the likelihood of future terrorist attacks. By this measure, there's evidence that the Radcons' go-it-alone strategy is backfiring. Senior counterterrorism officials interviewed by the *New York Times* more than a month after the fall of Saddam Hussein said Al Qaeda benefited from a spike in recruitment after the U.S. invasion. New young leaders were moving into operational and planning roles. Training camps were opening up in Kenya, Sudan, Pakistan, and Chechnya.[20]

In other words, *the Radcons are making the world more, not less dangerous.*

I've spent enough time in Washington to know that unless you've got your facts and objectives straight, you're going to make big mistakes. It's perilously easy inside the Beltway to lose sight of the basics. Washington is an echo chamber in which small tactical decisions are intensely repeated, debated, and criticized for days at a time, even while the basics are quickly assumed away.

Remember that the Radcons who are now in charge formulated their strategy in the nineties—well before 9/11. Their objectives included overthrowing Saddam Hussein and waging preemptive wars with or without U.N. backing. In developing their goals, they overlooked several important facts that are by now well documented:

1. The so-called war against terrorism is nothing like a conventional war. The enemy isn't a hostile nation that can be defeated in some spectacular military action. It doesn't have an army that can be outgunned. We will never be able to declare clear and decisive victory over it. Terrorism is a *tactic*; it is not itself the enemy.

2. Al Qaeda is bent on destroying the West, especially the United States.

3. Al Qaeda is not the only terrorist network harboring such goals. Al Qaeda is part of a global insurgency that includes the Jamaah Islamiyah in Southeast Asia, Ansar al-Islam in the Middle East, Dhamat Houmet Daawa Salafia in Algeria, and Al-Ittihad al-Islamiya in Somalia, among many others.

4. Not every group using terrorist tactics is intent on destroying the United States. Chechnyan rebels, for example, want independence from Russia. But such groups could be lured into international terrorism against America and the West.

5. Terrorists are not easily identifiable. We have no means of knowing how many there are, or how many are being recruited into their ranks, or at what rate. They have no central registry.

6. Terrorists are not dependent on a few "rogue" nations. They recruit and train in unstable parts of the world with weak or nonexistent governments, and they can move their bases and camps easily—from Afghanistan to Kenya, Sudan, Pakistan, Chechnya, the southern Philippines (Mindanao), northern Indonesia, or any other place where governments are weak.

7. Terrorists inhabit many countries, including Germany, Great Britain, France, Japan, and even the United States.

8. There is no finite number of terrorists. At any given time, the number depends on how many people are driven by anger and hate to join their ranks.

9. Terrorists are willing to die in order to impose death and destruction. We have been shown that a relatively small number of them can cause a large number of civilian deaths.

10. America's borders are fairly porous. In a single year, 475 million people cross them, as do 125 million vehicles. More than 20 million shipments arrive at 3,700 terminals located in 301 ports of entry. In recent years, more than 1.7 million undocumented immigrants have walked or ridden across the Mexican and Canadian borders.[21]

Given these facts, our priority shouldn't be attacking and occupying hostile nations. Fighting terrorism by taking over unfriendly regimes is comparable to fighting cancer by removing affected organs. Sometimes it can help, but it's dangerous and it often comes too late. Taken to its logical extreme, this approach would require America to assert control over many of the world's unstable regions. We would have to be a permanent occupying force, fighting guerilla wars over vast segments of the globe.

To some Radcons, this outcome would be just fine. Max Boot, former editorial page editor of the *Wall Street Journal*, claims that

"Afghanistan and other troubled lands today cry out for the sort of enlightened foreign administration once provided by self-confident Englishmen in jodhpurs and pith helmets."[22]

Well, I have my doubts that the inhabitants of the world's "troubled lands" cry out for an American version of British imperialism. But even if they did, it seems unlikely that most Americans are willing to bear the financial and human costs of empire. Moreover, an openly imperial America that occupied most of the "troubled lands" of the world would become an even larger target for terrorism than it is now.

The Radcons' priority is wrong again. Our goal should be making the whole body more resistant, by reducing the likelihood that weapons of mass destruction, especially nuclear devices, end up in terrorist hands. At its core, fighting terrorism isn't about vanquishing and occupying hostile nations; it's about policing the globe against dangerous and hostile groups. Radcon unilateralists don't understand how much our success in accomplishing this depends on the cooperation of the rest of the world.

Radcons are erecting a missile shield around the United States, at huge cost. But this is no real protection from terrorism. A single terrorist could carry a suitcase into the United States containing nuclear material. Or highly toxic bacteria could be hidden away in a shipment of fruits and vegetables—or in a bale of marijuana. In fact, a missile is the *least* likely way a weapon would enter the United States. Missiles are difficult and costly to produce, hard to hide, and they leave unambiguous return addresses.

Terrorists intent on setting off a nuclear device in the United States don't need to wait until a nuclear power sells or gives them the necessary material. They could steal or buy it on the black market. In 1999, Italian police seized enriched uranium from an organized-crime group trying to sell it to someone with presumed ties to terrorists. The uranium came from a U.S.-supplied research reactor in the former Zaire—presumably stolen or illegally purchased. Russia still has an arsenal of thousands of poorly maintained and guarded nuclear weapons, and enough highly enriched uranium and plutonium to make almost 70,000 more.[23] A lot of this is still not adequately secured against theft or black-market sale. As of this writing, the United States spends only $1 billion a year helping Russia and other former Soviet republics secure it, out of our total defense budget of some $400 billion. This is absurd.

America is focused on the so-called axis of evil—an occupied Iraq, Iran, and North Korea. Yes, these are dangerous places; the last two are developing nuclear weapons. But we're not spending nearly enough time, energy, and resources preventing illegal distribution of thousands of nuclear weapons already in existence in Russia, Pakistan, India, and other nuclear powers. And we're paying almost no attention to highly enriched uranium and plutonium in many other countries that terrorists could turn into nuclear weapons.

Radcons have their priorities backwards still again. What's needed is a tough global standard for preventing distribution (by theft, sale, or other means) across any national border of nuclear devices or material, or of biological or chemical weapons capable of mass destruction. And we need adequate resources to secure nuclear material, inspect to make sure it's secure, and apply force when necessary.

Effective policing involves "cops on the beat"—highly trained intelligence agents who can gain the confidence of people likely to know where trouble looms, get ongoing information about the locations of terrorist networks, directly infiltrate terrorist groups, and find out where dangerous materials are on the move. This requires the active cooperation of intelligence units and counterterrorism squads all over the world—exchanging information, sharing know-how, monitoring flows of money, tracking dangerous materials, intercepting communications, stopping transactions. So far in the war on terror, the biggest breaks have come from intelligence specialists in Pakistan, Britain, Spain, and Germany.[24]

But if we seem more like a global bully than a world leader, we won't get this cooperation.

FIGHTING TERRORISM BY GETTING THE WORLD ON OUR SIDE

Consider the following two fables. In important ways, America's security depends as much on which fable most people around the world come to believe as it does on our military strength.

Fable 1: The world is blessed with an advanced civilization renowned for its dynamism and freedom. Most of the world's peoples admire and emulate it. But this civilization fails to notice a primitive, diabolical force that emerges at its margins, intent on destroying it. Motivated by envy and hate, this force exploits the openness of the civilization to wreak havoc. Only in the nick of time does the civilization find the strength and moral fiber necessary to destroy this force and thus save humanity.

Most Americans believe this describes the United States, but quite a number of our traditional allies have started to doubt it, and most of the Islamic world and many of the world's poorest people don't believe it at all.

Fable 2: The world is ruled by a giant corporatist power that exerts control through spiritless technologies and materialist comforts. This sinister force acts to seduce, brainwash, monitor, and intimidate the world's people. But a few descendants of a former, more spiritual world, hidden away in mountains and teeming cities, keep the old faith alive. Through their cunning and bravery, these outlaws discover weaknesses in the system, and they exploit those weaknesses to destroy it and thereby liberate humanity.

Fable 2 is absurd, of course. But most terrorists believe it. And they want millions of others to believe it, too. Their job is easier if the entire Islamic world believes it; still easier if the entire Third World believes it. Then they can recruit almost a limitless supply of people willing to die to kill Americans and those who collude with them, and they can foil attempts to sabotage their plans. Their work is harder to accomplish if most of the world believes Fable 1, and almost impossible if the Islamic world comes to believe it.

Part of fighting terrorism is consciously reducing the credibility of Fable 2. Yet the Radcons' unilateral "you're either with us or against us" militarism does just the opposite, playing into terrorist hands.

Radcons claim that hostility toward America is rooted in envy of America's success and, in the words of Robert Kagan and William Kristol, "the inescapable reality of American power."[25] Wrong. It is precisely the Radcons' insistence on moving preemptively and unilaterally, and using military power to deal with so many obstacles and threats, that's fomenting anti-Americanism almost everywhere outside the United States.

Hostility to America was already there, of course, long before the Radcons embarked on their imperialist mission. America's Cold War history of support for anti-communist dictators didn't leave an endearing legacy in many parts of the world. As the world's last remaining superpower, moreover, we're automatically the object of envy, blame, and suspicion.

Yet in the months immediately following September 11, 2001, the world was mostly on our side. You probably heard it and saw it. Maybe, like me, you got e-mails from friends elsewhere around the world who expressed outrage at the deed and solidarity with the United States. Two hundred thousand Germans marched in Berlin to show solidarity with Americans; *Le Monde*, France's most prestigious newspaper, ran a banner headline proclaiming, "We Are All Americans."

As tragic as the events of 9/11 were, the aftermath offered a critical opportunity for global cooperation. Yet during the following two years that sympathy largely vanished. By acting as though world opinion didn't matter, Radcons squandered that good will.

Not since the Vietnam War has there been such a profound loss of faith in the moral authority of America. A survey of international opinion in some twenty countries after America invaded Iraq, undertaken by the Pew Research Center, found that the war "has widened the rift between Americans and Western Europeans, further inflamed the Muslim world, softened support for the war on terrorism, and significantly weakened global support for . . . the U.N. and the North Atlantic alliance." For example, in 2002, before the Iraqi war, 61 percent of Indonesians had a favorable impression of the United States; after the invasion, only 15 percent did. Majorities in Indonesia, Jordan, and areas administered by the Palestine Authority expressed "at least some confidence" in Osama bin Laden.[26]

If we behave more like the world's bully than its beacon light, why should we expect our friends to help us reduce the odds of further terrorist attacks here? If Fable 2 offers the world's destitute and angry a more convincing explanation for their condition, how can we prevent the ranks of terrorists from growing?

An American public scarred by 9/11 and fearful of future terrorist attacks is especially susceptible to demagoguery about America's unalloyed virtue and a worldwide conspiracy of evil that threatens our survival. A similar narrative captured the American mind in the 1950s when communism seemed poised to obliterate us—and, remember, in the fifties we hadn't been traumatized by thousands of civilian deaths on American soil. The consequences this time around could be a more uncompromising American militarism abroad that gives the rest of the world even more reason to believe Fable 2.

History provides abundant examples of how extremists gain power when politics becomes polarized around opposite views of reality. Each of these fables reinforces its opposite: The more one fable is believed and acted upon, the more plausible the opposite fable becomes to those who thereby feel threatened by the "evil" on the other side. And as those who are threatened act upon the opposing fable, they confirm the fears of those who cling to the other. Al Qaeda and other terrorist groups would like nothing better than for America to pursue a go-it-alone militarist mission. As the two fables gain credibility among opposing camps, the danger is that they both become greater realities.*

HOW TO BE THE WORLD LEADER RATHER THAN THE WORLD BULLY

Radcons say we have no obligation to anyone beyond our borders and should act only where our national interest is directly at stake — mainly to enhance our power and to control events outside America. This is a fundamental premise of their negative patriotism, but it's utter nonsense. Liberals have long understood that power is different from influence. And influence is what we need most right now. Liberals have also known the difference between leadership and control. We need to lead the world; we can't possibly control it. The only way America can get active cooperation from other nations is if we act in their interests, too.

Herein lies the basic tenet of liberal internationalism. In an interdependent world, America's efforts to relieve human suffering and spread prosperity around the globe serve our national interest. They also increase our legitimacy as world leader. This is the lesson we applied

---

* Talk by American officials about satanic forces in the Muslim world does not help our cause. When the general put in charge of the effort to capture Osama bin Laden and Saddam Hussein told a religious audience that America's real enemy is "a guy called Satan," declared that "they're after us because we're a Christian nation," and talked of his reaction to hearing a Muslim warlord in Somalia brag that he would be protected by Allah, as "I knew my God was bigger than his"—and then received only the mildest of rebukes and kept his responsibilities—it confirmed some of the worst fears of moderate Muslims around the world about America's intentions. See Douglas Jehl, "Bush Says He Disagrees with General's Remarks on Religion," *New York Times*, Oct. 23, 2003, p. A7.

after World War II when the Soviet threat made us take a broader view of national security. Not only did we rebuild Europe and Japan, but we also created and supported new international institutions—the United Nations, World Bank, International Monetary Fund, and General Agreement on Tariffs and Trade (which became the World Trade Organization)—to advance our interests *and* to promote peace and prosperity around the globe. The two goals are mutually reinforcing.

The current terrorist threat should cause us to think no less broadly and generously.

Think about these numbers: While the global economy has grown at an average of 2.3 percent a year during the past three decades, the gap between the best- and worst-off countries is ten times wider now than it was thirty years ago.* Of the six billion inhabitants of the planet today, almost half are struggling to survive on less than $2 a day. And the number of poor are growing faster than the number of rich.[27]

What are we doing about this? In many cases, the opposite of what we should be doing. America has turned its back on liberal internationalism. For example, we take care of domestic producers at the direct expense of the world's poor. The George W. Bush administration increased subsidies to America's corporate agribusinesses and hiked up import barriers on steel. These actions made it harder for poor nations to export food and steel to us—and earn the cash they need to pay their debts and build their economies. The yearly subsidy we give just to our own cotton farmers is three times our total foreign aid to Africa. (I should emphasize that on the issue of economic protectionism, Democrats are no better than Republicans and often worse.)

---

* Because this measurement is based on per capita gross national product—which, as I've noted, leaves out environmental quality, public health, public safety, and other aspects of a true measure of standard of living—it's likely to understate the real gap. As I've said, the world's poorest nations have among the worst environments and poorest public health because they can't afford better.

Meanwhile, we don't adequately support international efforts to reduce the debt burdens of poor nations, thus condemning them to years of crushing payments that suck up about 60 percent of their budgets. And our direct aid to poor nations is a joke. Even though we're the richest nation in the world, we give poor nations the equivalent of about $29 a year per each American, or one-tenth of one percent of our national product. This places us next to last among twenty-two donor countries in aid as a share of income—roughly one-third of European levels.[28] In 2003 the President asked for $200 million for the Global Fund to fight AIDS, tuberculosis, and malaria. That was equal to about one and a half days of the cost of the U.S. occupation of Iraq.

I'm not suggesting that global poverty is the direct cause of terrorism or that helping to spread prosperity will itself deter it. But we fool ourselves if we think there's no relationship between Third World poverty and the spread of Islamic fundamentalism—even to a remote island like Mindanao in the Philippines, where corn farmers are desperate because they can't compete with corn produced by American agribusinesses generously subsidized by the U.S. government.[29] While it's true that a lot of terrorists around the world are educated and middle class, they come from societies where there is general despair. And this despair provides fertile ground for new recruits and tactical support. If we sit back and allow the gap between the world's haves and have-nots to continue to widen into an unbridgeable chasm, we invite hundreds of millions more to despise us and we make Fable 2 all the more convincing.

America has more muscle than any other kid on the block. But leadership doesn't depend on brute strength. It depends on moral authority—setting an example for other nations to follow; providing a vision that's widely endorsed because it's likely to benefit everyone; and using our power to advance broad goals that help the planet survive.

The liberal tradition of American foreign policy has followed this moral principle. But the Radcons have opposed it. Rather than try to amend treaties we don't like, they reject them out of hand. They walk away from the Kyoto Protocol on global warming and choose to do almost nothing about greenhouse gases. They reject the biodiversity convention, the International Criminal Court and the World Court, the treaty on land mines, the treaty on small arms, and the Comprehensive Test Ban Treaty.

Radcons thumb their noses at the Geneva Conventions for treatment of war prisoners. Those conventions require, among other things, that prisoners of war be given accommodation and medical care equal to that of the troops guarding them, and that if a war prisoner is charged with a war crime—such as a terrorist attack on the United States—he be tried in a military court with the same procedural protections accorded troops who are court-martialed. In the "war against terrorism," these conventions are being ignored.

Radcons also turn their backs on nuclear arms control and decide to develop America's own low-yield "mini-nukes." They reject the U.N. charter, which bans the use of force except in self-defense or under a Security Council mandate. They scoff at the Nuremberg judgments, which treat preemptive attacks as war crimes.

When it comes to reconstructing Iraq, Radcons limit the contracts to a few major U.S. companies. They award the first major contract to the Bechtel Group, a politically connected company whose board includes a former U.S. secretary of state, and another to Halliburton, whose former chief executive is the vice president of the United States.

This isn't the conduct of a world leader. It's the behavior of an arrogant bully that cares nothing about the opinions of a skeptical world. Liberals should identify it for what it is.

All are by-products of negative patriotism, the idea that America's well-being and security depend on having more wealth and power than anyone else—so much wealth and power that we can simply ignore world opinion. From the Radcon perspective, foreign policy is a contest for dominance, where there can be only one winner. But this view overlooks America's growing interdependence with the rest of the globe—economically, ecologically, strategically, and politically.

A positive, liberal approach to global leadership would use our power to advance broadly shared goals around the world. It would see the struggle against global terrorism less like a war against a hostile foreign nation than a continuing international police action against global criminals. It would work with other nations, and through international organizations, to block dangerous weapons and their components from moving across borders. It would seek a global system for sharing intelligence and infiltrating terrorist networks. It would treat captured troops either as prisoners of war under the Geneva Conventions or as criminals under criminal law. Simultaneously, it would try to reduce global poverty, disease, hunger, and hopelessness—the soil in which terrorist hatreds take seed. As a result, the well-being and security of Americans would be enhanced, as would the well-being and security of most others on the planet.

IT'S YOUR COUNTRY

What should be asked of individual American citizens in this emergency? Radcons don't ask much more than uncritical support for their policies. That's the peculiar thing about Radcon patriotism—how little it really asks of Americans. I listened recently to a Radcon radio talk-show host fulminate against liberal "anti-American traitors" who criticize American foreign policy. Within a minute, he was on to another one of his favorite topics—taxes. "It's *your* money," he thundered, repeating the Radcon line we've heard so many times before. "It's not the government's money!" He bloviated on about why it was perfectly okay for citizens to use every tax dodge they could find to avoid paying Uncle Sam.

"It's *your* money" makes it sound as if citizens have no duty to support America. But how can we afford to fight terrorism if everyone tries to avoid paying taxes? What kind of patriotism is this? Real patriotism requires real sacrifice. Those who honestly love America feel a strong sense of responsibility to it. Displaying an American flag is easy. Paying your fair share of the cost of the nation requires some sacrifice.

We don't know exactly how much the fight against terrorism will cost in the years ahead, but it's bound to be far more than the $400 billion now budgeted annually for the Defense Department. I remember a White House meeting years ago when the President's national security adviser asked for billions of dollars more than had been budgeted for the Defense Department in order to go into Bosnia. It struck me as odd. I'd assumed the whole reason for spending hundreds of billions each year on defense was so the military could take military action. But it turned out that the purpose of the defense budget is to be *ready* for military action. Military action itself costs much more. "Battles are *extra*," I remember him saying.

We have to spend hundreds of billions more rebuilding Iraq, Afghanistan, and other countries we've pledged to help. We'll need to spend a bundle policing against terrorism around the world, even if other nations are also pitching in, too. Helping Russia and other nations secure all nuclear fissile materials will be a further major expense. Add to that the substantial cost of beefing up homeland security. As I've noted, exercising true world leadership is also expensive: It will require far more money, as well as attention, than we devote to it today.

Who's going to pay for all this? And for everything else the nation has to do? In 2003 almost 20 cents of every federal dollar was spent on national defense, including intelligence and homeland security. More than 40 cents went to Social Security, Medicare, and Medicaid. About 9 cents was for interest on the national debt. What remained—about 30 cents—was for everything else, including high-ways, schools, the environment, law enforcement, criminal justice, and veteran's benefits.

Of course government can and should be more efficient. I don't like the idea of paying for the equivalent of gold-plated toilet seats in military installations or $200 hammers. We need to keep pressure on military contractors, school administrators, and bureaucrats to weed out unnecessary expense. But even after you subtract "waste, fraud, and abuse," there's still a huge tab. We can't have a great nation on the cheap.

"It's *your* money?" It's your country! If you weasel out of what you owe in taxes, either someone else has to pay more taxes to make up the difference or there's less of what's required—roads, hospitals, troops, cops, safety inspectors, teachers—to keep it great.

Billionaire Steve Forbes, scion of the Forbes family fortune and publisher of *Forbes* magazine, speaks of taxes' "corrosive impact on our civic life." Well, taxes may corrode our wallets, but one thing they don't corrode is our civic life. If we didn't pay taxes, we wouldn't *have* a civic life. The eminent Supreme Court justice Oliver Wendell Holmes, Jr., got it right when he said, "Taxes are what we pay for civilized society."[30]

For years now, Forbes has been peddling a "flat" tax. His idea is that everyone should pay the same percentage of his income. In other words, chuck the graduated income tax. This may be a fine idea for people like Forbes, who would end up paying a lot less. But if the rich pay less, citizens of more modest means will have to pay more.

If we're serious about patriotism, the principle ought to be equal sacrifice. That's been the liberals' goal since the graduated income tax was introduced in 1913. I don't see why we should abandon it now, especially in wartime.

Equal sacrifice means that in paying taxes, people ought to feel about the same degree of pain—regardless of whether they're wealthy or poor. Logically, this means that someone earning $2 million a year should pay a larger proportion of his income in taxes than someone earning $20,000 a year. Even Adam Smith, the eighteenth-century guru of free-market conservatives, saw the wisdom of a graduated tax: "The rich should contribute to the public expense, not only in proportion to their revenue, but something more in proportion."[31]

Traditionally during wartime, taxes were raised on top incomes to help pay for the extra costs of war. The estate tax was imposed by wartime Republican presidents Lincoln and McKinley. It was maintained through World War I, World War II, the Korean War, and the Cold War. Only in 2001 did Radcons start to phase it out.

During World War I the income tax rate on the richest Americans rose to 77 percent. During World War II it was over 90 percent. In 1953, with the Cold War raging, Republican president Dwight Eisenhower refused to support a Republican bill to reduce the top rate, then 91 percent. By 1980, the top rate was still at 70 percent. Then Ronald Reagan slashed it to 28 percent. Because Reagan kept spending record sums on the military, the federal deficit ballooned. A few years after that, the Berlin Wall came down, ending the Cold War. We congratulated ourselves, and then faced the largest budget deficit since World War II.

Now we're back at war. But instead of raising taxes on the wealthy to pay for it, the Radcons want to cut them. Pardon me for asking, but where, exactly, is the patriotism in this?

Radcons say it's only fair and logical that the rich benefit most from income tax cuts because they pay most income taxes. What should be clear by now is that the rich pay so much in taxes in the first place because their incomes have skyrocketed in recent years, much more than everyone else's.

Liberals must do the arithmetic for the American public. Compare the *after-tax* earnings of families in the top one percent with the after-tax earnings of families in the middle. Between 1980 and 2000, the after-tax earnings of families at the top rose more than 150 percent, while the after-tax earnings of families in the middle rose about 10 percent. The Bush tax cut of 2003 raised the after-tax incomes of most Americans by a bit over one percent, but raised the after-tax incomes of millionaires by 4.4 percent. Apparently, in this time of national emergency, the wealthy have less of a patriotic duty to provide for the financial support of their country than do families of more moderate means.

Even if you're a billionaire, it's not just *your* money. You earned it because you live in America. As multi-billionaire Warren Buffett put it, "If you stick me down in the middle of Bangladesh or Peru or someplace, you'll find out how much this talent is going to produce in the wrong kind of soil. I will be struggling thirty years later."[32] President Theodore Roosevelt made the case in 1906, when arguing in favor of continuing the wartime inheritance tax. "The man of great wealth owes a particular obligation to the state because he derives special advantages from the mere existence of government."[33]

It's your *country*. And right now your country needs every American to sacrifice, in fair proportion. Liberals embrace this sacrifice. Radcons want to evade it.

Pointing out that the wealthy are paying less and less proportionally to support the nation isn't inviting class warfare, as Radcons often charge. It's exploring a deeper meaning of patriotism. The basic question is what we owe one another as citizens. That question is especially pertinent in a newly dangerous world in which we have to pull together. "Tax avoidance," FDR once quipped, "means that you hire a $250,000-fee lawyer, and he changes the word 'evasion' into the word 'avoidance.' "[34]

An acquaintance from law school is now a partner in one of Washington's biggest and wealthiest law firms, with offices in many different countries. With great glee he explained to me one day over lunch how he and his partners use tax rules to create offsetting taxable gains and losses, then allocate the gains to the firm's foreign partners who don't pay taxes in the United States. That way, they keep the losses here in the United States and shelter their income abroad.

I noticed he had an American flag lapel pin. "You're supporting our troops," I said, referring to it. "Yup," he replied, entirely missing my point. "And I can't stand all those naysayers who are knocking America. We stand or fall together."

Radcons think of patriotism in the symbolic terms of flags, Pledges of Allegiance, and non-dissent. But if patriotism isn't about taking on a fair share of the burden of supporting the nation, it doesn't count for much.

DOING YOUR FAIR SHARE

True patriots not only pay their fair share of taxes to support America; they also *do* their fair share to defend the nation and keep it strong. Here again, Radcons don't seem particularly interested in having everyone pull his or her weight. A liberal, positive patriotism would ensure that. If America is serious about patriotism, we should require that every young person spend two years in the military or in some other form of public service.

The United States has what's called an "all-volunteer" army, but the term is misleading. You don't "volunteer" for the military the way you volunteer to work in a homeless shelter. The job of soldiering is voluntary the same way any paid job is voluntary—you're not forced to do it; you're paid to do it. "All-volunteer" means there's no draft. People enlist because serving in the military is the most attractive job available to them.

Sure, some who serve in the military do so because of patriotic feelings, but pay is the major motivator. When military salaries and benefits are raised, more people sign up, the caliber of recruits is better, and they remain longer. That's why Congress lifted pay and benefits through the 1980s and 1990s, and why, by the late nineties, the average enlistee had higher scores on standardized tests than in 1973 when the draft ended. It's also why, during the George W. Bush administration, Congress pushed military pay scales even higher. By 2003, signing bonuses for jobs in high demand, like helicopter mechanics, reached $20,000. The army was paying recruits up to $50,000 to offset education costs and repaying up to $65,000 in student loans.

Paying for your army, by the way, has a long tradition in America. In the first American draft, during the Civil War, those who were called but didn't want to serve could hire a substitute to take their place. The market price varied from a few hundred dollars to $1,500 per substitute. When the variation in pay caused discontent among the ranks, Congress established a flat fee. If you were called and didn't want to serve you'd have to pay someone else $300 to replace you, roughly the year's wages of a laborer. Still, it struck many at the time as unseemly that the richer could buy their way out of military service.

Although the current system is better than the Civil War one because it puts the costs of hiring on society as a whole rather than only on people unlucky enough to be drafted, that's just a difference of degree. When taxpayers foot the bill, young Americans with better job prospects don't have to serve.

As a practical matter, this means the military is composed of fewer young people from rich families than the population as a whole. In the first Gulf war (no data are as yet available for the Iraqi war), enlistment rates for children of the richest 15 percent were one-fifth of the national average. When compared with other groups of the same age, the military also has more southerners and fewer northeasterners, and a higher percentage of blacks.[35] Black women in the army outnumber white women.[36] Only 3.5 percent of enlisted men and women have four-year college degrees. Most come from the same kind of blue-collar households whose incomes have gone nowhere for more than two decades.

Most of the children of America's elite don't serve in the military. Most children of journalists, lawyers, doctors, politicians, and investment bankers don't come near a fighting front. Charles Moskos, a sociology professor at Northwestern and an expert on military affairs, notes that in Princeton's class of 1956, from which he graduated, 450 of 750 men served in the military. In those days, America still had a draft. In 2002 only 3 of Princeton's 1,000 graduates served.[37]

Two years of required public service would exemplify positive patriotism at its best, and liberals should embrace this notion. The service could take many forms. Homeland security will require a large number of inspectors, monitors, and border patrols, as well as people trained to guide the public during an attack. Other young men and women will be needed for missions around the globe (the current war on terrorism is already straining the military and putting large burdens on reservists). The Peace Corps could be revived and expanded, offering young Americans ways to help people directly and maybe even improve America's image. AmeriCorps should be expanded on the home front, including more opportunities for young people to "Teach for America."

Recruits would be paid a modest stipend—at least living expenses plus interest payments on any education loans. That would be less than the current pay of "all-volunteer" army recruits.

Some might object that the wealthiest and best-connected young people would still end up with the safest and cushiest jobs. That's something to try to guard against. But of course it was an issue even when America had a draft. Young men from well-to-do families often seemed to end up at the safe desk jobs. At least under a system of universal public service every young person would have to put in two years.

Some object that compulsory service will create disciplinary problems. They point to the Vietnam War, when young men were still being drafted. In those days, the military was overwhelmed with desertions, AWOLs, and drug abuse. "Fragging"—the killing of officers by enlisted men—took at least a thousand lives between 1969 and 1972.[38]

But the draft itself wasn't the culprit. The problem was the Vietnam War. Many conscripts detested it. So, obviously, did the millions who avoided the draft. By the end of 1972, more than thirty thousand American draft resisters were living in Canada. More than a half million young men violated the draft laws, including a quarter million who never registered and thousands more who burned their draft cards. College students got deferments during their studies, and most young graduates continued to evade the draft with a variety of ailments or subterfuges.[39]

Vice President Dick Cheney got four separate deferments to stay out of harm's way during Vietnam. His explanation? He "had other priorities in the sixties than military service."[40] Cheney wasn't alone. The entire Radcon defense brain trust—Paul Wolfowitz, Richard Perle, and Bill Kristol—also managed to avoid military service during Vietnam, although they were prime for the picking.[41]

Bill Clinton famously got a graduate deferment based on entering ROTC after Oxford, until he drew a high number in the draft lottery and no longer needed an excuse.[42] George W. Bush jumped over a long waiting list to get into the Texas National Guard in 1968, far out of harm's way, and then apparently skipped more than a year of National Guard service.[43] Rush Limbaugh avoided the draft on account of a persistent boil on his buttock.[44] Howard Dean had a bad back. As for me, I failed the physical—two inches too short.

Soon thereafter, Richard Nixon officially ended the draft and created a paid military. He did it mainly to take the wind out of the sails of the anti-war movement, and he succeeded.

Now that we're in a permanent struggle against terrorism—a struggle that, unlike Vietnam, has already caused thousands of civilian deaths in the United States and threatens our very survival—universal public service should be the norm.

Many Radcons are firmly opposed. They blocked George W. Bush's modest proposal to expand AmeriCorps; in 2003 the House even failed to come up with enough money to maintain current levels. "The entire concept of paid volunteerism is an oxymoron," grumbled the editorial page of the *Wall Street Journal*,[45] apparently oblivious to America's "all-volunteer" paid army. Dick Armey, as House majority leader, refused even to schedule a vote on Bush's proposal, calling it "obnoxious" and suggesting he'd fight any attempt to move it through Congress. "We give least well when we give at the direction and supervision of the government," he told the *Washington Times*. "[T]he idea that government can teach charity to America rings very hollow with me."[46] With no strong push from the White House, the proposal died.

Universal service isn't about government teaching charity. It's about practicing love of country. The virtue of universal service—like that of a truly progressive tax—is that every family bears an equal share of the burden, regardless of income or social class. And it enables young Americans of different social classes to get to know one other. Supporting America in these ways should be considered part of the responsibilities of citizenship. They reflect an understanding that we're all in it together. They give each of us a direct stake in what this nation stands for and in what it does.

Positive patriotism—a direct descendant of our liberal tradition—offers us the best chance of being relatively secure in a world becoming less predictable and more perilous. The Radcons' bullying, negative version of patriotism is making us less secure by the day.

CHAPTER FIVE

WINNING:
IT WILL TAKE MORE THAN REASON

REASON AND VALUES

In the battle for America, liberals shouldn't recoil from morality, prosperity, and patriotism. The Radcon versions imperil our future. But unless they're met head-on by a bold liberal alternative, Radcons win by default. What is this alternative?

To recap:

Morality is important. Here, Radcons have it right. But they confuse public with private morality. A sensible public morality doesn't try to impose on Americans any particular religious notions about private sexual behavior; it vigilantly separates church and state. It focuses instead on immoral behavior that has unambiguously public consequences. Abuses of power and trust at the highest reaches of American business and government are undermining confidence in our economic and political systems. We need broad changes in laws to prevent corporate fraud, limit the exorbitant pay of top executives, and reduce the flow of money into politics. And these laws have to be backed not only by significant penalties but by strong public condemnation of people who abuse their authority.

Economic growth is essential, too. Again, Radcons are correct in emphasizing it (although we need to be careful about how it's measured, lest we become mesmerized by the gross domestic product). It's the Radcons' solution that's wrong. A proper vision of prosperity doesn't shower tax breaks on the rich and squeeze services for everyone else, especially now that the gap between the rich and the rest of us is wider than it's been in some eighty years. In a global economy, human capital is at least as important as financial capital—in many ways, more so. Our future prosperity depends uniquely on the productivity of our people. This means rejecting supply-side "trickle-down" economics in favor of "bubble-up" economics. We should oppose privatization of social insurance, and make broad-scale investments in the education and health of all Americans. At the very least, repeal Bush's tax cut for the top 2 percent, and go into debt if necessary, to have enough resources to equip all Americans for better jobs.

Patriotism is at the core of the American character, and we need to respond vigorously to the threat of terrorism and weapons of mass destruction. Radcons are right about this, too. But the Radcons' military solutions aren't working, and won't work. Instead of waging "pre-emptive" wars that leave us occupying hostile lands, we should work with our long-term allies to gather intelligence, infiltrate terrorist networks, and act as global "cops on the beat." We should lead world efforts to reduce global poverty and environmental decay. Positive patriotism also means protecting civil liberties at home, and insisting that all Americans bear their fair share of the burden of financing and serving the nation.

These liberal positions don't draw their moral urgency from blaming or demonizing anyone. They're about us, about what we make of ourselves. They come from a clear-eyed view of where America is, where we need to be, what we must do. Radcons' policies, by contrast, are based on ideology, not reason.

PASSION

But it's not enough to have reason on our side. To win, liberals also need fire in our bellies. Passion is necessary to gather resources, build organizations, and energize participants. Radcons have been passionate about their mission for more than twenty years.

Passion is also necessary in order to be heard. We need to show the strength and courage of our convictions. Unless we put our ideas out there aggressively, we leave the public arena to the likes of Rush Limbaugh, Heritage Foundation pundits, editorial writers and columnists for the *Wall Street Journal, Weekly Standard, Washington Times,* religious zealots, racists, and screamers.

Passion is required in order to counter Radcon propaganda with the truth. And since Radcons mislead the public over and over again, the truth has to be told repeatedly—through letters to the editor and opinion pieces, on web sites, through e-mail "trees," and, wherever possible, on radio and television. Consider, for example, how Radcons misled Americans on the estate tax by calling it the "death tax" and causing the public to think that almost everyone had to pay it at death when, in fact, only the richest 2 percent had to pay. As a result of this concerted deception, and liberals' failure to counter it, most Americans favored the estate tax's repeal. Among those were Americans earning less than $50,000, who told pollsters that they were concerned about increasing inequality in America and that the rich weren't paying their fair share of taxes.[1]

Passion doesn't mean irrational bile. Liberals don't need to be nasty to be heard. Rants based on nothing more than self-righteous indignation or religious dogma might generate good sound bites, but they coarsen public discourse and discourage rational argument. Perhaps that's why many Radcons prefer to push their opinions on talk radio and yell television, or in screed-like books and op-ed pages, without subjecting them to full civil debate. They don't want to debate, because they'd lose more often than not. Common sense and reason are not on their side. They'd rather prevent or close off dialogue.

The passions aroused by radical conservatives are fueled by anger and resentment, not by reason. They've taken the fears of many Americans caught in a long-term economic downdraft and twisted them into hatred of "them." They've blended cultural, economic, and nationalistic populism into an ideology based on conquering an "evil" with a mutable definition. Their evil exists as sexual deviance, sloth, and demonic forces outside America. The stakes are so high that the end justifies any means.

Radcons disguise their radical agenda behind these simple targets. And they offer oversimplified, lowest-common-denominator solutions (cut taxes on the rich, cut spending on the poor, cut regulations, ban abortions, put prayer in the schools, put more people in prison, invade and occupy hostile countries, find and kill all terrorists) and ridiculously simplistic choices (sexual deviance versus family values, big government or small government, blame America or love America). They thereby make their unreasonableness sound like reason. But most of this is fatuous nonsense.

Radcons claim they're standing up for average Americans and traditional values against so-called liberal elites who court these evils. But these "liberal elites" exist only in the Radcons' fevered imaginations. The elites are no longer liberal, if they ever were. Radcons now dominate government; they monopolize talk radio and television; and they inhabit most Washington-based policy institutes. Wall Street bankers and CEOs—hardly a liberal elite—run the economy.

Radcons rail against the fading ghosts of the furthest fringes of the sixties, phantom far-left limbs that disappeared long ago. They conjure up these apparitions in order to convince average working people that Radcons are on their side. But they're just distracting Americans from the real challenges ahead. And they're dividing us from one another and from our friends around the world.

Liberals have to reclaim from Radcons the populist mantle. Radcon apologists for concentrated wealth and power shouldn't be allowed to claim they're representing average working Americans. Long before the sixties, it was liberals who stood up for the little guys. Radical conservatives of America's Gilded Age represented big business and the wealthy. At the turn of the twentieth century, liberal Republican Theodore Roosevelt railed against the "malefactors of great wealth"—the price gougers and monopolists who owned large swathes of American industry. Decades later, FDR decried the "economic royalists"—the speculators who manipulated markets for their own benefit.

Wealth itself wasn't what provoked liberal ire. It was the special privilege, influence, and irresponsible behavior that habitually accompanied it. Liberals managed the economy on behalf of average working people—regulating business where necessary; spending more than was coming in and cutting taxes when the nation needed to prevent the economy from sinking and unemployment from rising; cutting deficits when they got out of control. Internationally, liberals were the ones who led the fights against tyranny, totalitarianism, and fascism, on behalf of human rights and common decency. Conservatives were isolationists.

But in the last several decades, liberalism lost its populist roots. It lost the language and passion of populism. It stopped standing up for ordinary Americans against the bullies; for people without wealth and power against those who have it and misuse it. Liberals who lived through the Depression and World War II moved into retirement and old age. Many of the student activists of the sixties, who had rejected liberalism in favor of New Left activism, fought their fights—winning some, losing some—and then retreated. Those who followed them turned inward, to "self-improvement" or to the "identity politics" of race, feminism, and gay rights. Many grew disillusioned with politics altogether. Some understandably shied away from the growing abusiveness of political discourse.

Yet if there was ever a time for liberals to reclaim the moral urgency of their mission, it is now. The concentration of wealth and power in our country invites abuses. It undermines trust in our economy and our government; showers huge financial awards on a small minority while subjecting many of the rest of us to financial insecurity; invites xenophobic and racist scapegoating; and propels a jingoistic, arrogant, and ultimately dangerous foreign policy. Radcons embrace all of this. The battle must be joined.

ORGANIZATION

Some liberals have tried to fight back. Every four years they throw themselves behind a presidential candidate they believe will deliver us from the steadily rising Radcon tide. But even if liberal-leaning presidents get elected from time to time, they can't accomplish much without a movement behind them. During the presidential campaign of 1936, a voter asked Franklin D. Roosevelt to push harder for certain New Deal measures. "Good idea," he responded, "but you've got to *make* me do it."[2] What he meant was that a president who wants to effect change needs citizens to mobilize support and keep the pressure on.

In 1994, when Bill Clinton was battling for his health care proposal, he was handicapped by the absence of an actively engaged political movement demanding the same thing. His formidable powers of persuasion weren't enough to overcome radical conservative organizing on the other side. By contrast, George W. Bush got his massive tax cuts through Congress (even though Americans were ambivalent about them, at best)[3] because he had a political movement behind him. Big business and evangelical Christians gave him the political support he needed.

Other liberals are embroiled in single-issue politics—the environment, abortion rights, campaign finance reform, the war. These are all important, but single-issue skirmishes don't build a political movement, either. Issues rise and fall, depending on which interests are threatened and when, and what makes the news. Sometimes they even divide liberals rather than unite them, as each issue-advocacy group scrambles after the same set of liberal donors, and competes for the limited attention of the media.

That isn't to say presidential campaigns are unimportant; all campaigns for elective office are important. Turning out voters is essential. And I can get as passionate about particular issues as anyone else. My point is that these isolated efforts use up huge amounts of energy and resources, but they don't build a permanent infrastructure that can be used for the *next* election campaign or for *another* issue. They don't mobilize people over the long term, and keep them mobilized for the long haul. The whole is less than the sum of the parts because these efforts don't build on one another.

I can't tell you how many solicitations I get every week from candidates and single-issue advocacy groups in Washington. Don't you? Liberals have become adept at direct mailings and at sticking checks in envelopes. My e-mail is brimming with new left-leaning sites and ways to zip money to this or that liberal cause at a keystroke. But a real movement requires ongoing organization beyond specific candidates or issues, based on shared values. It depends on networks of people who meet regularly at the local level, and periodically connect with others in different locales.* It requires the patience to build a disciplined national organization. A real political movement helps particular candidates and pushes specific issues, of course, but it does so out of the ongoing strength and commitment of its members. As it moves from battle to battle, it makes sure to accumulate greater and greater organizational heft, mobilizing liberal activists state by state, district by district, chapter by chapter.

Radcons began organizing two decades ago around a set of common values, with an eye on the long term. They recruited people

---

* The Internet may be helping in this regard: Meetup.com offers an efficient way for ordinary Americans who share certain interests to find one another. And MoveOn.com has proven to be a highly effective means of raising funds.

who share their beliefs and who would run for local, state, or federal office. They supported the campaigns of these people and held them accountable once in office. They found people with money who also shared their beliefs, and used that money to expand their organization, both in state capitals and in Washington. They recruited broadcast pundits and writers, and supported them and spread the word. They created long-term alliances and coalitions with the religious right, small businesses, trade associations, and key lobbyists in Washington.

And with their passion and their organization, they grabbed the mantle of populism right from under our liberal noses.

Americans are ready for a bold, new liberalism that reins in abuses of unconstrained power and greed, that widens the circle of prosperity, and that unites much of the world against terrorism and hate. This isn't the agenda of the sixties left, nor is it the Republican Lite politics peddled by Democratic centrists who think elections are won in the upscale suburbs. It's a liberalism grounded in public morality, in a commonsense program for prosperity, and in love of America. It's a liberalism that's both passionate and hardheaded.

But it needs to be organized.

DEMOCRATS JUST LOOK DEAD

Can liberals reclaim America through the Democrats?

I've served under two Democratic presidents, run for office as a Democrat, and attended hundreds of interminable conferences about "The Future of the Democratic Party." The truth is, there is no Democratic Party. Yes, I know: Millions of people call themselves Democrats and several hundred thousand show up at Democratic state and national conventions. A Democratic National Committee raises money. But there's no real national Democratic Party. At least nothing like what the Republicans have. They have discipline and organization. They decide on a party line and stick with it. What do

Democrats have? Conferences on "The Future of the Democratic Party."

The Radcons who have taken over the Republican Party may be dead wrong on the issues that matter to this country, but they have the courage of their convictions. And they've built a strong organization. Democrats have neither.

The only time there's even a semblance of a national Democratic Party is when Democrats come up with a presidential candidate. But if you look closely you'll see that Democrats don't actually come up with a presidential candidate. Instead, six to ten people who call themselves Democrats come up with themselves. Then, about a year before election day, as the Democratic primaries approach, the field is winnowed to a handful of contenders who have raised the most money and claimed the most headlines. At this point, a small group of Washington-based Democratic political consultants, pollsters, and marketers decide whom they'll place their bets on. Meanwhile, you and I are still sitting in some "The Future of the Democratic Party" conference.

From the 1930s through the 1970s, Democrats were in almost continuous control of the executive branch, the House of Representatives, the Senate, most governorships, and most state legislatures. Democratic presidents presided for thirty-two of the forty-eight years spanning 1932 and 1980. But in the 1980s, Democrats began losing ground in all these branches and all these levels of government. In the twenty-four years between 1980 and 2004, Democrats controlled the executive branch for exactly eight. Now Republicans have taken it all over, including most governorships. And Radcons are in the driver's seat.

Some people tell me to forget about the Democrats and join the Green Party, or maybe even help start another party. Third parties have a long history in American politics. Most notable, for our purposes, was the Liberal Republican Party of 1872 (which conspicuously launched the term "liberal" into American politics); the Populist Party of 1892; Teddy Roosevelt's Bull Moosers of 1912; Robert La Follette's Progressive Party of 1924; Henry Wallace's 1948 presidential bid; George Wallace's, of 1968; Ross Perot's Reform Party of 1992; and Ralph Nader's Greens of 2000.

But the history of these and other third-party efforts in America shows that they rarely displace either of the two dominant parties. They sometimes roil the waters and put new ideas into play, and in these ways they have made important contributions. But they also draw votes away from the major party that's closest to them, ideologically. In other words, third parties help the major party most opposed to their values. That's what happened in 1992, when H. Ross Perot pulled enough votes away from George H. W. Bush to hand Bill Clinton the election, and then again in 2000, when Ralph Nader drained enough votes away from Al Gore to give George W. Bush an electoral college victory.

Our Constitution created a "winner-take-all" system, where the presidential candidate with the most votes gets all a state's electors, and the party with the most senators or representatives runs that branch of Congress. This almost guarantees that politics will be dominated by only two major parties. When the winner takes all, only one party will take over. It's different in a parliamentary system, where smaller parties are represented in the legislature in proportion to the number of votes they get out of the total, and may have a part in forming the next government if (as is likely) no single party gets a majority. America could move to a different system. For example, "instant-runoff" voting, by which voters decide their order of preference for various candidates, is used in some American communities. But changing our Constitution isn't easy—the Founding Fathers didn't mean it to be—and it's far from clear any new system would be better than the one we have.

So as a practical matter, liberals need to work through the Democratic Party if we want to effect major political change in America. That shouldn't be a cause for despair. After all, look what Radcons accomplished in the Republican Party. They worked diligently for over twenty years and finally remade the GOP in their image.

The Democratic Party only looks dead.[4] It can be reawakened. What's needed is a real, ongoing Progressive Democratic Party that takes firm hold at the grass roots; the capacity to think through new ideas and market them; and a passionate commitment to social justice. The party has to be turned into a political movement that embraces all the people who have been left out, who have been mowed over by big corporations in cahoots with government—the people who are working their backsides off but aren't earning much more than they did a dozen years ago, people who have grown cynical about every institution in American society but still love America with all their hearts.

THE SHAM OF CENTRISM

Some blame the Democrats' steady eclipse on the party's being out of step with an American electorate grown more conservative and suburban. But this is more assertion than explanation. It doesn't say why voters have shifted their allegiances. Suburban life may be quieter than city life, but it's not intrinsically more Republican.

The biggest losses for Democrats since 1980 have been from America's giant middle and working classes—mostly, white workers without four-year college degrees, and especially white men. They were part of the old Democratic base. Some became "Reagan Democrats" in the 1980s. Since then, many of them have moved steadily into the Republican camp.

Not incidentally, these are the same people who have lost the most economic ground since the late 1970s, as the American economy shifted.[5] Naturally, they've been anxious and frustrated. Many of them were also appalled at the student radicals of the sixties—their casual sex, loud opposition to the Vietnam War, and apparent rejection of traditional American values. And they were put off by a Democratic

Party that seemed all too eager to help poor minorities and advance the aspirations of college-educated women, but do little or nothing for them.

Radcons have eagerly stepped into the void, blaming Democrats and "liberal elites" for coddling blacks and other new immigrants, welfare cheats, anti-American traitors, communists (now, terrorists), gays and lesbians, criminals, feminists, and the rest. They've repeated these charges so often that they've become a mantra. Broken down piece by piece, the allegations start to crumble. But left unexamined, they offered a simple explanation—and an easily proffered solution to a complex problem.

Democrats could have responded with bold plans for getting all Americans better and more secure jobs, better schools, more afford- able health care and child care, and better retirement security. They could have delivered a populist message about the responsibility of corporations to help their employees in all these respects, and of wealthy elites not to corrupt politics with money. They could have embraced serious and far-reaching campaign finance reform. But Democrats did very little of this. In some respects, they did just the opposite. Many Democratic candidates, dependent for campaign contributions on the same corporate and Wall Street interests as Republicans, didn't want to offend their sponsors. Others were intimi- dated by the rising clamor of radical conservatives who accused them of "taxing and spending." By the nineties, Democrats were promot- ing tax cuts and balanced budgets.

Many Democrats claim they have to move to the "center" to be elected, and that polls show that Americans have become cynical about government. Well, yes, Americans have grown cynical. But the cynicism is largely because government has been so ineffective in responding to the crisis faced by a large portion of working Ameri- cans. And that cynicism is fed by a steadily growing cacophony of radical conservative pundits and talk-show hosts.

It takes no conviction and less courage to move to the political "center," as defined by prevailing polls of likely voters. If you want to be a malleable politician, you campaign from the center. But if you want to be a leader, you *define* the center. You don't rely on polls to tell you where to go.* At best, polls tell you where people are, and it's pointless to lead people to where they already are. The essence of political leadership is focusing the public's attention on the hard issues that most would rather avoid or dismiss. We know the problems that need fixing.

Centrism is bogus. There's no well-defined, consistent political center in America. The rush by many Democrats in recent years to the so-called center is a pathetic substitute for clear thinking and candid talking about what the nation needs to do, and why. And then, once in office, doing it. Meanwhile, the "center" keeps shifting further right because Radcons stay put while Democrats keep meeting them halfway.

In the months leading up to the 1996 election, I frequently ran into Dick Morris in the White House. Morris, you may remember, was Clinton's pollster and political adviser who famously advised him to "triangulate"—that is, to find positions equidistant between Democrats and Republicans. I argued that this robbed Clinton of any mandate for a second term. Morris argued there wouldn't be a second term unless Clinton moved to the center. I still believe Morris was wrong. Clinton could have told Americans the truth— that the economic boom of the nineties was mainly enriching a small minority; that most Americans were doing only slightly better than before; that when the boom went bust we'd still have to face the underlying structural challenges of an economy and society concentrating more and more wealth and power in fewer hands. He could have said that America in the mid-nineties finally had the wherewithal to do what the nation couldn't do before—expand prosperity

---

* The polls in Appendix A are not intended to guide candidates or aspiring politicians, but only to reassure them that Americans are able to hear a liberal message.

by investing in our people, especially in their education and health. I think Clinton could have been reelected on this mandate. But he was reelected without any mandate. As a result, the nation was confused about what needed to be accomplished, and easily distracted by Radcon fulminations against a president who lied about sex.

By the late nineties, the federal budget was showing large surpluses. But the only thing Clinton or Al Gore, and most other Democrats, could think to do with the extra money was to pay off the national debt a year earlier. Polls showed that's what the suburban "swing" voters wanted.

But that's over now. What isn't over is the political nonsense of centrism. Supposedly 40 percent of Americans lean liberal and 40 percent lean conservative. If I hear another pundit say the real action is with the 20 percent upscale suburban "swing" in the middle who have no strong political commitments, I'm going to scream. When Democrats mute their message to attract these "swingers," Democrats lose more potential voters who decide that driving to the polls isn't worth the cost of the gas to get there.

Much of the old Democratic base that didn't become Republican has just stopped voting. The largest political group in America isn't Democrats or Republicans or even upscale suburban "swing" voters. It's people who don't vote. In 2002 only 33 percent of eligible voters cast ballots in races for the House. Republicans got 17 percent of eligible voters; Democrats, 15 percent. The turnout of core Democratic constituencies plummeted, even among minorities and the poor. What did Democrats talk about in 2002? They hardly talked about the poor economy, or the dwindling and overstressed middle class, or the widening gap between the rich and everyone else. They didn't focus on irresponsibility in executive suites, or rail against tax breaks mainly for the rich. They didn't warn of the perils of unilateral preventive wars. They didn't build support in poor and working-class communities. They did none of this because they were courting the upscale suburban swing voters and wooing money from the big boys.

In the presidential election of 2000, three-quarters of voters with family incomes over $75,000 a year went to the polls. But the lower down the income ladder, the lower percentage of people who voted. Sixty-nine percent of those earning $50,000 to $75,000 a year bothered. Only 38 percent of households earning less than $10,000 did.[6] If voters with family incomes under $25,000 had cast their ballots at the same rate as those above $75,000, more than 6.8 million more voters would have gone to the polls in 2000. Most of them would have voted for Al Gore, and Gore would have won handily—not just the popular vote, but also more states, which would have given him the election for sure.

Interestingly, turnout in the Republican primaries of 2000 actually surged. Republicans temporarily tapped into traditional nonvoters because John McCain wooed them with his moral heroism and energized them with his anti-establishment, tell-it-like-it-is, give-'em-hell message. The message wasn't the xenophobic bile of Ross Perot or Pat Buchanan. It was about grabbing government back for the people. Bill Bradley was the Democrat's anti-establishment candidate, but he didn't mobilize the nonvoters because his message had no "give 'em hell" in it. Nonvoters know you can't change a corrupt system by being polite. The only way to speak truth to power is with the moral fervor of a true reformer.

The big differences in American politics today are between those with courage and those without it, those who can inspire and those who can't. Among the former are the late Paul Wellstone and John McCain—politicians with deeply held views who are passionate about what they believe. They don't care much about the polls, they love this country, and they have a fair degree of contempt for Americans who are powerful but don't really give a damn about America or about most other Americans. On the other side is a large group of hard-boiled poll-watchers and ass-kissers who spend most of their time raising money from people and groups with a lot of it.

When he died tragically in a plane accident, Wellstone was

locked in a tight race for the Senate. Just weeks before, he had voted against Bush's carte blanche resolution to go to war in Iraq. Most people in his home state of Minnesota had backed the President, so Wellstone's vote was politically risky. I phoned him to say I admired his courage and hoped it wouldn't cost him the election. "Not a chance," he said, with his characteristic buoyancy. "My polls rose after the vote." I asked him why. He explained that the people of Minnesota supported him because he stood up for what he believed and was always ready to lay out the arguments behind his beliefs. "Besides," he added, "I wouldn't be an effective candidate otherwise. Saying and doing what I believe is right energizes me."

Democrats have to stand up and be counted. And while they're at it, Democrats also need to have fun, and conduct their politics with a sense of hope and humor. All the negativism and anxiety is a bummer. Who wants to join a funeral procession? We need a new generation of happy warriors. The world does not have to go to hell. Taking the long view, the achievements of the last century were extraordinary—largely because of reforms liberal Democrats championed. I'd hate to be a Radcon Republican because Radcon Republicans hate government, and now they run it. Can you imagine being in total control of something you detest?

THE GROUND TROOPS

To reignite the Democratic Party and transform it into a political movement will require the time and energy of a lot of people who are fired up enough to make this sort of commitment over a long term. Where are they?

Radcons have found many of their ground troops in the religious right. Can liberal Democrats find their own ground troops in the religious left? Large numbers of people who are active in their churches or synagogues are deeply concerned about the moral breakdown at the highest levels of business and politics and the widening gap between have-mores and have-lesses. They're distressed by the emergence of the belligerent, negative patriotism I've described. But their congregations are scattered and disorganized, and often reluctant to engage in politics directly. Quakers do demonstrate against the war. Unitarian Universalists organize food co-ops and homeless shelters. Catholic bishops, once a clear and strong voice for social justice, are mired in sexual-abuse scandals and anti-abortion politics. Jews watch out for Israel. Black Baptist churches try to keep their children out of trouble. Methodists and Presbyterians run bake sales and take up collections.

I don't want to be unfair. Liberal-leaning religious groups are doing a lot of good in their communities. But most are afraid of getting involved in anything resembling "politics" because they don't want to appear to be partisan or divisive. They don't want to risk that some prominent members may withhold contributions, or bolt. They worry about losing their not-for-profit tax status. All this is perfectly understandable, but wrong. Many of these same congregations and denominations had no compunctions about being politically active three decades ago. The National Council of Churches—the fifty-million-member group representing mainline Protestants, Orthodox churches, and the major African-American churches—effectively mobilized support for civil rights and against the Vietnam War. The Catholic Church, in the wake of Vatican II, was deeply involved in workers' rights, affordable housing, and social justice. Jewish congregations steadfastly supported the Civil Rights Act of 1964 and the Voting Rights Act of 1965.

The stakes today are as high, if not higher, as they were then.

If liberal ideals are to prevail, or even come into reasonable balance with those of radical conservatives, those who constitute America's religious left will need to become more active, more cohesive, and more directly engaged with politics. They have to understand that evangelical Christian fundamentalists are waging political war. The Christian right is intent on imposing its views on the rest of us about abortion, homosexuality, prayer in the public schools, creationism, and the inherent evil of Islam. They're energizing the Republican Party across the South, Midwest, and many western states. Now is the time for the religious left to join forces with liberals and Democrats, and speak and act with the moral urgency our times deserve.

Members of organized labor have been ground troops for the Democratic Party for many decades, but unionized workers continue to shrink as a proportion of the total workforce—now making up less than 10 percent of the private sector, as I said earlier. The recent efforts of the AFL-CIO to put more resources into union organizing drives is encouraging. Still, too many unions are bent on preserving old jobs at any cost, and have cast free trade as their major nemesis. Unions need to get behind a broader reform movement to salvage American politics from the Radcons.

The Service Employees International Union (SEIU) and the Hotel Employees and Restaurant Employees International Union (HERE) are representing just those who are most marginalized in the emerging economy—hotel workers, hospital workers, workers in large retail stores, janitors. And they're succeeding, with some huge victories over the last few years. The SEIU, in particular, is the closest we have to a "movement" union. It's the most diverse union in the AFL-CIO. Its ranks are full of Latinos and blacks, as well as whites. Its leadership is young. It's organizing like mad. It's recruiting and training a lot of young people. If it can keep growing and show some more political muscle, it could have a major role in transforming the Democratic Party.

Minorities—blacks, Latinos, and Asians—are becoming a larger portion of the American population and a significant liberal Democratic voting bloc. They were only about a tenth of the voting electorate in 1972, but grew to almost a fifth of all voters by 2000. At this rate, they'll account for nearly a quarter of voting Americans by 2010. They need to be mobilized and made a permanent part of this new political movement. If the venom that Radcons continuously spew into the airwaves about these minorities hasn't been enough to get them involved — they mustn't be allowed to be intimidated — a bold program focused on economic development of poor cities, affordable housing, good schools, and good jobs should be.

Working, single, and well-educated women constitute other potential ground troops. Most already vote Democrat. Most oppose the Radcons' position on abortion and contraception; they want help with child care and health care; they often feel badly treated by businesses that fail to accommodate the need to balance work and family; they oppose big tax breaks for the rich; and they disapprove of bullying militarism. While they don't have a lot of time to put into grassroots politics — their jobs and families consume them — they'd make time if they felt it was well spent.

Liberals need to be careful not to place too much reliance on the elderly. Over the next two decades, the "greatest generation" retirees will be replaced by aging boomers, who'll be the largest, noisiest, and most demanding political constituency in American history. Tens of millions of boomer bodies will all be corroding simultaneously. If you think prescription drug coverage is a big deal now, wait until medical science promises boomers we can look young, have sex like rabbits, and party until we drop at the age of a hundred. Across the land there'll be outcroppings of Med-Meds — think of Club Med combined with a medical facility: snorkeling all morning followed by extra oxygen in the afternoon. Worse yet, most boomers haven't saved a dime for retirement. All their equity is in their homes. And home prices will take a dive when the boomers all go to sell at about the same time.

In other words, brace yourself. We'll be lucky if the Democrats (as well as a lot of Republicans) don't sell out completely to aging boomers. Increasingly, the fault line in American politics will be generational. Who will represent the young? Who will inspire them? Who will enable them to discover the joy of politics?

Young people between the ages of eighteen and twenty-five are doing more voluntary work in their communities than any generation in living memory. They're tutoring poor kids, staffing after-school programs in poor schools, helping in soup kitchens, teaching in disadvantaged school districts. All this, yet they're cynical as hell about politics. We've got to get them involved.

I have this debate all the time with my sons, especially Adam, who has been working for the last few years with juvenile prisoners and parolees in Providence, Rhode Island. Adam believes that the best way to change America is through local organizing that brings people directly together to improve their communities. I value what Adam does and I'm proud he has the courage of his convictions. I also tell him that if he and his friends turn their backs on national politics they're ceding it to the Radcons—with disastrous consequences for every poor and working-class community in America.

As I told you, I lost the race for governor of Massachusetts in 2002. I got in too late to organize a grassroots effort that might have made up for my lack of campaign funds. Maybe I'm just not a very good politician. But I did at least inspire a lot of young people to get involved. They worked tirelessly in my campaign. They saw how politics can affect the lives of ordinary people in very practical ways. They felt the joy and excitement of politics, and also its disappointments. I wouldn't have done nearly as well as I did without them.

Here's some really hopeful news, and I learned it while running for governor. Liberal idealism isn't dead. It's just waiting to be ignited (among young people, minorities, the poor) or reignited (among the middle-aged and jaded). Millions of people are yearning to get involved and change the way politics is practiced. It doesn't matter whether they call themselves Progressives, Greens, Democrats, or Independents. They want the system cleaned up. They want government to work better and for more people. They yearn for political leaders who are authentic, who'll stand up for what they believe in, who aren't afraid to take on sacred cows and tell it like it is, who have new ideas that are commonsensical. They're deeply worried about where the Radcons are taking the country.

There's the kindling and the lighter fluid. All it will take is a match.

This is much bigger and more important than the future of the Democratic Party or even the future of liberalism. It's really about the future of our democracy. Our democracy is in terrible trouble right now. Power is in the hands of a tiny group of people who are using the threat of terrorism to impose their crimped vision of a corporate commonwealth. Large corporate entities are more politically potent than they've been at any time in living memory.

Parties are means, not ends. The question is: Can Democrats turn themselves into a national movement to take back our democracy? Can they give voice to those without a voice? Can they regain their passion, courage, and soul?

The Radcons dominating the Republican Party know exactly what and whom they stand for. Democrats don't. And when you know who you are and what you believe, you've got a much better chance of winning, even if you're wrong.

Some people say we don't need a vital politics to be a vital society. All we need is grassroots moral activism, spearheaded by community groups, socially responsible businesses, not-for-profits, religious organizations, and compassionate volunteers. All these forms of "civic engagement" are important, but they do not comprise an alternative to politics.

Throughout our history, civic activism has been the precursor, and the propellant, of political movements. A bit more than a century ago, American liberalism appeared similarly eclipsed, despite mounting social problems. As today, vast fortunes were being amassed, yet median wages had stopped growing and the poor were getting poorer. New technologies (steam engines, railway locomotives, the telephone, steam turbines, electricity) were transforming America, pulling families off the farms and immigrants from abroad and depositing many into fetid slums. Robber barons and Wall Street magnates were consolidating their empires. The richest one percent of the population owned more than the remaining 99 percent put together. Government was effectively up for sale to the highest bidder and politics had sunk into the swamp of patronage. The broad public was deeply cynical. "What do I care about the law: Hain't I got the power?" huffed Cornelius Vanderbilt.[7]

All seemed perfectly justified, as we've seen, by the convenient doctrine of social Darwinism. Some Americans turned to blaming immigrants and foreigners. The American Protective League was formed—viciously anti-Catholic, anti-Semitic, and anti-immigrant. The Ku Klux Klan was revived. America also turned imperialistic. With the sinking of the *Maine* in 1898, Spain, a third-rate colonial power in Cuba, was depicted by the McKinley administration as the world's most wicked despot. America quickly conquered the Philippines, another Spanish domain, and spent the next several years trying to quell a guerilla resistance that claimed the lives of four thousand Americans. Those who opposed the Spanish-American War were attacked as "ultra-pacifists." As the century closed, America seemed to be turning its back on liberal democratic ideals.

But as the new century dawned, the air began crackling with reform. Muckrakers such as Lincoln Steffens and Ida Tarbell exposed corruption, and the middle class demanded fundamental change. Small businessmen had had enough of the monopolies, and joined forces with trustbusters. Wisconsin's crusading governor, Robert La Follette, enacted legislation regulating health and safety in factories; Oregon limited the hours of work for women (no more than ten per day). Suffragists marched. Campaigns were organized for pure food and drug laws, workers' compensation, a minimum wage, a graduated income tax, and civil service reform. A progressive movement began to emerge. Liberal politics gained new life and meaning.

What happened? Indignation, which had been rising steadily, suddenly exploded and flooded the country. Morality and common sense simply couldn't abide the way things were going. Yet instead of opting for revolution and radical change, Americans preferred to spread the benefits of the emerging industrial economy, thereby saving capitalism from its own excesses.

If I'm right, and the historic parallel holds, another era of liberalism is on its way. Liberals will indeed win the battle for America because they are closer than Radcons are to the true American ideals. If Democrats can see and feel this resurgence, they will be the party of the future. If not, well, it will bubble up some other way, although maybe not with the same speed or force.

The most important thing for each of us to know is we're not alone in all this. There are tens of millions just like us—Americans who have had enough of the radical conservatives: their intolerance, their mean-spiritedness, their moral righteousness, their arrogance toward the rest of the world. But they see little or no alternative—many are almost as fed up with comatose Democrats: their lack of conviction, their spineless shift toward a rightward moving "center," their weak-kneed incapacity to tell it like it is.

The most important thing for us to do is get involved. We may not all call ourselves "liberals," but we share the same liberal values. We have reason on our side, and we need fire in our bellies. And when you and I join with others, and commit ourselves to the long-term struggle to revive our democracy and rededicate this nation to the liberal ideals on which it was founded, we will win.

APPENDIX A:

AMERICANS ARE NOT RADCONS

Public opinion polls give, at best, a snapshot of what Americans believe at any point in time. The following polls, from every major polling organization, paint a picture of an America that's far more liberal on social, economic, and foreign policy than the radical conservative positions on these issues. (All results are large enough to be statistically significant. Some totals may exceed 100 percent because of rounding.)

1. PUBLIC MORALITY

"Do you think homosexual relations between consenting adults should or should not be legal?"

SHOULD %	SHOULD NOT %	NO OPINION %
50	44	6

CNN/USA *Today*/Gallup poll. July 25–27, 2003.

"Which of the following best represents your views about abortion? The choice on abortion should be left up to the woman and her doctor. Abortion should be legal only in cases in which pregnancy results from rape or incest or when the life of the woman is at risk. OR, Abortion should be illegal in all circumstances."

WOMAN AND DOCTOR %	RAPE, INCEST, LIFE OF WOMAN %	ALWAYS ILLEGAL %	NOT SURE %
59	29	9	3

NBC News/*Wall Street Journal* poll conducted by the polling organizations of Peter Hart (D) and Robert Teeter (R). Jan. 19–21, 2003.

"Which ONE of the following three statements comes closer to your view? The United States is a Christian nation. The United States is a Biblical nation, defined by the Judeo-Christian tradition. OR, The United States is a secular nation in which religious belief, or lack of it, isn't a defining characteristic."

	%
A Christian nation	29
A Biblical nation	16
A secular nation	45
Don't know	10

Newsweek poll conducted by Princeton Survey Research Associates. June 27–28, 2002.

"Which comes closer to your view: Government can promote the teachings of a religion without harming the rights of people who do not belong to that religion, OR, any time government promotes the teachings of a religion, it can harm the rights of people who do not belong to that religion?"

	%
Can promote religion without harming rights	40
Promoting religion can always harm rights	54
No opinion	6

CNN/USA *Today*/Gallup poll. Sept. 19–21, 2003.

"And now a question about the power of different groups in influencing government policy, politicians, and policymakers in Washington. Do you think [see below] have/has too much or too little power and influence on Washington?"

	TOO MUCH %	TOO LITTLE %	ABOUT RIGHT (VOL.) %	DON'T KNOW/ REFUSED %
Big companies	80	10	4	5
Political action committees, which give money to political candidates	78	12	4	6
The news media	72	17	6	5
Political lobbyists	69	15	4	12
TV and radio talk shows	54	29	7	10
Labor unions	45	37	8	10
Opinion polls	33	48	8	11

Appendix A: Americans Are Not Radcons

	TOO MUCH %	TOO LITTLE %	ABOUT RIGHT (VOL.) %	DON'T KNOW/ REFUSED %
Churches and religious groups	27	53	10	10
Racial minorities	20	59	10	11
Public opinion	19	69	6	6
Small business	4	88	3	5

The Harris poll. Feb. 12–16, 2003.

"When it comes to dealing with the problems of the financial markets and major corporations, which do you think is the greatest danger: that regulators will go too far and impose restrictions on business that will hinder the economy, OR that they will not go far enough toward raising the standards of accountability and restoring confidence in the markets and U.S. corporations?"

	%
Will go too far	36
Will not go far enough	59
Not sure	5

NBC News/*Wall Street Journal* poll conducted by the polling organizations of Peter Hart (D) and Robert Teeter (R). Latest: July 19–21, 2002.

"Do you think that the current cases of wrongdoing among chief executives of major businesses represent a problem of a few corrupt individuals in a system that is mostly honest and aboveboard, OR a widespread problem in which many business executives are taking advantage of a system that is failing?"

	%
A few corrupt individuals	33
A widespread problem	61
Depends	4
Not sure	2

NBC News/*Wall Street Journal* poll conducted by the polling organizations of Peter Hart (D) and Robert Teeter (R). Latest: July 19–21, 2002.

"As you know, last year Congress passed and President Bush signed into law a bill which restricted the way candidates and political parties could raise and spend money. Based on what you have read or heard about the bill, do you think it is a good thing for the country, or a bad thing for the country?"

GOOD THING %	BAD THING %	NOT SURE %
58	18	24

Time/CNN poll conducted by Harris Interactive. Sept. 3–4, 2003.

"As you may know, the first amendment to the Constitution gives all Americans the right to free speech. Do you think the first amendment also gives Americans the right to contribute as much money as they want to political parties and candidates, or don't you think so?"

DOES GIVE THAT RIGHT %	DON'T THINK SO %	NOT SURE %
40	52	8

Time/CNN poll conducted by Harris Interactive. Sept. 3–4, 2003.

2. PROSPERITY AND ECONOMIC POLICY

"Which of these do you think should be the top priority for any surplus money in the federal budget: cut federal income taxes, put it toward reducing the national debt, strengthen the Social Security system, or increase spending on other domestic programs such as education or health care?"

	%
Education / health care spending	37
Strengthen Social Security	24
Cut federal income taxes	20
Reduce the national debt	18
No opinion	1

ABC News/*Washington Post* poll. Latest: Mar. 22–25, 2001.

"Do you think the new tax cut law [enacted in 2003] will or will not help your family's financial situation?"

WILL %	WILL NOT %	NO OPINION %
35	56	9

CNN/USA *Today*/Gallup poll. May 30–June 1, 2003.

"Do you think the tax cut is generally fair as to how it is divided between the rich, middle class or poor, or is it generally unfair?"

	ALL %	REPUB-LICANS %	DEMO-CRATS %	INDEPEN-DENTS %
Generally fair	34	53	24	31
Generally unfair	54	32	67	59
Not sure	13	15	9	10

The Harris poll. June 10–15, 2003.

"Do you think that the tax cut will help the [see below] a lot, some, only a little, or not at all?"

	A LOT %	SOME %	ONLY A LITTLE %	NOT AT ALL %	NOT SURE %
"The rich"	42	30	12	6	10
"The middle class"	11	39	31	11	8
"Low-income workers"	13	21	28	32	7

The Harris poll. June 10–15, 2003.

"Do you think federal spending on education should be increased, decreased, or kept about the same?"

	%
Increased	65
Decreased	8
Kept the same	26
No opinion	2

ABC News/*Washington Post* poll. Mar. 30–Apr. 2, 2000.

"Would you support or oppose a plan to reduce federal education funding to school districts whose students don't improve on standardized tests?"

	%
Support	36
Oppose	61
No opinion	3

ABC News/*Washington Post* poll. Mar. 30–Apr. 2, 2000.

"There is always a lot of discussion about the best way to finance the public schools. Which do you think is the best way to finance the public schools: by means of local property taxes, by state taxes, or by taxes from the federal government in Washington?"

	ALL %	PUBLIC SCHOOL PARENTS %
Local property taxes	21	19

	ALL %	PUBLIC SCHOOL PARENTS %
State taxes	33	31
Federal taxes	37	41
Don't know	9	9

Phi Delta Kappa/Gallup poll. June 5–23, 1998.

"Would you be willing or unwilling to pay more taxes to provide funds to improve the quality of the nation's inner-city public schools?"

	ALL %	PUBLIC SCHOOL PARENTS %
Willing	66	64
Unwilling	30	34
Don't know	4	2

Phi Delta Kappa/Gallup poll. June 5–23, 1998.

"Now turning to the subject of the environment: When it comes to regulating the environmental and safety practices of business, do you think the federal government is doing enough, should it do more, or should it do less?"

	ALL %	REPUBLICANS %	DEMOCRATS %	INDEPENDENTS %
Doing enough	25	38	20	21
Should do more	62	46	72	67

	ALL %	REPUB- LICANS %	DEMO- CRATS %	INDEPEN- DENTS %
Should do less	7	12	4	6
Don't know	6	4	4	6

CBS News/*New York Times* poll. Nov. 20–24, 2002.

"Do you agree or disagree with the following statement? Protecting the environment is so important that requirements and standards cannot be too high and continuing environmental improvements must be made regardless of the cost."

	ALL %	REPUB- LICANS %	DEMO- CRATS %	INDEPEN- DENTS %
Agree	57	41	66	62
Disagree	36	52	30	30
Don't know	7	7	4	8

CBS News/*New York Times* poll. Nov. 20–24, 2002.

"What do you think is more important: producing energy, or protecting the environment?"

	ALL %	REPUB- LICANS %	DEMO- CRATS %	INDEPEN- DENTS %
Producing energy	29	44	23	23
Protecting environment	57	41	66	62
Don't know	14	15	11	15

CBS News/*New York Times* poll. Nov. 20–24, 2002.

3. PATRIOTISM AND THE WAR ON TERROR

"How concerned are you that new measures to fight terrorism in this country could end up restricting our individual freedom? Are you very concerned, somewhat concerned, not too concerned, not concerned at all?"

VERY CONCERNED %	SOMEWHAT CONCERNED %	NOT TOO CONCERNED %	NOT CONCERNED AT ALL %	DON'T KNOW %
34	32	19	14	1

Associated Press poll conducted by ICR. Sept. 4–8, 2003.

"The Department of Defense is developing a program which could compile information from sources such as phone calls, e-mails, web searches, financial records, purchases, school records, medical records, and travel histories to provide a database of information about individuals in the United States. Supporters of the system say that it will provide a powerful tool for hunting terrorists. Opponents say it is an invasion of individual privacy by the government. Based on what you just heard, are you inclined to support this program, or inclined to oppose it, or haven't you heard enough about it to say?"

	ALL %	DEMOCRATS %	INDEPENDENTS %	REPUBLICANS %
Inclined to support	31	18	30	50
Inclined to oppose	36	42	40	22
Haven't heard enough	28	34	26	25
Don't know	5	6	4	3

Los Angeles Times poll. Dec. 12–15, 2002.

"As a result of the U.S. military action against Iraq, do you think the threat of terrorism against the United States has increased, decreased, or stayed about the same?"

INCREASED %	DECREASED %	SAME %	DON'T KNOW %
25	17	55	3

Newsweek poll conducted by Princeton Survey Research Associates. Sept. 18–19, 2003.

"In the long term, do you think having gone to war with Iraq will increase or decrease the risk of further terrorism in the United States?"

INCREASE %	DECREASE %	NO DIFFERENCE (VOL.) %	NO OPINION %
48	40	8	4

ABC News poll. Sept. 4–7, 2003.

"In the long run, do you think the U.S. military action against Iraq will do more to increase or decrease the risk that large numbers of Americans will be killed or injured in a future terrorist attack — or do you think that it won't make much difference either way?"

INCREASE %	DECREASE %	WON'T MAKE MUCH DIFFERENCE %	DON'T KNOW %
36	25	34	5

Newsweek poll conducted by Princeton Survey Research Associates. Aug. 21–22, 2003.

"Please tell me if you agree or disagree with the following statement: Because the world is so interconnected today, the U.S. should participate in efforts to maintain peace, protect human rights, and promote economic development. Such efforts serve U.S. interests because they help to create a more stable world that is less apt to have wars and is better for the growth of trade and other U.S. goals."

	%
Agree	78
Disagree	18
Don't know	4

Program on International Policy Attitudes. Oct. 21–29, 1999.

"Please tell me if you agree or disagree with the following statement: It is nice to think that joining in international efforts makes a more stable world. But in fact, the world is so big and complex that such efforts only make a minimal difference with little benefit to the U.S. Therefore, it is not really in the U.S. interest to participate in them."

	%
Agree	39
Disagree	58
Don't know	3

Program on International Policy Attitudes. Oct. 21–29, 1999.

"I'm going to read you two statements. Please tell me which comes closer to your point of view.

"(A) As the world becomes more interconnected, and problems such as terrorism and the environment are of a more international nature, it will be increasingly necessary for the U.S. to work through international institutions.

"(B) International institutions are slow and bureaucratic, and often used as places for other countries to criticize and block the U.S. It is better for the U.S. to try and solve problems like terrorism and the environment on our own instead."

	%
Statement A	56
Statement B	39
Don't know	5

Program on International Policy Attitudes. Oct. 21–29, 1999.

"Please tell me if you agree or disagree with the following statement: I regard myself as a citizen of the world as well as a citizen of the United States."

	%
Agree	73
Disagree	25
Don't know	2

Program on International Policy Attitudes. Oct. 21–29, 1999.

"Please tell me whether you agree or disagree with the following statement: As one of the world's richest nations, the United States has a moral responsibility toward poor nations to help them develop economically and improve their people's lives."

	%
Agree	68
Disagree	30
Don't know	2

Program on International Policy Attitudes. Oct. 21–29, 1999.

APPENDIX B:

RECOMMENDED READING

RADCONISM

I have found the following books especially helpful for understanding the major ideas of radical conservatism in modern America, and their origins:

Bennett, William J. *The Broken Hearth: Reversing the Moral Collapse of the American Family* (New York: Broadway Books, 2001).

Bloom, Allan. *The Closing of the American Mind* (New York: Touchstone, 1988).

Bork, Robert H. *Slouching Towards Gomorrah: Modern Liberalism and American Decline* (New York: ReganBooks, 1996).

Buckley, William F., Jr. *Up from Liberalism* (New York: Honor Books, 1965).

Charen, Mona. *Useful Idiots: How Liberals Got It Wrong in the Cold War and Still Blame America First* (Washington, D.C.: Regnery, 2003).

Friedman, Milton, and Rose Friedman. *Free to Choose* (New York: Harcourt Brace Jovanovich, 1980).

Gilder, George. *Wealth and Poverty* (New York: Bookthrift, 1984).

Goldwater, Barry M. *The Conscience of a Conservative* (Washington, D.C.: Regnery, 1990).

Appendix B: Recommended Reading

* Harding, Susan Friend. *The Book of Jerry Falwell: Fundamentalist Language and Politics* (Princeton, N.J.: Princeton University Press, 2001).

Hayek, Friedrich von. *The Road to Serfdom* (Chicago: University of Chicago Press, 1944).

Herrnstein, Richard, and Charles Murray. *The Bell Curve: Intelligence and Class Structure in American Life* (New York: Free Press, 1999).

Himmelfarb, Gertrude. *One Nation, Two Cultures: A Searching Examination of American Society in the Aftermath of Our Cultural Revolution* (New York: Vintage, 2001).

* Hofstadter, Richard. *The Paranoid Style in American Politics, and Other Essays* (Chicago: University of Chicago Press, 1979).

* ———. *Social Darwinism in American Thought* (Boston: Beacon, 1955).

Kagan, Robert. *Of Paradise and Power: America and Europe in the New World Order* (New York: Knopf, 2003).

Kirk, Russell. *The Conservative Mind* (Washington, D.C.: Regnery, 1953).

Murray, Charles. *Losing Ground: American Social Policy, 1950–1980* (New York: Basic Books, 1984).

Podhoretz, Norman. *The Present Danger* (New York: Simon & Schuster, 1980).

Rand, Ayn. *Capitalism: The Unknown Ideal* (New York: New American Library, 1986).

Strauss, Leo. *Natural Right and History* (Chicago: University of Chicago Press, 1953).

Wanniski, Jude. *The Way the World Works* (Morristown, N.J.: Polyconomics, 1989).

---

* An asterisk on this and the following list denotes an author who provides a historical account or analysis, rather than an argument about what the nation should do or become. The distinction between the two types of book is not always easy to draw, of course.

Appendix B: Recommended Reading

THE LIBERAL TRADITION IN AMERICA
*The following books are helpful for understanding the major ideas
of American liberalism that dominated the twentieth century:*

Beard, Charles A. *The Idea of National Interest* (New York: Macmillan, 1934).

Brandeis, Louis D. *Other People's Money* (New York: Macmillan, 1914).

Croly, Herbert David. *The Promise of American Life* (1909; New York: Transaction Books, 1993).

Dewey, John. *The Public and Its Problems* (New York: Holt, 1927).

Fulbright, J. William. *The Arrogance of Power* (New York: Random House, 1967).

Galbraith, John Kenneth. *The Affluent Society* (Boston: Houghton Mifflin, 1958).

* Goldman, Eric F. *Rendezvous with Destiny: A History of Modern American Reform* (New York: Vintage, 1967).

Harrington, Michael. *The Other America* (New York: Macmillan, 1962).

* Hofstadter, Richard. *The Age of Reform* (New York: Vintage, 1955).

* Isaacson, Walter. *The Wise Men: Six Friends and the World They Made* (New York: Simon & Schuster, 1997).

Kennan, George F. *Memoirs, 1925–1950* (New York: Knopf, 1983).

Popper, Karl. *The Open Society and Its Enemies* (Princeton, N.J.: Princeton University Press, 1971).

Rawls, John. *A Theory of Justice* (Cambridge, Mass.: Belknap/Harvard University Press, 1971).

* Rorty, Richard. *Achieving Our Country: Leftist Thought in Twentieth-Century America* (Cambridge, Mass.: Harvard University Press, 1998).

Schlesinger, Arthur, Jr. *The Vital Center: The Politics of Freedom* (Boston: Houghton Mifflin, 1949).

* Schwarz, Jordan. *Liberal: Adolf A. Berle and the Vision of an American Era* (New York: Free Press, 1987).

Appendix B: Recommended Reading

* Steel, Ronald. *Walter Lippmann and the American Century* (New York: Vintage, 1980).

Tarbell, Ida. *The History of the Standard Oil Company* (New York: Macmillan, 1904).

Tawney, R. H. *The Acquisitive Society* (London: Macmillan, 1921).

Veblen, Thorstein. *The Theory of the Leisure Class* (New York: Macmillan, 1912).

THE CURRENT BATTLE

The following books provide useful insights into the battle over American politics and values that emerged full blown in the 1990s and continued into the first decade of the twenty-first century:

Alterman, Eric. *What Liberal Media?: The Truth About Bias and the News* (New York: Basic Books, 2003).

Blumenthal, Sidney. *The Clinton Wars* (New York: Farrar, Straus and Giroux, 2003).

Brock, David. *Blinded by the Right: The Conscience of an Ex-Conservative* (New York: Three Rivers Press, 2002).

Dionne, E. J., Jr. *They Only Look Dead: Why Progressives Will Dominate the Next Political Era* (New York: Simon & Schuster, 1996).

Krugman, Paul. *The Great Unraveling: Losing Our Way in the New Century* (New York: Norton, 2003).

Nye, Joseph S., Jr. *The Paradox of American Power: Why the World's Only Superpower Can't Go It Alone* (New York: Oxford University Press, 2002).

Teixeira, Ruy, and Joel Rogers. *Why the White Working Class Still Matters* (New York: Basic Books, 2000).

NOTES

1. PRELUDE: THE REVENGE OF THE RADCONS

1. *Labor Journal*, Oct. 17, 1941, p. 18.

2. This historical point can be found in William Safire, *Safire's New Political Dictionary* (New York: Random House, 1993), p. 407.

3. Roosevelt made this remark during his first campaign for president, in 1932. See *The Public Papers and Addresses of Franklin D. Roosevelt* (New York: Random House, 1938–50), 1:27–28. I was led to the remark by Gene Amole, "Dreaded 'L' Word Deserves Respect," *Rocky Mountain News*, Oct. 8, 1996, p. 5A.

4. Edmund Burke, *Reflections on the Revolution in France* (1790; London: Penguin, 1986), pp. 280–81.

5. Quoted in David Brock, *Blinded by the Right* (New York: Three Rivers Press, 2002), p. 59.

6. Burke, pp. 279–80.

7. Michael Savage, *The Savage Nation* (Nashville, Tenn.: WND Books, 2002), p. 23.

8. Ann Coulter, *Slander* (New York: Crown, 2002), pp. 2, 6.

9. Joseph Farah, WorldNetDaily, Oct. 8, 2002 (http://www.wnd.com/news/article.asp?ARTICLE_ID=29201).

10. Rush Limbaugh, cited in Brock, p. 61.

11. *The 700 Club*, Sept. 13, 2001, discussion with Pat Robertson. Falwell

quoted in John Harris, "God Gave U.S. 'What We Deserve,' Falwell Says," *Washington Post*, Sept. 14, 2001, p. C3.

12. Reverend Franklin Graham said this shortly after the 9/11 attacks. Despite protests from Muslim groups, Graham was invited to the Pentagon to hold a Good Friday service in April 2003. See Richard W. Stevenson, "For Muslims, a Mixture of White House Signals," *New York Times*, Apr. 28, 2003, p. A13.

13. The phrase originated with David Brock. See his "The Real Anita Hill," *American Spectator*, March 1992. Brock later retracted his allegations about Hill. See generally, Brock, *Blinded by the Right*.

14. G. Gordon Liddy, quoted in Eric Alterman, *What Liberal Media?* (New York: Basic Books, 2003), p. 70.

15. Robert H. Bork, *Slouching Towards Gomorrah: Modern Liberalism and American Decline* (New York: ReganBooks, 1996), pp. 21, 11.

16. Quoted in "Offensive Prayer Offensive," *New York Times* editorial, Aug. 1, 2003, p. A22.

17. Quoted in Kevin Johnson and Toni Locy, "Ashcroft to Refocus Law Agencies for 'Wartime,' " *USA Today*, Nov. 9, 2001, Final Edition, p. A9.

18. From speech of President George W. Bush, Sept. 20, 2001.

19. Philip Larkin, "Annus Mirabilis," in *High Windows* (New York: Farrar, Straus and Giroux, 1974).

20. The point has been made that Republican rhetoric exemplifies the notion of strict fathering, while Democratic rhetoric exemplifies the nourishing mother. See George Lakoff, *Moral Politics* (Chicago: University of Chicago Press, 1996).

21. Newt Gingrich, cited in Brock, pp. 66–67.

22. Savage, p. 98.

23. Gertrude Himmelfarb, *One Nation, Two Cultures* (New York: Knopf, 1999), p. 314.

24. William J. Bennett, *The Broken Hearth* (New York: Broadway Books, 2001), p. 17.

25. "No Guardrails," *Wall Street Journal* editorial, Mar. 18, 1993, p. A12.

26. Bork, pp. 20–21.

27. Mona Charen, *Useful Idiots* (Washington, D.C.: Regnery, 2003), p. 29.

28. Ibid., p. 31.

29. William J. Bennett, *Why We Fight* (Washington, D.C.: Regnery, 2003), p. 49.

30. Cited in *The Economist*, Apr. 26, 2003, p. 22.

31. The letter is found at http://www.newamericancentury.org/iraqclinton

letter.htm. See also Neil Mackay, "Rumsfeld Urged Clinton to Attack Iraq," *The Sunday Herald*, Mar. 16, 2003, p. 1.

32. Bork, p. 21.

33. Ibid., pp. 13, 17.

34. Ibid., pp. 34, 55.

35. Ibid., p. 2.

36. Quoted in Robert Shogan, "Clinton Is Ducking the Issues, Three GOP Conservatives Charge," *Los Angeles Times*, Jan. 31, 1998, p. A17.

37. William J. Bennett, *The Death of Outrage* (New York: Free Press, 1998), p. 130.

38. Quoted in Michael Lind, "The Texas Nexus," *Prospect*, April 2003, p. 33.

39. Quoted in Brock, p. 51.

40. Quoted in Robert Kuttner, *The Life of the Party: Democratic Prospects in 1988 and Beyond* (New York: Viking, 1987), p. 62.

41. Quoted in Brock, p. 134.

42. For these and other data on wages, benefits, and wealth distribution, see Lawrence Mishel et al., *The State of Working America, 2002–2003* (Ithaca, N.Y.: Cornell University Press, 2003).

43. On the real cost of middle-class life, see Elizabeth Warren and Amelia Warren Tyagi, *The Two-Income Trap* (New York: Basic Books, 2003).

44. Address to the Republican convention, Aug. 20, 1984.

45. Bennett, *Why We Fight*, p. 7.

46. See Chris Mooney, "Breaking the Frame," *The American Prospect*, Apr. 1, 2003, p. 27.

47. See William Safire, *Safire's New Political Dictionary* (New York: Random House, 1993), pp. 408–9.

48. Quoted in Alan Cooperman, "Santorum Angers Gay Rights Groups," *Washington Post*, Apr. 22, 2003, p. A4.

2. PUBLIC MORALITY

1. William J. Bennett, *The Broken Hearth* (New York: Broadway Books, 2001), p. 166.

2. Ibid., p. 168.

3. Ibid.

4. Ibid., pp. 124–25.

5. Robert H. Bork, *Slouching Towards Gomorrah* (New York: ReganBooks, 1996), p. 5.

6. James Q. Wilson, *The Moral Sense* (New York: Touchstone, 1993), p. 9.

7. William J. Bennett, *Why We Fight* (Washington, D.C.: Regnery, 2003), p. 62.

8. Ibid., p. 63.

9. Bennett, *Hearth*, p. 138.

10. Daniel Patrick Moynihan, "Defining Deviancy Down," *The American Scholar*, Winter 1993, p. 17.

11. Bennett, *Hearth*, p. 177.

12. "No Guardrails," *Wall Street Journal* editorial, Mar. 18, 1993, p. A12.

13. Radley Balko, "No Guardrails?" Fox News Channel, May 8, 2003.

14. Michael Savage, *The Savage Nation* (Nashville, Tenn.: WND Books, 2002), pp. 92–93.

15. Bork, p. 154.

16. Bennett, *Hearth*, pp. 18–19.

17. Ibid., p. 146.

18. Cited in Thomas Byrne Edsall, "Blue Movie," *Atlantic Monthly*, January–February 2003.

19. Elizabeth Hayt, "Surprise, Mom: I'm Against Abortion," *New York Times*, Mar. 30, 2003, Section 9, p. 1.

20. George W. Bush, campaign speech on education, Gorham, New Hampshire, Nov. 2, 1999.

21. David Harding and Christopher Jencks, "Changing Attitudes Toward Premarital Sex: Cohort, Period, and Aging Effects," *Public Opinion Quarterly*, 67 (2003): 211–26.

22. Tom W. Smith, "American Sexual Behavior: Trends, Socio-Demographic Differences, and Risk Behavior," National Opinion Research Center, University of Chicago. GSS Topical Report No. 25. Updated, December 1998.

23. See Brady E. Hamilton et al., Division of Vital Statistics, Centers for Disease Control and Prevention, *National Vital Statistics Reports* 51, no. 11 (June 25, 2003): 1.

24. Amara Bachu, "Is Childlessness Among American Women on the Rise?" U.S. Bureau of the Census, Population Division, May 1999.

25. On this point, see Elizabeth Warren and Amelia Warren Tyagi, *The Two-Income Trap* (New York: Basic Books, 2003).

26. "The Marriage Experiment," *Washington Post* editorial, Jan. 31, 2004, p. A20.

27. A study of census data by researchers at Princeton and Columbia found

that more than 33 percent of fathers of children born out of wedlock lacked a high school degree; 28 percent were unemployed; 20 percent had incomes of less than $6,000 a year; and roughly 38 percent had criminal records. See Michael Tanner, "Wedded to Poverty," *New York Times*, June 29, 2003, p. A27.

28. See, for example, Ronald Mincy and Allen Dupree, "Family Formation in Fragile Families," Center for Research on Child Well-Being, Princeton University, working paper.

29. General Social Survey, Tom W. Smith, "The Emerging 21st Century American Family," National Opinion Research Center, University of Chicago, General Social Survey Report no. 42, Nov. 24, 1999.

30. Bennett, *Hearth*, p. 142.

31. Ibid., p. 161.

32. In 1957, 9.2 percent of women who had been married were divorced; in 1965, 10.6 percent; 1975, 20.3 percent; 1980, 22.8 percent; 1990, 20.9 percent; 1995, 20.5 percent. National Center for Health Statistics, various years.

33. Savage, p. 95.

34. Mary Parke, "Are Married Parents Really Better for Children? What Research Says About the Effects of Family Structure on Child Well-Being," Center for Law and Social Policy, May 2003.

35. A majority of young adults think gay marriage should be legal, according to a *USA Today* poll taken June 18–29, 2003. See Charisse Jones, "Poll: Young Adults Back Gay Marriages," *USA Today*, July 1, 2003, p. A8.

36. Bennett, *Hearth*, p. 114.

37. Ibid., p. 119.

38. "A growing body of scientific literature demonstrates that children who grow up with one or two gay and/or lesbian parents fare as well in emotional, cognitive, social and sexual functioning as do children whose parents are heterosexual." Ellen C. Perrin et al., "Co-Parent or Second-Parent Adoption by Same-Sex Parents," *Pediatrics* 109, no. 2 (February 2002): 341–44.

39. Bennett, *Hearth*, p. 113.

40. Ibid., p. 115.

41. Alan Cooperman, "Santorum Angers Gay Rights Groups," *Washington Post*, Apr. 22, 2003, p. A4.

42. *Lawrence v. Texas*, decided June 26, 2003.

43. See www.nace-cee.org/presidentreport.htm.

44. Alan Cooperman, "Paige's Remarks on Religion in Schools Decried," *Washington Post*, Apr. 9, 2003, p. A6.

45. Tamar Lewin, "Arkansas School Is Accused of Harassing a Gay Student," *New York Times*, Mar. 25, 2003, p. A10.

46. On the increasing tendency of husbands and wives to change shifts of work and child care, see National Study of the Changing Workforce, 1997 (survey of more than 3,500 working men and women). See also Jacqueline Salmon, "A Tag-Team Approach to Wrestling with Child Care," *Washington Post Weekly Edition*, Apr. 10, 1998, p. 30.

47. For evidence, see Robert Putnam, *Bowling Alone* (New York: Simon & Schuster, 2001), p. 100.

48. Data from "Those Young Americans," *The Economist*, Sept. 6, 2003, p. 31.

49. Kathleen Deveny et al., "We're Not in the Mood," *Newsweek*, June 30, 2003, p. 40.

50. Bennett, *Hearth*, p. 26.

51. Ibid., p. 25.

52. Ibid.

53. *The Economist*, Sept. 6, 2003, p. 31.

54. "Mayhem over Martha," *Wall Street Journal* editorial, June 5, 2003, p. A16.

55. Interview with the president of the Securities Industry Association, Sept. 13, 2003.

56. See, generally, Robert Bryce, *Pipe Dreams: Greed, Ego, Jealousy and the Death of Enron* (New York: PublicAffairs, 2003); Peter Fusaro and Ross Miller, *What Went Wrong at Enron: Everyone's Guide to the Largest Bankruptcy in U.S. History* (New York: Wiley, 2003); Mimi Swartz and Sherron Watkins, *Power Failure* (New York: Doubleday, 2003).

57. See "Enron's Friends in Need," *New York Times* editorial, July 31, 2003, p. A24.

58. Floyd Norris, "Bankrupt Thinking: How the Banks Aided Enron's Deception," *New York Times*, Aug. 1, 2003, p. C1.

59. David Cay Johnston, "Wall Street Firms Are Faulted in Report on Enron's Taxes," NYTimes.com, Feb. 14, 2003.

60. Nanette Byrnes and Louis Lavelle, "The Corporate Tax Game," *BusinessWeek*, Mar. 31, 2003, pp. 79–87.

61. Richard Oppel, Jr., "Panel Finds Manipulation by Energy Companies," *New York Times*, Mar. 17, 2003, p. A12.

62. Jonathan Glater, "Financial Statements Rose to Record in 2003, Study Says," *New York Times*, Jan. 13, 2004, p. C2.

63. "Revenge of the Investor Class," *Wall Street Journal* editorial, Oct. 23, 2003, p A20.

64. Ben White, "Stock Doublespeak," *Washington Post Weekly Edition*, May 5–11, 2003, p. 20. Jack Grubman called SmartTalk a "screaming buy" and it went bankrupt a few months later. One retail broker writes: "Will [Grubman] come to arbitration with us when the lawsuits begin?"

65. Quoted in Don Aucoin, "Let's Be Honest," *Boston Globe Magazine*, Aug. 3, 2003, pp. 8, 9.

66. The survey of 112 money managers was conducted by Broadgate Consultants. See Gretchen Morgenson, "Wall Street Reform Falls Short, Survey Says," *New York Times*, Aug. 31, 2003, p. B6.

67. See Simon Targett, "Market Timing Abuses Seen as Systemic," *Financial Times*, Nov. 24, 2003, p. 1.

68. Gary Silverman, "Finance Sector Warned Over 'Conflict Crisis,'" *Financial Times*, Sept. 10, 2003, p. 1.

69. The U.S. General Accounting Office reported in October 2003 that illegal tax shelters were costing the Treasury tens of billions of dollars each year. See "Internal Revenue Service: Challenges Remain in Combatting Abusive Tax Shelters," GAO Report 04-104T, issued Oct. 21, 2003. See also "Wide Range of Tax Shelters Attracts Senate Inquiry," *New York Times*, Oct. 22, 2003, p. B1.

70. For an extended discussion, see David Callahan, *The Cheating Culture* (New York: Harcourt, 2004), pp. 5–8.

71. Kirstin Downey, "The Pension Gap Widens," *Washington Post Weekly Edition*, Apr. 21–27, 2003, p. 18. See also Brian Hall and Kevin Murphy, "The Trouble with Stock Options," *Journal of Economic Perspectives*, 2003.

72. Brian Hall and Jeffrey Liebman, "The Taxation of Executive Compensation," in *Tax Policy and the Economy*, National Bureau of Economic Research volume edited by J. Poterba (Cambridge, Mass.: MIT Press, 2000).

73. Joann Lublin, "Why the Get-Rich-Quick Days for Executives May Be Over," *Wall Street Journal Online*, Special Report: Executive Pay, Apr. 14, 2003.

74. Patrick McGeehan, "At Heinz, A Novel Way to Say the Boss Is Worth It," *New York Times*, Aug. 10, 2003, p. C4.

75. Louis Lavelle, Frederick Jespersen, Spencer Ante, and Jim Kerstetter, "Special Report: Executive Pay," *BusinessWeek*, Apr. 21, 2003.

76. Floyd Norris, "In U.S. Eyes, a Notably Bold Case of Health Care Fraud," *New York Times*, Mar. 20, 2003, p. B1.

77. Data from the *New York Times*, Apr. 6, 2003, section 3, p. 1.

78. Matt Murray, Rachel Emma Silverman, and Carol Hymowitz, "GE's Jack Welch Meets His Match in Divorce Court," *Wall Street Journal*, Nov. 27, 2002, p. A1.

79. Joseph Treaster, "As Hancock's Profit Declined, Chief's Pay Rose to $21 Million," *New York Times*, May 17, 2003, p. B1.

80. Holman W. Jenkins, Jr., "Who Decides How Much Is Too Much?" *Wall Street Journal*, Sept. 24, 2003, p. A21.

81. Carol Hymowitz and Joann Lublin, "Benefits: I'll Have What He's Having," *Wall Street Journal*, May 20, 2003, p. B1.

82. *Wall Street Journal*, Sept. 4, 2003, p. A18.

83. David Firestone, "Bush Loyalists Compete for Spots on President's A-Team by Raising Record Money for 2004," *New York Times*, June 21, 2003, p. A10.

84. These and other data from Federal Election Commission reports.

85. Ibid.

86. Grover Norquist, "Step-by-Step to Reform," *Washington Post Weekly Edition*, June 23–29, 2003, p. 26.

87. "Radical Birthday Thoughts," *The Economist*, special section on capitalism and democracy, June 28, 2003, p. 9.

88. Stephen Labaton and Jonathan Glater, "Staff of S.E.C. Is Said to Dilute Rule Changes," *New York Times*, Jan. 22, 2003, pp. A1, C1, C12.

89. Tom Hamburger, "U.S. Flips on Patents Show Drug Makers' Growing Clout," *Wall Street Journal*, Feb. 6, 2003, p. A4.

90. Thomas B. Edsall, "Money Trail Raises Questions About Energy Firm's Influence," *Boston Globe*, June 29, 2003, p. A18.

91. The study was prepared by the Center for Public Integrity. It was reported in Edmund Andrews and Elizabeth Becker, "Bush Got $500,000 from Companies That Got Contracts, Study Finds," *New York Times*, Oct. 31, 2003, p. A8.

92. Neil King, Jr., "Bush Has an Audacious Plan to Rebuild Iraq Within a Year," *Wall Street Journal*, Mar. 17, 2003, pp. A1, A6.

93. Peter Yost, "Top Lobbyist of Loan Giant Gave Assist to Lawmakers," *Boston Globe*, July 20, 2003, p. B6.

94. Jim VandeHei and Juliet Eilperin, "Targeting Lobbyists Pays Off for GOP," *Washington Post*, June 26, 2003, p. A1.

95. Jill Abramson, "The Business of Persuasion Thrives in Nation's Capital," *New York Times*, Sept. 29, 1988, p. A22.

96. Study by Center for Public Integrity. Cited in *New York Times*, Apr. 4, 2003, p. A18.

97. "Radical Birthday Thoughts," *The Economist*, p. 8.

98. William J. Bennett, *The Death of Outrage* (New York: Free Press, 1998), p. 11.

3. REAL PROSPERITY

1. Data from U.S. Bureau of Labor Statistics, "Labor Force Statistics from the Current Population Survey: Annual Average Tables from the January 2000 Issue of Employment and Earnings," and from Lawrence R. Mishel et al., *The State of Working America, 2002–2003* (Ithaca, N.Y.: Cornell University Press, 2003).

2. Quoted in Amity Shlaes, "Republicans Sample the Rhetoric of Confidence," *Financial Times*, May 22, 2001, p. 23.

3. Quotation from Frances Perkins, *The Roosevelt I Knew* (New York: Viking, 1946), pp. 282–83.

4. Robert Bork, *Slouching Towards Gomorrah* (New York: ReganBooks, 1996), pp. 162–63.

5. For the typical employee with family coverage, out-of-pocket spending for insurance premiums, deductibles, and drug co-payments rose to $2,790 in 2003, from $1,890 in 2000. See report on employer-sponsored health care by the Kaiser Family Foundation and the Health Research and Educational Trust, cited in Milt Freudenheim, "Employees Paying Ever-Bigger Share for Health Care," *New York Times*, Sept. 10, 2003, p. A1.

6. Kathleen Stoll, "Going Without Health Insurance: Nearly One in Three Non-Elderly Americans," Families U.S.A., prepared for the Robert Wood Johnson Foundation, March 2003.

7. Bork, p. 67.

8. Milton Friedman, *Free to Choose* (New York: Harcourt Brace Jovanovich, 1980), p. 127.

9. Ibid., p. 124.

10. Bork, p. 163.

11. A study of seven hundred women in four geographic areas who left welfare four years before revealed that most had found jobs but remained in poverty. See Bruce Fuller et al., "New Lives for Poor Families? Mothers and Young Children Move Through Welfare Reform," Growing Up in Poverty Project, Berkeley, Calif., April 2002, p. 102. See also Meredith May, "Welfare Reforms Not Ending Poverty," *San Francisco Chronicle*, Apr. 16, 2002, p. A1.

12. For data on families who left welfare between 2000 and 2002, see Pamela Loprest, "Fewer Welfare Leavers Employed in Weak Economy" and "Welfare Leavers Face Serious Threats," Urban Institute, Washington, D.C., August 2003. On the increase in child poverty, see U.S. Census Bureau, American Community Survey Change Profile 2001–02, www.census.gov/acs/www/Products/Profiles/Chg/2002/0102/index.htm.

13. Interviewed on *Think Tank* with Ben Wattenberg, Public Broadcasting Service, Oct. 14, 1994. At http://www.pbs.org/thinktank/transcript129.html.

14. Bork, p. 74.

15. This is because parental income has a direct bearing on the quality of schooling, health care, nutrition, intellectual stimulation, and psychological and physical security children have. See, generally, Rebecca Blank, *It Takes a Nation: A New Agenda for Fighting Poverty* (Princeton, N.J.: Princeton University Press, 1997), and Jody Heymann, *The Widening Gap: Why America's Working Families Are in Jeopardy—and What Can Be Done About It* (New York: Basic Books, 2000).

16. William Graham Sumner, *The Challenge of Facts, and Other Essays* (New Haven, Conn.: Yale University Press, 1914), p. 90.

17. Quoted in Eric Goldman, *Rendezvous with Destiny* (New York: Vintage, 1967), pp. 71–72.

18. See Jon Hilsenrath and Rebecca Buckman, "Factory Employment Is Falling World-Wide," *Wall Street Journal*, Oct. 20, 2003, p. A2.

19. See Robert B. Reich, "The Future of Information-Technology Jobs in an Age of Global Outsourcing," *Chief Information Officer*, Summer 2003; Amy Waldman, "More 'Can I Help You?' Jobs Migrate from U.S. to India," *New York Times*, May 11, 2003, p. A4.

20. Clare Ansberry, "Outsourcing Abroad Draws Debate at Home," *Wall Street Journal*, July 14, 2003, p. 2.

21. The distribution of benefits of these two taxes has been subject to a great deal of scrutiny. These estimates are derived from studies by Citizens for Tax Justice, and the Brookings Institution and Urban Institute, 2003.

22. Study by the Internal Revenue Service, cited by David Cay Johnston, "Very Richest's Share of Income Grew Even Bigger, Data Show," *New York Times*, June 26, 2003, p. A1.

23. George Gilder, *The Spirit of Enterprise* (New York: Simon & Schuster, 1984), p. 144.

24. Mishel et al., pp. 75–78. Even by the 1990s, a time of unbounded exuberance and opportunity, it was more difficult than ever for young workers to

surpass their parents' standard of living, the proverbial American dream. See Isabel Sawhill and Daniel McMurrer, "Declining Economic Opportunity in America," Urban Institute, Apr. 1, 1996.

25. A. Carnavale and S. Rose, *Socioeconomic Status, Race/Ethnicity, and Selective College Admissions* (New York: Century Foundation, 2003).

26. Peter Enrich, "Stalking Corporate Welfare," *Northeastern Law*, Summer 2003, p. 2.

4. POSITIVE PATRIOTISM

1. Program on International Policy Attitudes, "Americans on Globalization: A Study in U.S. Public Attitudes," University of Maryland, 1998, p. 8.

2. Michael Savage, *The Savage Nation* (Nashville, Tenn.: WND Books, 2002), pp. 69.

3. Robert Bork, *Slouching Towards Gomorrah* (New York: ReganBooks, 1996), pp. 298–99, 304.

4. William J. Bennett, *Why We Fight* (Washington, D.C.: Regnery, 2003), pp. 162–63.

5. Cited in Max Boot, "America and the U.N., Together Again?" *New York Times* op-ed, Aug. 3, 2003, p. 11.

6. Quoted in an interview with G. M. Gilbert during the Nuremberg trials, Apr. 18, 1946. See G. M. Gilbert, *Nuremberg Diary* (New York: Farrar, Straus, 1947), p. 279.

7. Bennett, *Why We Fight*, p. 154.

8. Mona Charen, *Useful Idiots* (Washington, D.C.: Regnery, 2003), p. 257.

9. Bennett, *Why We Fight*, p. 48.

10. Charen, pp. 54, 257.

11. Attorney General John Ashcroft, Senate hearing, December 2001, quoted in "Ashcroft's Policy Role Is Steadily Increasing at Justice Department," *New York Times*, Mar. 15, 2003, pp. A1, A9.

12. Quoted in David Smyth, "Pop-Star Chicks Turn Country on Its Head," *The Evening Standard*, London, Mar. 11, 2003, p. 1.

13. MSNBC *Reports* with Joe Scarborough, Apr. 10, 2003.

14. Ibid.

15. Quoted in Jim Rutenberg, "Cable's War Coverage Suggests a New 'Fox Effect' on Television Journalism," *New York Times*, Apr. 16, 2003, p. B9.

16. Neil Cavuto, "Common Sense," Fox News, Apr. 9, 2003.

17. Bill O'Reilly, "Talking Points," commentary, *The O'Reilly Factor*, Fox News, Feb. 26, 2003.

18. CBS News, *See It Now*, Mar. 9, 1954.

19. Robert Kagan and William Kristol, "The Present Danger," *The National Interest*, Spring 2000, pp. 58, 67.

20. "U.S. Officials See Signs of a Revived Al Qaeda," *New York Times*, May 17, 2003, pp. A1, A8.

21. Data from Joseph S. Nye, Jr., *The Paradox of American Power* (New York: Oxford University Press, 2002), p. 56.

22. Quoted in Alan Murray, "Warning Is Sounded as Empire-Building Gains New Cachet," *Wall Street Journal*, July 15, 2003, p. A4.

23. On this and other facts about the ease with which terrorists could obtain the makings of a nuclear bomb, see Martin Rees, *Our Final Hour: A Scientist's Warning: How Terror, Error, and Environmental Disaster Threaten Humankind's Future in This Century—on Earth and Beyond* (New York: Basic Books, 2003).

24. Michael Ignatieff, "Why Are We in Iraq?" *New York Times Magazine*, Sept. 7, 2003, pp. 38, 85.

25. Robert Kagan and William Kristol, "The Burden of Power Is Having to Wield It," *Washington Post* op-ed, Mar. 19, 2000, p. A27.

26. Cited in Christopher Marquis, "World's View of U.S. Sours After Iraq War, Poll Finds," *New York Times*, June 4, 2003, p. A19.

27. See *Human Development Report 2003: Millennium Development Goals: A Compact Among Nations to End Human Poverty* (New York: Oxford University Press, for the U.N. Development Program, 2003). See also Strobe Talbott, "The Other Evil," *Foreign Policy*, November/December 2001, pp. 75–76.

28. *Human Development Report 2003*.

29. See "Rigged Trade Game," *New York Times* editorial, July 20, 2003, p. A10.

30. *Compañía de Tabacos v. Collector*, 275 U.S. 87, 100 (1904).

31. Adam Smith, *An Inquiry into the Nature and Causes of the Wealth of Nations*, vol. 2, ed. R. H. Campbell et al. (Oxford, Eng.: Clarendon, 1976), p. 840.

32. "Warren Buffett Talks Business," University of North Carolina, Center for Public Television, Chapel Hill, 1995, cited in Janet Lowe, *Warren Buffett Speaks* (New York: Wiley, 1997), p. 164.

33. President Theodore Roosevelt, speech to Congress, Dec. 4, 1906.

34. Quoted in Arthur M. Schlesinger, Jr., *The Politics of Upheaval* (Boston: Houghton Mifflin, 1960), p. 333.

35. Larry Tye, "All-Volunteer Force No Mirror of Society," *Boston Globe*,

Feb. 2, 1991, pp. 1, 3; Steven A. Holmes, "Is This Really an All-Volunteer Army?" *New York Times*, Apr. 6, 2003, Section 4, p. 1.

36. David Halbfinger and Steven A. Holmes, "Military Mirrors a Working-Class America," *New York Times*, Mar. 30, 2003, pp. A1, B12.

37. James Traub, "All Go Down Together," *New York Times Book Review*, Mar. 2, 2003, pp. 21, 22.

38. M. B. Norton et al., *A People and a Nation* (Boston: Houghton Mifflin, 1996), p. 608.

39. Ibid.

40. Senate confirmation hearing for secretary of defense, 1989. Cited in Mead Gruver, "School, Parent Deferments Keep Cheney from Draft," *Chattanooga Times Free Press*, July 28, 2000, p. A5.

41. "Personal Wars," *Los Angeles Weekly*, Sept. 20, 2002, p. 12.

42. David Maraniss, *First in His Class* (New York: Simon & Schuster, 1995), pp. 185–205.

43. Walter Robinson, "One Year Gap in Bush's Guard Duty, No Record of Airman at Drills in 1972–1973," *Boston Globe*, May 23, 2000, p. A1.

44. Joe Conason, "Selective Service," Salon.com News, July 13, 1999.

45. *Wall Street Journal*, July 30, 2003, p. A13.

46. Ibid., p. 9.

5. WINNING: IT WILL TAKE MORE THAN REASON

1. See Larry Bartels, "Homer Gets a Tax Cut: Inequality and Public Policy in the American Mind," Woodrow Wilson School of Public and International Affairs, Princeton University, August 2003.

2. Arthur M. Schlesinger, Jr., *The Politics of Upheaval* (Boston: Houghton Mifflin, 1960), p. 503.

3. For relevant polls, see Appendix A.

4. The phrase has been used before in reference to liberals and progressives. See E. J. Dionne, Jr., *They Only Look Dead* (New York: Simon & Schuster, 1996).

5. See data in Ruy Teixeira and Joel Rogers, *Why the White Working Class Still Matters* (New York: Basic Books, 2000).

6. "Voting Registration and the Election of November, 2000," U.S. Census Bureau, Current Population Reports, February 2002, Table B, pp. 6–7.

7. Quoted in Eric Goldman, *Rendezvous with Destiny* (New York: Vintage, 1967), p. 3.

ACKNOWLEDGMENTS

I want to thank several people who were especially helpful to me in writing this book. John Heilemann, Jack Donahue, Ken Dornstein, John Isaacson, Doug Dworkin, Nancy Schwartz, Rozann Kraus, Dick Leone, Perian Flaherty, Ron Axelrod, Emily Axelrod, and Richard Parker read early drafts and offered thoughtful suggestions. Mike Pujals provided ever-ready research assistance. Margaret Post, Brian Giacometti, and Jessica Herman did additional research. My assistant, Michelle Browning, watched over the preparation of the manuscript. I'm also indebted to my colleagues at Brandeis University and its Heller School, at the University of California at Berkeley and its Goldman School, and at *The American Prospect* magazine, for their continuing insights into the worlds of policy, politics, and social values. Special thanks are due my literary agent and friend, Rafe Sagalyn, for his persistent encouragement; to my editor and comrade, Jonathan Segal, for his enduring wisdom; and to my wife, Clare Dalton, who not only read and commented on earlier drafts but also provided enthusiastic support throughout.

INDEX

Index

Index

Index

A NOTE ABOUT THE AUTHOR

Robert B. Reich is University Professor at Brandeis University and Maurice B. Hexter Professor of Social and Economic Policy at Brandeis's Heller Graduate School. He has served in three national administrations, most recently as secretary of labor under President Bill Clinton. He has written nine books, and his articles have appeared in *The New Yorker, Atlantic Monthly, New York Times, Washington Post,* and *Wall Street Journal.* Mr. Reich is co-founder and national editor of *The American Prospect* magazine. He lives in Cambridge, Massachusetts, with his wife, Clare Dalton. They have two sons.

A NOTE ON THE TYPE

The text of this book was set in Electra, a typeface designed by W. A. Dwiggins (1880–1956). This face cannot be classified as either modern or old style. It is not based on any historical model, nor does it echo any particular period or style. It avoids the extreme contrasts between thick and thin elements that mark most modern faces, and it attempts to give a feeling of fluidity, power, and speed.

Composed by Creative Graphics, Allentown, Pennsylvania
Printed and bound by R.R. Donnelley & Sons, Harrisonburg, Virginia
Designed by Robert C. Olsson